Alternative Ideas in Real Estate Investment

RESEARCH ISSUES IN REAL ESTATE

Sponsored by
The American Real Estate Society

Volume I

APPRAISAL, MARKET ANALYSIS, AND
PUBLIC POLICY IN REAL ESTATE
edited by
James R. DeLisle and J. Sa-Aadu

Volume II

ALTERNATIVE IDEAS IN
REAL ESTATE INVESTMENT
edited by
Arthur L. Schwartz, Jr. and
Steven D. Kapplin

Alternative Ideas in Real Estate Investment

edited by

Arthur L. Schwartz, Jr.
University of South Florida

and

Steven D. Kapplin
University of South Florida

The American Real Estate Society

Kluwer Academic Publishers

Boston / Dordrecht / London

Distributors for North America:
Kluwer Academic Publishers
101 Philip Drive
Assinippi Park
Norwell, Massachusetts 02061 USA

Distributors for all other countries:
Kluwer Academic Publishers Group
Distribution Centre
Post Office Box 322
3300 AH Dordrecht, THE NETHERLANDS

Library of Congress Cataloging-in-Publication Data
Alternative ideas in real estate investment/edited by Arthur L. Schwartz and Steven D. Kapplin.
p. cm.—(Research issues in real estate; 2)
Includes index.
ISBN-13:978-94-010-6651-8 e-ISBN-13:978-94-009-0367-8
DOI: 10.1007/978-94-009-0367-8

1. Real estate investment. I. Schwartz, Arthur L. II. Kapplin, Steven D. III. Series: Real estate research issues; 2.
HD1382.5.A45 1995
332.63'24—dc20 94-23019
CIP

Printed on acid-free paper.

1995
AMERICAN REAL ESTATE SOCIETY

PRESIDENT'S COUNCIL

Appraisal Institute
Bomi Institute*
Institutional Real Estate. Inc.
International Association of Corporate Real Estate Executives
LaSalle Advisors Limited*
MIG Realty Advisors
Price Waterhouse

REGENTS

Equitable Real Estate Investment Management
The Roulac Group
The RREEF Funds

INSTITUTIONAL SPONSORS

AEtna Realty Investors
American Agricultural Investment
Boston Financial Group
Business One Irwin
CIGNA Investments
CB Commercial Real Estate Group
Citadel Realty
Cornerstone Real Estate Advisers
Counselors of Real Estate
Davis & Associates
Dearborn Financial Publishing
The Dorchester Group
Ernst & Young
Federal National Mortgage Association
Freddie Mac
Heitman/JMB Advisory Corporation
International Development Research Council
International Council of Shopping Centers
Korpacz & Associates
Lambda Alpha International
The Liquidity Fund
MetLife Realty Group
MetLife Real Estate Investments*
Mortgage Banker's Association
National Association of Industrial and Office Parks
National Association of Real Estate Investment Trusts
National Association of REALTORs
Prentice Hall, Inc.
Prudential Realty Group
The REIS Reports
Real Estate Research Corporation
Society of Industrial and Office REALTORS[R]
Summa Corporation
Urban Land Institute

*New for 1995

1995 FELLOWS
THE AMERICAN REAL ESTATE SOCIETY

Joseph D. Albert
James Madison University

Dennis H. Anderson
L. W. Ellwood & Co.

John S. Baen
University of North Texas

Stan Banton
Banton Associates

John D. Benjamin
American University

J. Thomas Black
Urban Land Institute

Donald H. Bleich
California State University at Northridge

Waldo L. Born
Eastern Illinois University

Donald W. Conley
Appraisal Institute

James R. Cooper
Georgia State University

Charles G. Dannis
Crosson Dannis, Inc.

James R. DeLisle
Equitable Real Estate Investment Management

Mark G. Dotzour
Wichita State University

John T. Emery
Louisiana Tech University

Donald R. Epley
Mississippi State University

John L. Glascock
Louisiana State University

William C. Goolsby
Washington State University

G. Hayden Green
University of Alaska at Anchorage

D. Wylie Greig
The RREEF Funds

Karl L. Guntermann
Arizona State University

Richard L. Haney
Texas A&M University

Jerome R. Jakubovitz
MAI

Linda L. Johnson
Miller & Mosley

G. Donald Jud
University of North Carolina at Greensboro

Steven D. Kapplin
University of South Florida

George R. Karvel
St. Cloud State University

James B. Kau
University of Georgia

William N. Kinnard, Jr.
Real Estate Counseling Group of Connecticut

Ed G. Lane
Lane Consultants

Donald R. Levi
Wichita State University

Joseph B. Lipscomb
Texas Christian University

Chris Manning
Loyola Marymount University

Thomas E. McCue
Duquesne University

Willard McIntosh
MIG Realty Advisors

John McMahan
McMahan Real Estate Advisors

Ivan J. Miestchovich, Jr.
University of New Orleans

Philip S. Mitchell
Mitchell & Associates

Glenn R. Mueller
Alex Brown Kleinwort Benson Realty Advisors

F. C. Neil Myer
Cleveland State University

Theron R. Nelson
University of North Dakota

Hugh O. Nourse
University of Georgia

Thomas D. Pearson
The Thomas D. Pearson Company

Kenneth Posner
Morgan Stanley Realty

(continued)

EDITORIAL REVIEW BOARD
RESEARCH ISSUES IN REAL ESTATE: VOLUME 2

CONTENTS

* Deceased.

About the Editors

Arthur L. Schwartz, Jr.

Arthur L. Schwartz, Jr. is Professor of Finance and Real Estate at the University of South Florida in Saint Petersburg. He holds a B.B.A. and a M.B.A. degree from the University of Michigan and a Ph.D. in Finance from the University of Oregon. He has also held faculty positions at California Polytechnic State University, San Luis Obispo, and at the University of Hawaii, Manoa. He was a Distinguished Visiting Scholar at Lincoln University, New Zealand, in 1988.

Professor Schwartz's articles have appeared in journals such as *Journal of Real Estate Research, Journal of Real Estate Literature, Journal of Finance, Journal of Financial and Quantitative Analysis, Financial Review,* and *Journal of the American Real Estate and Urban Economics Association*. He is co-editor of the special issue of *The Journal of Real Estate Research* on International Investment, and was a co-editor of the *Research in Real Estate* monograph series, Volume 3 and *Real Estate Research Issues* monograph series, Volume 2. He is also the co-editor of the International Section of the *Journal of Real Estate Literature*, as well as an associate editor of the Case Studies and the Review Article sections of that journal. Finally, he is an editorial board member of both the *Journal of Real Estate Research* and the *Journal of Real Estate Portfolio Management* and is the real estate editor for the *Financial Services Review*.

Professor Schwartz is one of the founders of the American Real Estate Society (ARES) and has served on its Board of Directors every year since its founding except one. He is the immediate past president of ARES and was the ARES vice president for programs at the 1992 Annual Meeting in San Diego. He is the ARES meeting planner and he, Professor James

Webb, and Professor Theron Nelson have managed ARES Annual Meetings since 1988. He is also a founder and the executive director of the International Real Estate Society (IRES).

Steven D. Kapplin, Ph.D.

Steven D. Kapplin is a tenured Professor of Finance and Real Estate at the University of South Florida and directs the real estate program, which he was instrumental in developing. Dr. Kapplin received his BA in English Literature in 1970 and his doctorate in Real Estate and Urban Affairs in 1979 from Georgia State University. His disseration on real estate investment trusts received first prize in the American Real Estate and Urban Economics Association dissertation competition in 1980.

Dr. Kapplin has authored more than 50 articles and three books on rseal estate investment analysis and valuation, including the best selling textbook *Real Estate Investment: Strategy, Analysis, Decisions*. His articles have appeared in such journals as *Journal of Real Estate Research, Journal of American Real Estate and Urban Economics Association, Housing Finance Review, Appraisal Journal, Real Estate Review, Real Estate Issues, The Real Estate Appraiser, Appraisal Review Journal, and Journal of the American Association of Individual Investors*. He is a candidate in the Appraisal Institute, a national instructor of Appraisal Institute courses, and is nationally recognized for his research on real estate limited partnerships. He is a past director of the American Real Estate Society, serves on the editorial board of the *Journal of Real Estate Research* and is the 1994–5 President of the American Real Estate Society.

Dr. Kapplin began his career in real estate as a broker in Atlanta and was a partner in the firm which originated Underground Atlanta in 1965. He continues an active involvement in the Atlanta area real estate market.

INTRODUCTION

Arthur L. Schwartz, Jr. and Steven D. Kapplin

The focus of this volume of the ARES Monograph Series is new ideas in real estate investment. Within this volume, empiricial studies, literature reviews, and tutorials examine a broad range of important investment issues. Many new and innovative ideas are presented. This volume should be a rich source of real estate investment ideas for many years to come.

Kapplin and Schwartz examine the returns of two types of REITs, as well as that of Master Limited Partnerships (MLP), over the 1987–1989 time period. Their sample consisted of 54 real estate securities; they conclude that these entities did not provide an effective inflation hedge. MLP returns exceeded that of the overall stock market, but the two REIT types did not provide rates-of-return in excess of the marked.

An extensive review of the commercial real estate return literature is presented by Fletcher. He focuses upon studies that utilize commingled real estate fund (CREF) data. His detailed overview of the subject provides a much needed synthesis of the current literature.

Roulac presents an extensive discussion of the differences in the perspectives of individual versus institutional investors. In his essay, he considers such factors as scale, diversification, and related issues. Additionally, he examines a wide range of literature from within academia, as well as the opinions of various real estate gurus. He concludes that behavioral factors override economic considerations.

A very detailed review of the real estate investment performance literature is presented by Liu, Grissom, and Hartzell. Their paper examines the return premia earned by such real estate risk factors as inflation, illiquidity, thin trading, indivisibility, and market segmentation. They suggest that a CAPM world is compatible with real estate performance studies.

The impact of unbundling asset returns for portfolios containing both real estate assets and financial assets in examined by Webb and Rubens. Optimal portfolios are constructed and multiple sets of optimal portfolio allocations are examined to determine the sensitivity of the portfolios to unbundled asset return estimates.

In his empirical study, Williams investigates the portfolio effects of including properties with significantly different cash flow patterns. Utilizing pension fund data, he examines the impact of various income and reversion patterns upon the portfolio. He concludes that diversification by cash flow patterns can improve the performance of income property portfolios.

Leggett examines the risk premia for real property investments. He provides an overview of the relevant risk/return literature and discusses the theoretical liquidity risk premium necessary for real estate investments. His empirical analysis suggests that a sufficient risk premium does exist to compensate investors for the illiquidity and market segmentation present in most real estate investment.

The inflation hedging ability of farmland is examined by Rubens and Webb. They examine aggregate and individual state farmland returns during periods of inflation and periods of deflation. They conclude that farmland is an effective inflation hedge, but a very poor deflation hedge.

Glascock and Davidson's study is an analysis of the returns for 31 exchange-listed real estate companies, including 15 real estate investment trusts (REITs) during the 1977–1986 time period. These authors conclude that publicly traded real estate companies do not appear to provide unique inflation hedging returns.

Dotzour and Levi's tutorial on partitioning income property returns is a valuable teaching tool for a graduate real estate investments course, as well as for real estate investors to use in analyzing potential acquisitions. These authors review the literature on the various components of a property's rate-of-return and illustrate the marginal impact of each return component upon the internal rate-of-return.

Real estate researchers often use event study methodologies to analyze the impact of a variety of events upon real estate returns. Glascock and

Karafiath's paper contains an illustration of a useful dummy variable procedure that can aid in obtaining accurate event study results. They demonstrate how this technique can be employed for both calendar event studies and firm-specific event studies.

The co-editors thank the authors and the editorial review board for their contributions to this edition. Their hard work made this interesting and useful volume of new ideas in real estate investment possible.

This Volume is dedicated to Professor Jack H. Rubens (1956–1994). Jack was an excellent teacher, thoughtful scholar and a good friend. He will be missed by the Co-Editors and all his colleagues at the American Real Estate Society.

Arthur L. Schwartz, Jr.
University of South Florida
Steven D. Kapplin
University of South Florida

1 RECENT PERFORMANCE OF U.S. REAL ESTATE SECURITIES

Steven D. Kapplin and Arthur L. Schwartz, Jr.

Introduction

Investors can include real estate in a diversified portfolio in two ways. They can acquire direct investment in real property, or they can acquire a security backed by direct real estate investment. This paper examines the benefits of the latter—investment in real estate securities. Presently, there are four types of real estate securities: Real Estate Limited Partnerships (RELPs), Real Estate Investment Trusts (REITs), Finite Life REITs (FREITs), and Master Limited Partnerships (MLPs). This study examines only REITs, FREITs, and MLPs. Real Estate Limited Partnerships (RELPs) have been omitted from this study because RELPs are not publicly traded as are REITs, FREITs and MLPs (Kapplin and Schwartz, 1988a,b, 1989, 1986; Kensinger and Martin, 1986; *The Stanger Register*, 1989).

Numerous studies have examined the performance of real estate assets, including REITs, FREITs, and RELPs. However, the RELP studies were limited by available data to examining internal rates of return rather than monthly holding period returns. Further, those RELP studies did not analyze securities traded on public stock exchanges nor did they compare the performance of trusts and MLPs. Goebel and Kim analyzed the comparative performance of FREITs and REITs. Their study concluded that trusts under performed the market index over a study period extending from December 1983 through December 1987 and demonstrated little inflation hedging capability (Goebel and Kim, 1989).

For real estate securities to be reasonable substitutes for direct real estate investment, they should provide investment characteristics similar to those of direct investment. These characteristics are assumed to be: 1) competitive return/risk relationship; 2) hedge against inflation; 3) low correlations with the security market's returns over time. Although studies have examined these characteristics for MLPs, REITs, and FREITs separately, previous studies have not analyzed the comparative performance of REITs, FREITs, and MLPs. The purpose of this paper is to analyze the recent investment performance of the three publicly-traded real estate securities, MLPs, REITs, and FREITs, and to determine whether or not real estate securities' returns are uncorrelated with the stock market and provide a hedge against inflation. The study covers a time period of analysis from January 1987 through July 1989.

Our analysis confirms Goebel and Kim's findings that REITs and FREITs underperformed the market index over the study period. Further, we find that MLPs outperformed the market index during the study period and that none of the three real estate securities showed any evidence of inflation hedging ability. All three real estate securities evidenced low correlations with the market.

Institutional characteristics

REITs and FREITs invest in real estate activities and are similar to closed-end mutual funds. They differ principally in that FREITs provide for termination of the trust at the end of a period of time or in connection with a defined event. Whereas trusts may pass through only profits, limited partnerships have the advantage of being able to pass through both profits and losses to investors. Investors may hypothesize that MLPs provide higher expected returns than trusts because of the added current benefit of loss pass-throughs (Collins and Bey, 1986; Kensinger and Martin, 1986). On the other hand investors may prefer trusts because of expected higher current cash flow. Many MLPs have provided for guaranteed minimum returns to investors to enhance the MLP's desireability.[1]

Master limited partnerships

MLPs differ from ordinary limited partnership investments in that they are openly traded on major stock exchanges. This feature makes the MLP a significantly more liquid investment than the ordinary limited partnership.[2] Distributions may consist of cash flows, taxable income, or returns of capital. As with limited partnerships, all MLP income and capital losses or gains are passed through to the investor, where they are taxed at the investor's ordinary tax rate. Under the 1987 Tax Reform Act, most MLPs continued to be taxed as partnerships. However, MLPs which were actually operating companies rather than passive investment companies will be taxed as corporations beginning in 1997. MLPs are no longer as attractive a tax shelter vehicle, although they retain the benefit of having only one level of taxation, because MLP income or loss is considered as portfolio income or loss. Currently, liquidity is the MLP's primary benefit to the investor.

Real estate MLPs can be placed in three general categories based upon the origin of the partnership. A "roll-up" MLP is created by combining the partnership interests of several existing limited partnerships into a new MLP. In general, the roll-up is the least common type of real estate MLP. A number of roll-ups were created in 1989 in an effort to combat declining investor interest in real estate MLPs due to poor performance during the 1986–88 period. Unfortunately, real estate markets declined nationwide during the 1988–90 period, and interest in real estate MLPs continued to deline.

The "roll-out" MLP is a common type of real estate MLP. A roll-out MLP is the sale or transfer of existing corporate real estate to a master partnership sponsored by the corporation. The corporation receives either cash or MLP units in exchange for assets. If the company receives MLP interests in the exchange, it can sell the units via an underwritten offering. This type of transaction is often called a "carve-out." If the corporation elects to distribute the interests to its shareholders, the transaction is often called a "spin-off." There are several benefits to the corporate roll-out MLP sponsor. First, the corporation may be able to realize better value for its real estate assets while retaining control of the assets. Secondly, the roll-out could be used as a tactic for warding off corporate raiders. Thirdly, the corporation earns substantial fees for sponsoring the MLP. Investor benefits include the ownership of mature real estate assets with long term leases.

The third and most common type of real estate MLP is the roll-in. This term applies to corporate conversions to MLPs, as well as to new issues of MLPs to raise capital for the purchase of assets. Corporate conversions often lead to revaluing real estate assets which have low book values but high market values and avoid corporate income taxes. Additionally, the leading syndicators sponsor MLP initial offerings to raise funds to invest in mortgages or developed real estate.

MLPs are managed by the general partner who may hire an investment advisor, or the partner may provide that service him- or herself. The general partner usually receives fees associated with the acquisition of property for the portfolio, management fees associated with the daily operational requirements of partnership, and real estate brokerage commissions from the sale or acquisition of property. The general partner will also share in cash flows and capital gains.

Real estate investment trusts (and FREITs)

REITs were initially created under a 1960 amendment to the Internal Revenue Code.[3] At that time REITs could only be organized as an unincorporated business association. This requirement was amended in 1976. REITs are accorded beneficial tax treatment provided they meet certain requirements. The most significant ones are summarized below:

1. At least 95% of earnings must be distributed to shareholders.
2. At least 75% of assets must be in real estate, loans secured by real estate, shares in other REITs, government securities, and cash.
3. At least 75% of revenues must derive from rents, mortgage interest, and gains from selling real estate.
4. REITs must have at least 100 shareholders. Not more than 50% of outstanding shares may be held by five or fewer individual shareholders.
5. REITs must contract with outside professionals to carry on certain management activities. Property management must be delegated. Major decisions must be made by Board of Trustees, with operational decisions delegated to Trust Advisor or officers.
6. REITs cannot engage in speculative activities nor engage in short-term holding of real estate for quick profit.

If the REIT meets the distribution requirements along with the other qualifications, then income is passed through to investors, avoiding corporate tax. Although a REIT may shelter distributions through depreciation or other losses, it cannot pass net losses through to the shareholder, and net losses may only be carried forward. The tax treatment distinguishes the REIT from the MLP. Whereas a MLP may pass through both profits and losses, a REIT may only pass through profits. Otherwise, REITs and MLPs are quite similar. They both provide a marketable security, pooled investment in real estate, single taxation at the individual level, and limited liability. Of course, partnerships generally have a limited life, whereas REITs may have an unlimited life. However, the finite-life REIT (FREIT) is similar to the partnership in that it contains provisions for liquidation after a specified time period.

Typically, a REIT has a board of trustees responsible for major decisions. Day-to-day operations are delegated to the trust advisor and/or internal management. Trust advisors are independent contractors, but may be separate entities controlled by the REIT's sponsors. Trust advisors typically earn fees of 0.5 to 1.5% of invested assets. Property management must be delegated to an outside entity. However, the property manager may also be a subsidiary of either the sponsor or the advisor. Property managers are compensated on a percentage of gross revenue which can vary from 1 to 5%.

Data

Price and dividend data were collected for three portfolios of real estate securities. Samples consisted of 26 REITs, 15 MLPs, and 13 FREITs. The REITs and FREITs were selected from the *National Association of Real Estate Investment Trusts* (NAREIT) listings of currently active and trading REITs and FREITs. To be included, the securities had to have traded on one of the major exchanges (NYSE, AMEX, NASDAQ), had to have continuously traded over the study period of January 1, 1987 through July 1989, and their prices and dividends were available from Compuserve's *MicroQuote* database. NAREIT identified 171 REITS, of which 117 were qualified REITs during the study period.[4] Of the 117 qualified REITs, 92 had a continuous trading history during the study period. NAREIT identified 54 FREITs, all of which traded on the major exchanges. Of the 54 FREITs, only 30 qualified as a FREIT during the study period, due to continuous trading. The sample of MLPs was selected from the listing of 51 MLPs published in *The Stanger Register* for May 1989. Of the 51 MLPs listed, 33 had a continuous trading history over the study period. Thus, the sample sizes used in this study represent 28%, 24%, and 45% of the respective REIT, FREIT, and MLP populations which met the selection criteria.

In addition to the real estate securities, data were collected on the Standard and Poor's *500 Stock Index* (S&P 500), the *Consumer Price Index* (CPI), and 90-day Treasury Bill rates (T-Bills). Data were collected from Compuserve's *MicroQuote* database. A summary of the breakdown of each sample is appears in Table 1.

Limitations

The results of this study are subject to several limitations. First, the sample sizes are small. Sample sizes were constrained by the relatively few qualifying FREITs and MLPs that were in existence longer than three years at the time of this study. The small sample sizes also prevent grouping the securities based on their investment portfolios, e.g., equity versus mortgage. Second, the data were obtained from a public dial-up database, Compuserve *MicroQuote*, which maintains a database of prices and dividends on a substantial number of traded securities. However, not all of the real estate securities which are traded were in the MicroQuote database. Those securities not in the *MicroQuote* database had to be eliminated from eligibility. Third, the study uses monthly data. *MicroQuote*

Table 1. Sample Makeup

Trust type	*Real Estate Investment Trusts** *FREITs*	*REITs*
Equity	9	7
Mortgage	4	11
Hybrid	0	6
Total	13	24

*Real Estate Master Limited Partnerships*** *MLP Type*	
Equity:	6
Mixed Equity	3
Hotel/Motel	2
Restaurant	
Mortgage	4
Total	15

* *Source*: *REIT Facts*, National Association of Real Estate Investment Trusts.
** *Source*: *Stanger Register*, May 1989.

provides monthly prices and dividends, which are recorded on the last trading day of each month. Thus, the monthly periods extend from the first trading day of the month to the last trading day of the month. Fourth, some MLPs offered guaranteed minimum returns to investors. While it is not known whether the MLPs in our sample provided for guaranteed returns, the provision of guaranteed minimum returns would bias results. Finally, the time period of analysis is short. The short period of analysis is the result of several factors. Few FREITs and MLPs have been in existence long enough to develop portfolios of reasonable size. The difficulty of assessing the impact of the 1986 Tax Reform Act on the behavior of these securities caused the study to look at performance after the Tax Reform Act. Third, the time period of analysis spans the October 1987 stock market crash. The impact of the crash may significantly bias the results of the study. In an attempt to overcome that bias this paper analyzes the portfolios' performance subsequent to the crash. However, the time period is then limited to only 19 months. Therefore, the results of this study may be biased by the fact that the time period of analysis does not adequately reflect either historical or future performance (the volatility of and changes in the real estate market make it difficult to select an appropriate, recent time frame for study).

Methodology

This paper will test (1) whether real estate securities provide higher returns at lower risks than the stock market; (2) whether real estate securities provide a hedge against inflation; and (3) whether real estate securities are uncorrelated with the stock market.

The first question is answered by comparing the returns performance of the three real estate securities' portfolios. The comparisons were performed using both simple descriptive analyses and the market model. The descriptive analysis compares only the returns performance, but does not explicitly consider risk. The market model provides the framework for examining the risk-adjusted performance of the real estate securities. The *S&P 500 Stock Index* is used as the market index in the market model. Returns for the portfolios were computed as follows:

$$R_{pt} = \frac{(P_{pt} - P_{pt-1}) + D_{pt}}{P_{pt-1}}$$

where

R_{pt} = return on portfolio, p, in period t ($t = 1, 2, 3, \ldots, n$)

P_{pt} = price of portfolio, p, in period t
P_{pt-1} = price of portfolio, p, in previous period
D_{pt} = dividends for portfolio, p, in period t.

The resulting periodic returns are pretax.

The market model equation used is

$$R_{pt} = \alpha_p + \beta_p R_{mt} + \epsilon_p,$$

where
R_{pt} = monthly return of portfolio p, in period t
α_p = portfolio intercept
β_p = portfolio beta (regression coefficient)
R_{mt} = monthly return on the S&P 500 Index in period t
ϵ_p = portfolio error term.

The second question is answered by analyzing the correlation matrix of returns between the real estate portfolios and the CPI, where the CPI is used as the proxy measure for the rate of inflation. The last question is answered partly through the results of the market model analyses and partly by examining the correlation matrix of returns between the real estate portfolios and the market index.

Analysis and results

Tables 2 and 3 present the descriptive information on the three real estate portfolios and the S&P *500 Index*. Table 2 covers the full time period of analysis of 31 months from January 2, 1987 through July 31, 1989. Table 3 covers the time period from January 4, 1988 through July 31, 1989. The latter time period eliminates the 12 months of 1987, during which the October crash occured. MLPs had the highest mean monthly return, 1.435% per month. This was slightly higher than the S&P 500 and substantially higher than either REITs or FREITs. However, the standard deviations of returns differ substantially amongst the three securities and the market index. We used the coefficient of variation (CV) to provide a relative risk/return ranking.[5] MLPs provided the best risk/return performance of the three real estate securities and the S&P *500 Index* for the time period of analysis. The performance superiority of MLPs is evidenced in both the full time period of analysis and the limited time period. REITs and FREITs underperformed the S&P *500 Index* during the time period of analysis. The results of paired t-tests are reported in the notes

Table 2. Descriptive Statistics for Three Real Estate Portfolios and the S&P 500 Index (for period 1/2/87–7/31/89)

Asset	*Mean monthly return*	*Standard deviation*	*Coeff. of variation*	*Minimum*	*Maximum*
FREIT**	−0.418	4.987	−11.93	−10.225	12.964
MLP*	1.435	5.502	3.83	−13.232	19.351
REIT**	0.069	3.387	48.81	−11.364	7.778
S&P 500	1.346	6.031	4.48	−21.763	13.177

* A paired *t*-test showed that MLP returns were significantly higher than those of REITs and FREITs at the 0.05 level or better, but not significantly different from the S&P 500 return.

** A paired *t*-test showed that REIT and FREIT returns were significantly lower than the S&P 500 return at the 0.10 level or better.

Table 3. Descriptive Statistics for Three Real Estate Portfolios and the S&P 500 Index (for period 1/4/88–7/31/89)

Asset	*Mean monthly return*	*Standard deviation*	*Coeff. of variation*	*Minimum*	*Maximum*
FREIT**	0.067	4.674	69.66	−7.815	11.930
MLP*	2.271	3.693	1.63	−2.577	13.344
REIT**	0.430	2.336	5.44	−3.039	7.526
S&P 500	1.847	3.518	1.90	−3.860	8.837

* A paired *t*-test showed that MLP returns were significantly higher than those of REITs and FREITs at the 0.05 level or better, but not significantly different from the S&P 500 return.

** A paired *t*-test showed that REIT returns were significantly lower than the S&P 500 return at the 0.09 level, while FREIT returns were not significantly different than the S&P 500 return.

of Tables 2 and 3, respectively, for both time periods of analysis; they support the conclusion that MLPs significantly outperformed both REITs and FREITs, while REITs and FREITs underperformed the market as proxied by the S&P *500 Index*. MLP returns did not differ statistically from the S&P 500 return.

Tables 4 and 5 summarize the market model analyses for both time periods of analysis. For the full period of analysis, FREITs exhibited the least systematic risk, about 24% of the variation in return (total risk) as measured by the R^2, while REITs and MLPs exhibited systematic risk of

Table 4. Regression Results for Three Real Estate Portfolios on the S&P 500 Index for period 1/2/87–7/31/89 (*t*-statistics in parentheses)*

Portfolio	*Adjusted* R^2	α *Intercept*	β *Beta*	*DW test***
FREIT	0.238	−0.990 (1.234)	0.424 (3.221)	2.212
MLP	0.485	0.564 (0.776)	0.647 (5.410)	2.072
REIT	0.544	−0.496 (1.178)	0.420 (6.065)	1.651

* *t*-tests are all significant at the 0.003 level or better for 30 Degrees of Freedom.
** Not significant at the 0.05 level. There is no evidence of autocorrelation.

Table 5. Regression Results for Three Real Estate Portfolios on the S&P 500 Index for period 1/4/88–7/31/89 (*t*-statistics in parentheses)*

Portfolio	*Adjusted* R^2	α *Intercept*	β *Beta*	*DW test***
FREIT	0.024	−0.617 (0.513)	0.371 (1.197)	1.550
MLP	0.306	1.133 (1.413)	0.616 (2.987)	1.379
REIT	0.095	−0.037 (0.065)	0.253 (1.698)	1.193

* *t*-tests are significant at the 0.10 level or better for 18 degrees of freedom.
** Not significant at the 0.05 level. There is no evidence of autocorrelation.

about 50% of total risk. MLPs were the riskiest security in terms of beta, while REITs' and FREITs' betas were not statistically different.[6] Betas are significant at the 0.0001 level for MLPs and REITs, and significant at the 0.003 level for FREITs.

For the reduced period of analysis, the market model results are quite different from the period which included the October 1987 crash. FREITs and REITs exhibit very little systematic risk, less than 10% of total risk. MLP systematic risk is also less than that for the full period of analysis, dropping from nearly 50% of total risk to about 30% of total risk. Betas for all three securities are less than those for the full period. FREITs had the largest decline in beta from that of the full period of analysis. MLPs continued to exhibit a higher beta than the other two real estate securities, and this difference is statistically significant at the 0.05 level. Again, on a risk-adjusted basis, MLPs significantly outperformed FREITs and REITs. However, note that the beta for FREITs is not significant, while REITs' beta is significant at a 0.10 level. Beta for MLPs is significant at the 0.008 level.

Tables 6 and 7 contain the correlation matrices for the three real estate securities, the *S&P 500 Index*, the CPI, and the 90-day T-Bill rate. For the full period of analysis, the real estate securities exhibit little correlation with either the CPI or short-term interest rates. Short-term interest rates were negatively correlated with the real estate securities' returns. Similar results were obtained for the reduced time period of analysis where the correlation coefficients for the CPI and short-term interest rates were all negative. These results reject the assumption that real estate securities may provide a good hedge against inflation, at least in the short run.

The correlation of real estate securities' returns with the market index is mixed. During the full period of analysis MLPs and REITs exhibited correlation coefficients greater than 0.70, while the FREIT group was somewhat lower at 0.513. However, in the limited time period (post–October 1987 crash) the MLP group's correlation coefficient dropped to 0.587, and both REITs nor FREITs had correlation coefficients well below 0.50.

Table 6. Correlation Matrix of Returns on Three Real Estate Securities, S&P 500 Index, CPI, and 90-day T-Bill Rate for period 1/2/87–7/31/89

	FREIT	*MLP*	*REIT*	*S&P 500*	*CPI*	*T-Bill*
FREIT	1					
MLP	0.713	1				
REIT	0.701	0.807	1			
S&P 500	0.513	0.709	0.748	1		
CPI	0.209	0.077	0.002	0.086	1	
T-Bill	−0.163	−0.016	−0.110	0.104	0.152	1

Table 7. Correlation Matrix of Returns on Three Real Estate Securities, S&P 500 Index, CPI, and 90-day T-Bill Rate for period 1/4/88–7/31/89

	FREIT	*MLP*	*REIT*	*S&P 500*	*CPI*	*T-Bill*
FREIT	1					
MLP	0.456	1				
REIT	0.661	0.701	1			
S&P 500	0.279	0.587	0.381	1		
CPI	−0.011	−0.202	−0.041	−0.219	1	
T-Bill	−0.389	−0.244	−0.398	0.104	0.152	1

Summary and conclusions

The results of the study weakly suggest that only MLPs provided returns which outperformed the market index on a risk-adjusted basis over the time period of analysis. Neither REITs nor FREITs provided returns which exceeded or even approximated the market return. In addition, based on a comparison of coefficients of variation from Tables 2 and 3, both securities exhibited higher risk/return ratios (coefficients of variation) than the market or MLPs. Thus, we can conclude that only MLPs provided risk-adjusted returns which were competitive with the market index for the period of analysis.

For the full period of analysis only FREITs exhibited below average systematic risk (as measured by the R^2), while all three securities exhibit below average systematic risk during the period of analysis, which excluded 1987.[7] For the full period of analysis all three securities exhibit correlation coefficients above 0.50 with the S&P *500 Index*. However, for the reduced period, only MLPs exhibit a correlation coefficient above 0.50. We cannot conclude, based upon the evidence of this study, that real estate securities are uncorrelated with the stock market, and, hence, provide minimal diversification benefits. However, all three real estate securities exhibit betas less than 1.0.

Lastly, real estate securities exhibit little correlation with the rate of inflation, as proxied by the CPI, or with short term interest rates, as proxied by the 90-day T-Bill rate. This paper does not support an assumption that real estate securities provide a hedge against inflation. However, given the risk/return relationships demonstrated in this analysis, only MLPs appeared to be a good choice for inclusion in the investment portfolio during the study period. In a previous paper by Kapplin and Schwartz, MLPs were found to have outperformed the S&P *500 Index* during the period 1982–1986. (5) However, in that study, the portfolio size varied over the study period due to the few number of MLPs in operation prior to 1986. With reservations, this study provides continuing evidence that MLPs have provided better returns than the other two real estate securities over the study period. The performance advantage of MLPs appears to have been unaffected by the 1986 Tax Reform Act and the subsequent clarifications which appeared in 1987 and 1988.

It's difficult to explain why MLPs so outperformed REITs and FREITs during the study period given that MLPs suffered adverse public relations during the 1986–87 period. While information regarding the taxation of MLPs was still uncertain, MLPs lost favor with the market and performed poorly during that period such that one would have thought that REITs and FREITs would become preferred investments during this period. Unfortunately for investors, however, REITs and FREITs did not produce returns competitive with the market return during the study period.

Although the results of this study are constrained by the limited time period of analysis and small sample sizes, nevertheless, a picture emerges regarding the behavior of securitized real estate investment. This picture suggests that whatever special benefits real estate provides through direct investment in the hard asset, those benefits will not necessarily fall through to investors who purchase real estate by proxy through securitized investment vehicles such as investment trusts and limited partnerships. Furthermore, it appears that once real estate is securitized, risk/return performance becomes more dependent upon the behavior of securities' markets and less a function of the underlying assets in the securitized investment portfolio.

Notes

1. The 1986 Tax Reform Act diluted the tax sheltering benefits of loss pass-throughs from MLPs such that investors may no longer perceive a significant difference in the returns expected from either limited partnerships or trusts.

2. Because of the general partnership rules, the percentage of ownership traded in any one year must be kept below 50%. If more shares are traded in one year, the partnership is considered to be terminated for tax purposes. Although such an outcome is certainly a legal concern, it is not a practical concern, because the percentage of ownership available for public trade is usually much less than 50% of the MLP's total units.

3. *Internal Revenue Code*, Sections 856–860. Some provisions of the original rules were subsequently relaxed by §§ 661–669 of the Tax Reform Act of 1986.

4. The term "qualify" is here used to mean that the REIT or FREIT met Internal Revenue Service guidelines for qualifying as a real estate trust.

5. The coefficient of variation is computed as: $CV = \frac{\bar{S}}{\bar{X}}$. The CV provides a simple relative risk measure which may be used to rank investments having returns with different means and variances.

6. The difference in beta between FREITs and REITs had a *t*-statistic of 0.1252. However, the differences in betas between MLPs and FREITs and REITs had *t*-statistics of 4.699 and 7.733, respectively. These latter are significant at the 0.01 level.

7. Numerous studies have reported that most securities exhibit R^2s between 0.30 and 0.50.

References

Collins, J.M. and R.P. Bey. "The Master Limited Partnership: An Alternative to the Corporation." *Financial Management* (Winter 1986).

Goebel, P.R. and K.S. Kim. "Performance Evaluation of Finite-Life Real Estate Investment Trusts." *Journal of Real Estate Research* (Summer 1989).

Kapplin, S.D. and A.L. Schwartz, Jr. "Public Real Estate Limited Partnership Returns: A Preliminary Comparison with Other Investments." *Journal of American Real Estate and Urban Economics Association* (Spring 1988a).

Kapplin, S.D. and A.L. Schwartz, Jr. "A Preliminary Analysis of the Risk and Return Aspects of Real Estate Master Limited Partnerships." Unpublished paper presented at the annual meetings of the *American Real Estate Society* (April 1989).

Kapplin, S.D. and A.L. Schwartz, Jr. "Real Estate Investing Through Master Limited Partnerships." *American Association of Individual Investors* (September 1988b).

Kapplin, S.D. and A.L. Schwartz, Jr. "Investing in Real Estate Limited Partnerships." *American Association of Individual Investors* (September 1986).

Kensinger, J.W. and J.D. Martin. "Royalty Trusts, Master Partnerships and Other Organizational Means of 'Unfirming the Firm.'" *Midland Corporate Finance Journal* (Summer 1986).

Rogers, R.C. and J.E. Owers. "The Investment Performance of Real Estate Limited Partnerships." *American Real Estate and Urban Economics Journal* (Summer 1985).

The Stanger Register. Public Partnership Market Focus, September 1989, p. 18.

2 COMMERCIAL REAL ESTATE INVESTMENTS AND RETURNS: A REVIEW OF THE LITERATURE USING CREF DATA

Stuart Fletcher

Introduction

In the past decade, empirical studies of multimarket investments in commercial real estate have typically relied on data taken either from real estate investment trusts or commingled real estate funds (CREFs). In this review, the findings of studies using the latter, CREF data, are briefly summarized.

Commingled, or pooled, real estate funds are group ownership vehicles originated by insurance companies, large commercial banks, and real estate investment companies for pension fund investment in real estate. CREFs allow the tax-exempt pension funds to invest in diversified portfolios of real estate without incurring the responsibilities of managing the individual properties.

Many of the CREF studies are based on properties included in the *NCREIF/FRC Property Index* database, which is jointly maintained by the National Council of Real Estate Investment Fiduciaries and the Frank Russell Company. A few studies have merely used data taken from one or, perhaps, two CREF portfolios, while others have used CREF-specific data from as many as 20 different CREFs.

Studies relevant to returns on tax-exempt CREF investments fall into three major categories: (1) those of real estate returns versus returns on other asset classes such as stocks and bonds; (2) those of returns on individual properties within CREF portfolios; and (3) those of returns on CREFs.

The review is split into separate sections for each of the aforementioned categories, with general findings on real estate returns, as well as specific observations on CREF returns versus other assets, being included in the first section. The second section discusses CREF property indexes and the findings of property-specific studies using CREF data; the third section reviews what little data is available and what little research has been done on CREFs themselves.

Historical returns on real estate versus other assets

The literature on empirical examinations of real estate returns versus returns on other mediums of investment is comprehensively and thoroughly reviewed in a survey article by Sirmans and Sirmans (1987). In this article, the authors find mixed results on the relative performance of equity real estate investments versus other asset classes.

The authors point out that one of the major difficulties experienced by others in comparing real estate returns to returns on other assets is the complexity of making risk adjustments on equity real estate returns. The types of risk adjustments that have been previously used may be insufficient to make equity real estate directly comparable to stocks and bonds, due to measurement errors in real estate returns.

Specifically, many of the data sets used for calculating real estate returns are based on appraised values rather than market values. Also, returns based on actual real estate sales do not reflect the illiquidity of real estate relative to other asset classes. As a result, there is little consensus among authors of previous studies as to the relative risk of real estate in comparison to that of stocks and bonds.

There appears to be some consensus, however, on the relative qualities of real estate as an inflation hedge. Not only is real estate typically found to be a superior hedge against actual inflation when compared to stocks and bonds, but it is also found in some studies to be an effective hedge against unexpected inflation as well. Furthermore, returns on stocks and bonds are typically found to have relatively low or negative correlations with inflation. It is for these key reasons that CREFs have become an important consideration for the pension fund portfolio.

An earlier survey article by Zerbst and Cambon (1984) reviews and summarizes the results of over a dozen studies that focused on the historical return rates on real estate as well as the performance of real estate assets in diversified portfolios of alternative assets. Zerbst and Cambon also add their own analysis of returns on CREFs to the review. They find that the return results for pooled funds are quite similar to previously reported results for other mediums of equity real estate investment. The authors reach the following general conclusions on the basis of their analysis and their interapretations of the results of previous studies:

1. the real rate of return on equity real estate has averaged from 4 1/2% to 6% annually for holding periods of five years and longer over the past thirty years;
2. there is a low correlation between the returns on equity real estate and stocks; and
3. based on the two above observatiuons, real estate is an important medium of investment that should be seriously considered for institutional portfolio diversification.

A study by Brueggeman, Chen, and Thibodeau (1984), which also examines the gains from diversification of the traditional institutional portfolio by adding equity real estate, focuses specifically on CREFs. They investigate CREF returns from 1972 through 1983 to determine the inflation-hedging attributes that pooled funds provide to the traditional pension fund portfolio of stocks and bonds.

They estimate three alternative specifications of regression models that use market levels of returns, inflation, and Gross National Product as explanatory variables for excess returns. Using the returns on two of the oldest and largest CREFs, they find the risk-adjusted return performance of the two pooled funds to be most superior to the performance of highly diversified stock and bond indexes in an inflationary environment. They also find that the addition of these funds to porfolios of stock and bond indexes consistently reduces overall portfolio risk while increasing overall portfolio return. These findings are consistent with previously discussed results on the benefits of using equity real estate to diversify the traditional stock and bond portfolio.

Criticisms of this study include the use of quarterly data (rather than annual data), which may be affected by the frequency and timing of appraisals within each pooled fund, and the underspecification of the various returns models that are tested.

None of the studies that have been published to date has concluded that equity real estate should not be an integral part of the institutional portfolio. In fact, empirical results of more recent studies indicate that more than 20% of the total mixed-asset portfolio should be invested in equity real estate if risk-adjusted portfolio return is to be maximized.

For example, studies such as those by Webb, Curcio, and Rubens (1988) and Firstenburg, Ross, and Zisler (1988), which specifically examine and identify several "efficient combinations" of stocks, bonds, and equity real estate assets, imply that equity real estate should be at least one-third of the total value of the mixed-asset portfolio, as weighted by asset class in the institutional portfolio. "Efficient combinations" or "efficient portfolios" are nothing more than combinations of assets in a portfolio that maximize risk-adjusted portfolio return.

The two studies each use historical returns on CREF investments (as well as returns on other types of real estate) in combination with historical returns on stocks and bonds in making their findings. Criticisms of this type of approach focus primarily on the construction of mixed-asset portfolios of real estate with other mediums of investment.

Specific concerns involve the use of appraised values for real estate returns combined with the use of market value returns for stocks and bonds. Also, alternative investments other than real estate, such as foreign stocks and bonds, are not included in the porfolios formed in these studies. Finally, differences in liquidity between real estate and stocks and bonds make this approach questionable, as well. "Within real estate" portfolio combinations that include real estate assets only are less subject to these criticisms, since the assets that are combined into portfolios are relatively more homogeneous than portfolios of mixed-asset classes.

CREF property indexes and property-specific studies

The most widely used index on equity real estate that reflects historical returns on various types of commercial real estate is the *NCREIF/FRC Property Index*[1], which was created in 1980 by the Frank Russell Company and the National Council of Real Estate Investment Fiduciaries. Though it originally included less than 250 properties, it is now made up of over 1200 properties selected from actual portfolios of participating CREFs. There are more than three dozen different participating pooled fund managers, each of whom contributes information on a quarterly basis for the properties in the index.

The *NCREIF/FRC Property Index* was created to be used both as a benchmark of historical rates of return for comparison to actual fund performance and to provide returns information on subcategories, based on property characterisitics, within the index. The broad index and its subindices provide rates of return on the aggregated portfolio of properties from the first quarter of 1978 to the present on a quarterly basis.

The subindices in the *NCREIF/FRC Property Index* are based on property type and property location. As is the case with the aggregated index, return rates for the categories within each of these subindices are also calculated on a quarterly basis. The original property type subindex is split into five descriptive categories, namely, retail, industrial, apartments, office buildings, and hotels. The original property location subindex is divided into the East, West, Midwest, and South regions of the country, along the lines of the four census regions. Total return rates on all of the categories are also split into income return and appreciation return, so that the relative impacts of these two components of total return can be separately evaluated.

One of the major criticisms of the *NCREIF/FRC Index* is that the included properties' values are all based on appraisals. Once a property is sold, it falls out of the index, and, furthermore, the actual selling price of the property is never reflected in the index.

Other criticisms focus on the dominance of a small number of participating funds in its earlier years (in terms of the number of properties they contribute to the index) and the continuous changes in the size and the makeup of the index. For example, at one time, over a quarter of the value of the index was made up of properties from a single CREF (the Prudential Insurance PRISA I CREF). Also, as previously mentioned, the original *NCREIF/FRC Index* contained less than 250 properties, while it is now made up of over 1000 properties. Although the index is now more broadly represented by a larger number of CREFs and properties than in the past, studies using the historical returns on the index and its subcategories should be viewed with caution due to the many changes in the index over time.

Standard & Poor's Corporation has also introduced a real estate index. The S&P *National Real Estate Index*, which was developed by Richard Wollack of the Liquidity Fund and then sold to Standard & Poor's, differs from the *NCREIF/FRC Property Index* in that it is based on samples of actual sales of commercial real estate from around the country. This index has been criticized for not being statistically meaningful, however, due to the small number and unrepresentative types of property sales that make up each quarterly calculation (Lowenstein, 1988).

Many studies have used historical property-specific returns data bases to analyze real estate investments made by pooled fund sponsors. For example, the Firstenburg, Ross, and Zisler (1988) study mentioned above makes use of the *NCREIF/FRC Property Index* and its subcategories from 1978 through 1985 to construct efficient portfolio combinations. They first use the subcategories of property location and type to construct efficient real estate portfolios, and they then use the aggregated *NCREIF/FRC Index* to form efficient combinations of stocks, bonds, and real estate.

As previously mentioned, efficient combinations are those combinations of assets in a portfolio that maximize risk-adjusted portfolio return. The manner in which efficient combinations are found is by creating all possible combinations of portfolios and plotting them on a graph using "return" on the vertical axis and "risk" on the horizontal axis. For each possible level of return, there will be a unique portfolio, or combination of assets, that minimizes risk, as measured by the standard deviation of return. The border that connects the many efficient combinations, or portfolios, across different rates of return is referred to as the efficient frontier. The dominant region of the efficient frontier is that region which maximizes return while minimizing risk.

In their analysis of diversification by geographic location, Firstenburg, Ross, and Zisler find that both the "East only" and "Midwest only" nondiversified portfolios fall on the efficient frontier, although the "Midwest only" portfolio is not on the dominant region where return is maximized for a given level of risk. Both the "South only" and "West only" portfolios, on the other hand, are clearly inferior in terms of risk-adjusted return over the same period, with the "South only" being farthest from the efficient frontier.

They also construct portfolios diversified by property type and find that "hotel only" and "industrial only" portfolios lie on the dominant region of the efficient frontier. "Apartments only" lies just beneath the dominant region of the efficient frontier and "retail only" lies on the frontier, but not on the return-maximizing dominant region. The "office only" portfolio is the least favorable of the individual property type portfolios on the basis of its being farthest in distance from the efficient frontier.

Several important observations can be made from the results of their study. First, little, if any, diversification across the broad categories of either property type or property location is necessary in order to maximize risk-adjusted portfolio return, since some of the region- or type-specific portfolios lie on the dominant region of the efficient frontier. Alternatively, many of the real estate portfolio combinations that are highly diversified across property type or region also maximize return while minimizing risk. Also, over the 1978 to 1985 sample period, the East was clearly the most favorable region of the country for real estate investing in terms of risk-adjusted return, and offices appeared to be the least favorable type of property in which to invest on the basis of historical returns. These latter observations, of course, are time-specific, and do not imply that future returns will be similarly determined.

Other earlier studies of returns on equity real estate also make use of individual property samples taken from pooled funds to construct real estate portfolios instead of utilizing the actual portfolio returns themselves. For example, two articles examining individual characteristics of properties held by a single CREF were published by Miles and McCue (1984a,b) to examine the benefits of diversifying within the pooled fund portfolio. In one of the papers (in the *Journal of Financial Research*), the authors focus on the number and type of properties needed in a real estate portfolio to diversify away unsystematic, or nonmarket, risk. In the other study (in the *AREUEA Journal*), they further examine the benefits of diversification by property type and location, as well as by lease structure.

In the former article, they examine the variation of return rates on different size portfolios of individual properties. They find real estate assets to have relatively low levels of systematic risk as compared to other asset classes such as stocks and bonds, suggesting that the benefits of diversifying within real estate portfolios are quite large relative to other mediums of investment. They also find that the gains from naive diversification within real estate portfolios may be just as great as from diversifying by type or region. This is due to relatively low systematic risk levels across and within these subgroups and to the nonhomogeneous nature of real estate investments. In terms of the gains from using real estate as a portfolio diversifier, they observe that real estate returns have low correlations with returns on stocks and bonds, yet are highly correlated with inflation.

In the latter article, the authors create subsamples of properties on the basis of similar property type and location characteristics, and they analyze the return distributions of the subsamples. They draw conclusions similar to those made in their first paper, in terms of the benefits of diversifying within a single category. They point out, however, that their "within real estate fund" findings may, in part, reflect uncontrolled differences and similarities between lease structures, yet they are unable to demonstrate the degree of influence that lease terms have on returns due to the lack of more detailed lease information. They conclude, and stress quite heavily, that the broad definitions of property type, location, and lease structure used in the sample fund's reports are too general to be of use for "within fund" portfolio diversification purposes.

Additional findings not discussed in the previous paper focus on the usefulness of real estate as a hedge against unanticipated inflation. Specifically, Miles and McCue examine correlations between property returns and inflation and find that their fund-specific real estate returns are highly correlated with actual and anticipated inflation, but not with unanticipated inflation. These findings are consistent with the results of most previous studies on equity real estate returns.

In a more recent article, Hartzell, Hekman, and Miles (1987) use a returns model similar to that used by Brueggeman, Chen, and Thibodeau (1984) to examine the inflation protection offered by different types of real estate in the portfolio. The sample of properties analysed in their study is taken from the same single pooled fund as was used in the Miles and McCue studies, but the period of analysis is from 1973 to 1983. Using portfolio returns constructed from this data base, they conclude that real estate is a good hedge against both expected and unexpected inflation, the one exception being that industrial properties do not clearly provide a hedge against unexpected inflation.

They attribute the fact that their findings are different from those of prior studies to their use of a longer sample period and, in part, to shortcomings of previous efforts. Specifically, they criticize the study by Brueggeman, Chen, and Thibodeau (1984), because pooled fund returns, and not property returns, were used as proxies for actual returns on real estate in that study. They criticize Miles and McCue (1984a) for using annual inflation rates and quarterly property return rates to analyze the relationship between inflation and real estate.

An earlier paper by Hartzell, Hekman, and Miles (1986) is aimed at finding additional characteristics other than location and property type that describe the returns and diversification benefits of commercial real estate. In this paper, which uses the same database as their inflation study discussed above, they examine property size, lease duration, and SMSA population growth as possible factors that influence return and diversification benefits. They employ a methodology similar to that of Miles and McCue (1984a) in that they construct subsamples of properties on the basis of similar property characteristics and analyze the return distributions of the subsamples. They also examine correlations of returns within their categories of property characteristics to returns on stocks and bonds.

Regardless of the subsample of real etate used (i.e., all large properties versus all small properties, all long-lease maturities versus all short-lease maturities, and all fast SMSA growth rates versus all slow SMSA growth rates), they find that stock and bond portfolios can benefit from the addition of any of the various combinationos of real properties, These benefits are both in terms of risk-adjusted return on the overall mixed-asset portfolio and in terms of protection against actual inflation.

After surmizing that the inclusion of virtually any type of equity real estate in the traditional institutional stock and bond portfolio is beneficial, they then examine the benefits of diversifying within the real estate portfolio itself. They find little advantage in diversifying across either property type or location, and they conclude that diversifying in this manner is little more than naive diversification. This particular finding is consistent with previously discussed results.

In terms of mean returns and diversification characteristics based on property size, they observe that properties of greater than $20 million in value tended to outperform those properties with values of between $1 million and $20 million. The smallest properties with values of less than $1 million appeared to do well, too, relative to midsized properties. Upon further examination, however, the statistics revealed the superior performance of small properties to be driven by outliers, since the mean quarterly return rates on the smallest properties exceeded the median quarterly rates of return by more than 2%.

In comparing properties located in areas with fast versus slow SMSA growth rates, they find that the slow growth areas outperformed the fast growth areas over the sample period, but not necessarily on a risk-adjusted basis. They also find the correlation of returns between fast-growth and slow-growth areas to be low, suggesting that diversification across growth rates would be beneficial.

Comparisons of returns on properties on the basis of lease maturities were inconclusive. The authors state that this latter finding may be due to the many lease characteristics other than maturity, such as escalator clauses and expense stops, that are not reflected in their study. In conclusion, Hartzell, Hekman, and Miles suggest that more precise subcategories of real estate should be developed so that truly scientific diversification within portfolios of equity real estate propertiess can be accomplished.

As a result of articles stressing greater need for precision in describing differences among properties, many recent papers have focused on establishing more narrowly defined and more meaningful subcategories of commercial real estate based on economic classification rather than upon grouping by broad regional similarities. Also, more distinct definitions of property type, such as downtown office versus suburban office, have been suggested.

Examples of these studies include a paper by Hartzell, Shulman, and Wurtzebach (1987), which suggests that the United States be divided into eight distinct regions on the basis of similarities in economic activity within each region, and an article by Cole, Guilkey, Miles, and Webb (1989), which offers ten different intuitive subcategories of real estate that are simultaneously based on location, type, size, and economic similarities.

The results of both of these articles clearly demonstrate that a number of improvements can be made over the traditional classifications of equity real estate used in previous studies. Unfortunately, however, most publicly available databases remain organized by the broadly defined property type and location characteristics discussed earlier.

Theoretical and empirical papers examining the potential for error or bias in appraisal-based returns series on CREF properties are numerous and are not covered in this review.[2] Those studies examining the differences between appraised values of individual properties in pooled funds and their actual selling prices have not found any long-term evidence of systematic positive or negative bias in appraisal-based returns in the aggregate. They have, however, found substantial differences between appraisals and selling prices on individual CREF properties; they have also consistently found appraisal-based returns series on CREF properties to be far smoother over time than transactions-based returns.

In terms of appraisal accuracy, acceptable tolerance levels concerning their accuracy have not been established within the CREF industry. In practice, it would be very difficult to assess the accuracy of an appraisal without the sale of the property. However, a recent study by Guilkey, Miles, and Cole (1989) suggests that there are selling motives for properties that have sold which would bring into question straight comparisons of sales prices to appraised values. Furthermore, this study implies that there is potential for bias in transactions-based returns on CREF properties.

CREF fund-specific data and studies

The "Diversified Edition" of *Real Estate Profiles*, which is published quarterly by Evaluation Associates, Inc., or EAI, includes a wealth of information on diversified CREFs. Aggregate fund portfolio characteristics and historical returns data are covered in each report. There are 20 to 25 funds that have appeared in each of the reports since 1983.

The data set provides general information on numerous characteristics of the properties within each fund, such as property type and property location. Also included is a wealth of information on the characteristics of the open-end pooled fund itself, such as the fund's net asset value and its total asset value, the total number of properties and the total number of investors in each fund, and the percentage of the fund that is not invested in pure equity real estate such as cash reserves, real estate stocks, and hybrid equity mortagages.

A relative newcomer to CREF returns measurement is the Lowry Real Estate Fund Indexes. There are three indexes, two of which track returns on open-end and closed-end CREFs separately, and then a third that combines the weighted average results of the two types of funds into a broader measure of CREF performance. The Lowry Indexes appear on a quarterly basis in *Pension World* magazine.

Although these benchmark indexes first appeared in January 1989, they reflect returns data from the beginning of 1983 to the present. A comparison of the measures indicates that closed-end CREFs averaged a 2% higher annualized return than their open-end counterparts over the six-year period. The creators of the indexes, Michael Oliphant and John Corgel (1989), speculate that this difference in return may be due in part to the fact that closed-end CREFs use relatively greater leverage, are relatively less liquid, and are made up of fewer and larger properties on average than open-end CREFs.

These general differences between the two types of funds are averaged out in the combined fund, which places equal weighting on each of eight open-end and five closed-end fund managers. One serious drawback to the combined fund index, however, is that it measures the performance of a total of only thirteen open-end and closed-end fund managers; thus, its usefulness (as well as the usefulness of the "open-end only" and "closed-end only" indexes) as a reliable industry benchmark may be questioned due to its sample size. Also, the combined index reflects returns on both liquid and illiquid real estate investments, since closed-end CREF participation lasts for the duration of the existence of the closed-end fund.

The same originators of the Lowry Indexes, John Corgel and Michael Oliphant, recently published a paper on the benefits of diversifying across managers of CREFs (1989). They used quarterly returns on ten large, diversified open-end CREFs over the period from 1983 through 1987 to construct four different efficient portfolios of funds at various levels of risk and return.

The four efficient portfolios that they presented, with annual returns of 9, 10, 11, 12% and standard deviations of return of 1.01%, 1.13%, 1.39%, and 1.99%, respectively, each had at least three, and up to as many as six, different funds in them. The authors concluded, therefore, that portfolio diverification across CREFs is truly beneficial, since multifund portfolios outperformed all of the single funds on a risk-adjusted returns basis.

The authors attributed the benefits of diversifying across funds to differences in managment style, although they provided no evidence of any actual measures of style differences. They did, at least, offer half a dozen potential reasons why managers may not act in a similar fashion. Examples of these difficult to quantify hypothesized differences include research abilities and specialization skills, property management arrangements, and buying, selling, and financing policies.

Yet another reason for diversifying across CREFs, which was not discussed in this particular study, would be the reduction of liquidity risk for investors in pooled funds. This risk reduction would result not only from differences in liquidity among funds, but also from smaller withdrawal requests being made from any one fund in the case of investor liquidation of positions held in CREFs.

The only published empirical study that deals specifically with the relationship between return rates and fund-specific portfolio characteristics of CREFs was done by Mike Miles and Arthur Esty (1982). They analyzed fund-specific and aggregated property-specific data from published quarterly reports on 20 open-end pooled equity real estate funds as of year-end 1979.

The authors hypothesized that fund investment return was a function of the following five factors: the size of the fund; the age of the fund; and the type, location, and size of the properties within each fund's portfolio. Using year-end fund statistics as the explantory variables in a rank bivariate correlation analysis, they reached the following general conclusions:

1. returns are positively significantly correlated with both size and age of the fund;
2. returns are positively significantly correlated with the percentage of a fund's portfolio invested in the West, and negatively, but less significantly, correlated with the percentage of a fund's portfolio invested in the South;
3. returns are negatively correlated with the percentage of a fund's portfolio invested in properties under \$2 ½ million in value, and positively significantly correlated with the percentage invested in properties over \$5 million in value;
4. returns are positively correlated with the percentage of a fund's portfolio invested in industrial and retail properties, and negatively correlated with the percentage invested in office buildings; and
5. the size of a fund is positively significantly correlated with the value of the properties that it is invested in. (Relatively large funds typically hold relatively large properties.)

One drawback to the Miles and Esty study is that it is based on a single year of returns data. Thus, there is little likelihood that observations made on the basis of one year of returns will indicate future relationships between returns and portfolio characteristics, unless those observed relationships remain constant over time. Other admitted weaknesses of the study are the relative "newness" of many of the funds (since the sample period was 1979) and the fact that the two largest funds in their sample held more real estate assets than the remaining 18 funds combined.

A study by Fletcher (1993) examines the return rates and portfolio characteristics of 18 CREFs from 1983 through 1988 using regression analysis and paired comparisons of portfolios of CREFs. The most significant observation made in terms of property characteristics and return rates is that the size of the real estate investment was found to be strongly positively related to both appreciation and total return over the sample period. In terms of property type and location, it was found that the East was the most profitable region, and that offices were the least profitable type of real estate over the sample period.

Other specific conclusions from the empirical analysis are in regard to the many relationships between returns and various fund-specific characteristics. The level of cash balances within a pooled fund's portfolio was found to be positively related to total return, and the use of leverage by CREFs was found to be beneficial only when nominal return on the pooled funds was relatively high as compared to interest rates on mortgages. Fees charged by fund managers were found to be inversely related to return over the sample period, suggesting that managers may use high fees to compensate for poor performance. Finally, the size of the CREF was found to be negatively related to return over the sample period. This finding is opposite to findings in earlier studies, suggesting previously unobserved cyclical performance for pooled funds.

Conclusions

With regard to the major findings relating to equity real estate returns versus returns on other assets, real estate is virtually always found to have low or negative correlation of return with stocks and bonds and high correlation of return with actual inflation, thus, making its inclusion in the institutional portfolio very advantageous in terms of overall diversification benefits. However, real estate has sometimes, but not always, been found to be a good hedge against unanticipated inflation, depending on the method of analysis and the time period examined.

Examinations of real estate returns and property-specific characteristics indicate that property diversification "within real estate" by traditional subcategories, such as property type and location, amounts to little more than naive diversification, because the definitions of region and type are too broad to be of much use in constructing scientifically diversified portfolios. In fact, evidence suggests that property diversification across subcategories may, in some instances, be completely ineffective, while diversification within a particular subcategory may occasionally be very beneficial.

An example of this apparent contradiction can be seen upon examination of recent historical returns on properties in Denver and Los Angeles, which are included in the West region, and Houston, which is in the South. It has been highly publicized that typical returns on properties in both Denver and Houston were negatively affected in the first half of the 1980s, since both their economies were sensitive to falling oil prices. As a result, diversifying across these two regions in this manner alone would have been highly unsuccessful. A more satisfying real estate portfolio strategy would have been to diversify within the West region by investing in both Denver and Los Angeles, since prices in the latter local market were relatively insensitive to falling oil prices.

Nonetheless, in spite of the demonstrated need for newer, more narrowly defined subcategories of properties, it is possible to make a few generalizations on the basis of historical returns within existing subcategories of real estate over certain time periods. Specifically, studies of recent historical returns on property subcategories within pooled funds indicate that the Eastern region of the United States had the highest total rates of return among the four property locations until the late 1980s, and office buildings have had the lowest total return rates among the major property types. Also, the largest properties within CREFs, with values of at least $20 million, have tended to outperform midsized properties over the 1980s.

Of course, the observed temporal reltionships would not be expected to continue into the distant future. In fact, a more logical prediction under the assumption of efficient markets would be that previously observed relationships between commercial real estate investments and return rates would not continue. As investors seeking higher returns bid prices up (and yields down) on those investments yielding greater than average risk-adjusted rates of return, the returns on all investments should tend toward the mean.

Finally, it is quite likely that studies other than those discussed above have been undertaken by private consultants and by research department staff within firms that manage and/or invest in CREFs. It is also likely that such studies may have empirically investigated the relationships between commercial real estate investments by CREFs and the returns on those investments. Unforunately, it may also be the case that the results of these studies, if they do, indeed, exist, will never be made available to the public due to their proprietary nature.

Notes

1. The index is also referred to as the *Russell/NCREIF Index.*
2. See, for example, Cole, Guilkey, and Miles (1986, 1987); Giliberto (1988); Geltner (1989), (1990); Wheaton and Torto (1989); Gau and Wang (1990); Miles, Cole, and Guilkey (1990); and Fletcher and Diskin (1994).

References

Brueggeman, W.B., A.H. Chen, and T.G. Thibodeau. "Real Estate Investment Funds: Performance and Portfolio Considerations." *AREUEA Journal* 12 (1984), 333–354.

Cole, Rebel, David Guilkey, and Mike Miles. "Toward an Assessment of the Reliability of Commercial Appraisals." *The Appraisal Journal* 54 (1986), 422–432.

Cole, Rebel, David Guilkey, and Mike Miles. "Pension Fund Investment Managers' Unit Values Deserve Confidence." *Real Estate Review* 17 (1987), 84–89.

Cole, Rebel, David Guilkey, Mike Miles, and Brian Webb. "More Scientific Diversification Strategies for Commercial Real Estate." *Real Estate Review* 19 (1989), 59–66.

Corgel, John B. and Michael L. Oliphant. "Multifund Real Estate Strategy for Pension Funds." *Real Estate Review* 19 (1989), 67–70.

Firstenburg, Paul B., Stephen A. Ross, and Randall C. Zisler. "Real Estate: The Whole Story." *Journal of Portfolio Management* 14 (1988), 22–34.

Firstenburg, Paul B. and Charles H. Wurtzebach. "Managing Portfolio Risk and Reward." *Real Estate Review* 19 (1989), 61–65.

Fletcher, Stuart. "Portfolio Considerations in Commingled Real Estate Funds. *Journal of Real Estate Research* 8 (1993), 171–187.

Fletcher, Stuart and Barry A. Diskin. "Agency Relationships in Appraising for Institutional Assset Managers." *The Appraisal Journal* (1994), 103–112.

Gau, George W. Ko Wang. "A Further Examination of Appraisal Data and the Potential Bias in Real Estate Return Indexes." *AREUEA Journal* 18 (1990), 41–48.

Geltner, David. (1989). "Estimating Real Estate's Systematic Risk from Aggregate Level Appraisal-based Returns." *AREUEA Journal* 17 (1989), 463–481.

Giliberto, S. Michael. "A Note on the Use of Appraisal Data Indexes of Performance Measurement." *AREVEA Journal* 16 (1988), 77–83.

Guilkey, David, Mike Miles, and Rebel Cole. "The Motivation for Institutional Real Estate Sales and Implications for Asset Class Returns." *AREUEA Journal* 17 (1989), 70–86.

Hartzell, David, John Hekman, and Mike Miles. "Diversification Categories in Investment Real Estate." *AREUEA Journal* 14 (1986), 230–254.

Hartzell, David, John Hekman, and Mike Miles. "Real Estate Returns and Inflation." *AREUEA Journal* 15 (1987), 617–637.

Hartzell, David J., David G. Shulman, and Charles H. Wurtzebach. "Refining the Analysis of Regional Diversification for Income-producing Real Estate." *Journal of Real Estate Research* 2 (1987), 85–96.

Lowenstein, Roger. "The S&P Guide to Real Estate Investing: Index, Index, Index." *The Wall Street Journal* (November 8, 1988), p. 214, Cl.

Miles, Mike, Rebel Cole, and Guilkey David. "A Different Look at Commercial Real Estate Returns." *AREUEA Journal* 18 (1990), 403–430.

Miles, Mike and Arthur Esty. "How Well Do Commingled Real Estate Funds Perform?" *The Journal of Portfolio Management* 8 (1982), 62–68.

Miles, Mike and Tom McCue. "Historic Returns and Institutional Real Estate Portfolios." *AREUEA Journal* 10 (1982), 184–199.

Miles, Mike and Tom McCue. "Commercial Real Estate Returns." *AREUEA Journal* 12 (1984a), 355–377.

Miles, Mike and Tom McCue. "Diversification in the Real Estate Portfolio." *Journal of Financial Research* 7 (1984b), 57–68.

NCREIF Report. Washington, DC: The National Council of Real Estate Investment Fiduciaries and the Frank Russell Company.

Oliphant, Michael L. and John B. Corgel. "Real Estate Index Measures Performance of Open, Closed Funds." *Pension World* 25 (January 1989).

Real Estate Profiles. Diversified edition. Westport, CT: Evaluation Associates.

Sirmans, G. Stacy and C.F. Sirmans. "The Historical Perspective of Real Estate Returns." *Journal of Portfolio Managment* 13 (Spring 1987), 22–31.

Webb, James R., Richard J. Curcio, and Jack H. Rubens. "Diversifications Gains from Including Real Estate in Mixed-Asset Portfolios." *Decision Sciences* 19 (Spring 1988), 434–452.

Webb, James R. and Jack H. Rubens "How Much in Real Estate? A Surprising Answer." *Journal of Portfolio Management* 13 (Spring 1987), 10–14.

Wheaton, William C. and Raymond G. Torto. "Income and Appraised Values: A Reexamination of the FRC Returns Data." *AREUEA Journal* 17 (1989), 439–449.

Zerbst, Robert H. and Barbara R. Cambon. "Historical Returns on Real Estate Investment." *Journal of Portfolio Management* 10 (Spring 1984), 5–20.

3 IMPLICATIONS OF INDIVIDUAL VERSUS INSTITUTIONAL REAL ESTATE INVESTING STRATEGIES

Stephen E. Roulac

Investor status is often perceived as a proxy for sophistication, competence and performance. Whereas individuals once dominated corporate securities markets, institutional investors have recently emerged as the dominant power player (Welles, 1975). Institutional investors presumably gain market share at the expense of individuals, since the compounding effect of superior performance resulting from their competitive advantages provides then still more funds to invest (Train, 1982), which phenomenon is magnified by declining individual savings and increasing spending rates. The growing complexity, sophistication and competitiveness of the corporate securities markets combine to favor the institutional over the individual investor (Ellis, 1975; Welles, 1975).

Investor status is commonly linked to investor scale, with institutions perceived as being large and individuals small. While these relationships generally apply, significant large individual investors have been highly visible and influential in both corporate securities and real estate investing. Although scale considerations have important strategic implications in terms of access to investment opportunities as well as economy and power in investment decision making and management, investor status exerts dominant behavioral and legal influences on which strategies are elected, how they are implemented, and their viability. Although these factors and influences are common to both corporate and real estate investing, the legal and behavioral considerations have a relatively greater impact on real estate investing.

Significantly, both individual and institutional investors seem to embrace less than totally rational decision styles. Although there are common behavioral forces influencing individual and institutional irrationality (Herrnstein and Mazur, 1987), individual and institutional investors manifest their irrationality in markedly different ways. Although financial folklore popularizes the premise of wholesale individual financial miscalculation (Makay, 1841), institutional real estate investors are certainly not immune from such misperceptions, as reflected by past assumptions of continually escalating rental levels and property prices leading to extraordinary investor returns for real estate investments (Jaffe and Sirmans, 1984).

Modern portfolio theory, building from Harry Markowitz's classic portfolio selection work (Markowitz, 1991), is based upon an implicit bias favoring an institutional orientation. In his classic paper, Markowitz described an *investing institution* that was an open-end investment company or mutual fund. Markowitz argued for "mean and variances criteria in judging 'goodness'...this formulation turned out to be widely acceptable in practice as well as tractable analytically".

Markese has observed that "most investment theory has been developed for institutional investors" (Markese, 1992). Recently, Markowitz has acknowledged that individual investing differs from institutional investing. Notably, the conclusion that smaller stocks, generally held by individuals rather than institutions, outperform the market (represented by larger companies in the S&P 500), challenges the conventional thinking that individuals are at a competitive disadvantage to institutional investors (Markowitz, 1991).

As important as institutional and individual status is in influencing the strategy elected by investors, few studies have addressed comparative investment strategies and styles between individual and institutional real estate investors. Although textbooks on real estate investment acknowledge an array of investor objectives (Jaffe and Sirmans, 1989; Phyrr et al., 1989; Roulac, 1976), the implications of individual versus institutional status generally and the derivative scale consequences specifically are seldom addressed explicitly. Most real estate investment texts leave unexplored the implications of scale on the viability of various real estate investing strategies. Insights into the implications of scale on individual versus institutional investing strategies can guide practice, teaching, and research.

Scale implications

Many perceive that scale also is a direct proxy for sophistication and a primary determinant of investing strategies for individuals and institutional investors in real estate. Indeed, lessons from capital market theory on real estate investment performance suggest that superior returns can be realized by more sophisticated approaches (Roulac, 1978), which approaches are more readily implemented by institutional investors.

While scale is not considered to be a major impediment in the application of modern portfolio theory strategies to corporate securities investing (Fama, 1970), scale considerations do exert a profound influence on viable real estate investing strategies, but in ways that are very different than what might commonly be perceived.

Access to investment opportunities is a function of the interdependency of the relative scale relationships of investors' resources and the financial magnitude of the investments. The largest investors can consider the largest investment opportunities, as well as all smaller investment opportunities. Since smaller investors can consider only those investment opportunities that match their resources, their universe of possible investments is necessarily restricted, placing them at a competitive disadvantage to the larger investor in terms of the array of possible choices available for consideration. Through securitization, large investments are made divisible into small units, thereby vastly expanding the universe of eligible investors and introducing more parity in investment selection for investors of different scale.

Significant costs, pricing, and agency issues associated with securitization complicate the assessment of access parity relative to scale. Additionally, despite the equalizing consequences of securitization, because some investments at both ends of the size spectrum are inherently less appropriate for or amenable to securitization, both large institutional and small individual investors enjoy some competitive advantages in certain segments of the investment markets.

Whereas the fungibility and active trading markets that characterize corporate securities investing (Tinic, 1972), accommodate adapting institutional investing strategies and styles to corporate securities portfolios of divergent scale, such translations do not readily apply in real estate investing. The inherent indivisibility of non-securitized real estate interests, the extraordinary differences in managerial emphasis associated with different building sizes, and the limited liquidity of securitized real estate constrain the transferability of modern corporate securities investing strategies to real estate (Roulac and Friedman, 1993). Within the universe of real estate investing, scale has profound implications both on feasible investing strategies and also as a proxy for individual versus institutional objectives, constraints, and style.

An investor of modest means may acquire the same stocks and assemble the identical portfolio as the largest, most sophisticated institutional investor, albeit on a much smaller basis, with a timing difference. Unless participating through some fund arrangement whereby his or her capital is combined with other investors to create a larger pool, the small investor generally is denied access to certain specialized types of investing, such as private placements, risk arbitrage, takeover activities, commodities and futures, and certain Treasury debt issues. At the same time, large investors may find it difficult to commit a meaningful part of their portfolios to certain smaller size securities, with the consequence that the smaller investor may enjoy the opportunity to gain a greater relative portfolio concentration in smaller size issues. Although the smaller scale real estate investor enjoys comparable advantages over the large institutional investor (Porter, 1985), the relative paucity of securitized real estate investing opportunities affords the institutional investor a broader array of choices by way of property size and diversification opportunity (Retkwa, 1990).

Individual and institutional strategies

There has long been a literature oriented to individual direct real estate investing strategies. William Nickerson's classic *How I Turned $1000 Into One Million Dollars in Real Estate in My Spare Time* appeared in the 1950s, with subsequent editions updating the figure to three million dollars and then to five million dollars in the 1980 edition (Nickerson, 1980).

According to John Reed, until Nickerson promulgated his investing strategy, no one thought the average investor could get rich investing in real estate (Reed, 1993). Nickerson's strategy involved employing a modest down payment and mortgage borrowing to purchase a single family home on reasonable terms, increasing rental income and value through property improvements, pyramiding the property into a duplex, and then repeating the process to assemble an ever larger real estate portfolio (Reed, 1991).

Nickerson's legacy was taken over by Albert Lowery who extended, refined and broadly promoted Nickerson's basic strategy (Lowery, 1977). Subsequently, Mark Haroldsen repackaged Nickerson's concepts and aggressively promoted his own book through an extensive advertising campaign, featuring long narrative promotional copy, describing his investment success and his financial success, supported by testimonials from his accountant (Haroldsen, 1976). In fact, this type of pioneering promotion proliferated for other real estate and non-real estate information products.

The apparent success of Nickerson, Lowery, and Haroldsen attracted other investment gurus, the most visible of whom was Robert Allen, who, in a succession of books, seminars and late night television "infom-ercials", promoted the individual investing wealth-building strategy featuring "nothing down", high leverage, distressed-seller purchase, and cosmetic fix-up strategy (Allen, 1980). Allen's "nothing down" strategy presumes an improbable combination of seller distress, property and tenant quality, and market strength. Reed is highly skeptical of the validity of such assumptions, observing that "it is hard to do Allen's 'nothing down' strategy legally or ethically. If you can in fact buy a property for nothing down, it will likely have negative cash flow" (Reed, 1992).

These real estate guru, individual investing strategies presume direct involvement, with the associated time commitments, risk exposure, and tenant interactions. Many do not understand the concept of attributing a price to their individual effort, since they really are buying a second job, not an investment (Friedman, 1992). Although the attributes of this active investing strategy appeal to some, many are disinclined to pursue such approaches, either by preference or in recognition of their lack of the requisite attributes for success in direct real estate involvement (Reed, 1990).

Institutional investors face similar issues as do individuals in crafting a strategy involving varying emphases between active direct involvement and passive indirect involvement. Although some major institutional investors are self-contained and fully integrated in their approaches to real estate investing, institutional investors electing involvement in real estate investing increasingly lack a tradition of involvement, and so have no organizational structure and strategy in place. In 1976 Roulac recognized the importance of institutional considerations in *Modern Real Estate Investment: An Institutional Approach* (Roulac, 1976a) and other writings (Roulac, 1985, 1976b, 1978).

Interestingly, a symbiotic interdependence exists between individual and institutional investors. Ultimately, the vast majority of institutional funds are in fact linked to individual sources. Investment managers acting on behalf of pension funds are representing the collective individual interests of pension beneficiaries. Insurance companies participating as major institutional players are investing funds raised from the sale of life insurance policies. Managers acting on behalf of a real estate investment trust or limited partnership are representing the collective resources of individuals. The institutional investors are acting on behalf of a discrete element of an individual's portfolio.

An investor's status, by defining both sophistication and decision resources access, exerts a strong influence on investing strategies and styles. A Department of Housing and Urban Development study on multifamily housing concluded that organizations actively engaged in real estate as their primary business activity analyze potential investments and make final decisions on those investments themselves, whereas other participants "rely heavily on staff members for the analysis of the investment potential of a given project" (Touche Ross & Co., 1972). Insurance companies and REITs tend to involve outside advisors such as mortgage correspondents and fee appraisers (Touche Ross & Co., 1972).

While the literature of individual investing strategies has continued to expand, with real estate titles being among the most successful segments of the publishing industry, and writings on institutional real estate investing strategies have proliferated in both the academic and professional journals, the interdependencies of individual and institutional investing have been largely unexamined. Significantly, the emergence of securitization, specifically the expansion of public limited partnerships, real estate investment trusts, and commingled real estate funds, represents assembling resources on an individual basis to represent an aggregate that is the equivalent of institutional scale.

Property size and securitization

To the extent that the divergent circumstances and objectives of individual and institutional investors are considered, the assessment views individual real estate investors as favoring smaller, lower quality properties, often purchased under distressed circumstances with an objective to upgrade cash flow and thereby property value, through aggressive property management and cosmetic improvements, in highly leveraged tax-oriented transactions. Institutional investors, by contrast, are perceived to be conservative in their approach, emphasize institutional grade properties, purchased on all cash terms, reflecting their tax-exempt status, and simultaneously making inefficient use of the tax attributes of such opportunities.

Although divergent financial resources driving the determination of property size and divergent tax status are perceived as the dominant and defining differences between individual and institutional real estate investing, the subject is in fact more complicated. As with various phenomena, things are not always what they seem; scale advantages can be transformed by securitization, and tax benefits can be realized by financial engineering. Thus, securitization can allow the individual investor to compete with the large institutional investor, and financial engineering can enable the tax exempt institutional investor to capture the perceived tax shelter benefits traditionally reserved to the individual investor.

Basic to consideration of individual versus institutional investing opportunities is consideration of implications of investor resources on property scale. As highlighted in Figure 1, individual investors tend to have small amounts of resources where institutional investors have large amounts of resources. While investors with small amounts of resources can consider buying smaller properties, investors with larger amounts of resources can consider buying bigger properties as well as all other properties of a lesser size. Thus, the relative buying competition for a property is inverse to its size: few compete to buy big properties while many compete to buy small properties.

The scale of investing is significant by virtue of the property type eligibility that it implies, with large institutional investors concentrating their involvement on investment grade properties while individual investors are relegated to non-investment grade properties. Indeed, in some circles *investment grade* is code terminology for *professional* and *sophisticated*, while *non-investment grade* is code terminology for *unsophisticated* and

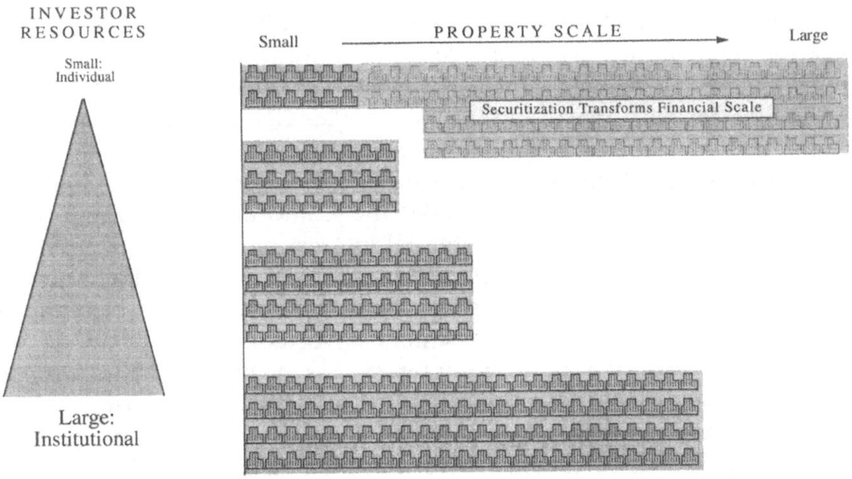

Figure 1. Scale of Implications for Universe of Individual Versus Institutional Investing Opportunities

lesser competence. Significantly, securitization, which combines the resources of individual investors to represent the financial capability of the institutional buyer, transforms financial scale.

Real estate securities rapidly emerged in the early 1980s to represent a major capital source for the real estate sector and an important investing vehicle for individual and smaller institutional investors (Roulac, 1988). The emergence of real estate securities, specifically public limited partnerships and real estate investment trusts, afforded individuals passive involvement, limited liability, and the opportunity both to gain access to the advantages of professional investment management and also to enjoy the power and economy of scale associated with larger scale involvement. Two decades ago Roulac described the advantages of the investor combining with others to improve his relative buying position, there being fewer large buyers than small buyers. Through a consolidation of resources a group of investors can consider both small and large properties and probably acquire a better property than would have the investor on his own. There may be less competition of larger properties while many competing buyers tend to drive up the prices on the smaller properties. With a larger property, further advantages are achieved through professional property management, which professional management may be uneconomic for smaller properties. Because the cost of expertise and professional service is spread over a number of partners, the syndicate can hire the very best talent, which cost would be prohibitive if this talent were to do similar work for a private investor (Roulac, 1988).

Various prominent properties are in fact held by individuals via securitization. Notable in this group are the Empire State Building, in which individual investors have quite a major stake via investments of $10,000 per unit in the early 1960s, and the Rockefeller Center, whereby investors acquiring shares in a real estate investment trust gained ownership of one of the world's great properties. But other major properties are available only to the largest investors. In 1990 the California Public Employees' Retirement System gained a substantial interest in what was then known as Santa Fe Realty, subsequently renamed Catellus, a portfolio of diverse holdings of prime West Coast properties. Indicative of the blending of individual and institutional investment involvement, however, is the consideration that the portfolio interest was acquired in the form of shares of common stock, so that the large pension fund now owns shares alongside many other investors. A further indication of this divergence is that The Irvine Company, the several billion dollar portfolio of prime developable land in Orange County, is in fact controlled by Donald Bren, an individual rather than an institution.

Reflective of the divergence between investment grade and non-investment grade properties is the assessment by Lachman that institutional grade properties are the largest and highest quality in the most advantageous locations, are the best maintained, enjoy the best occupancy, have the lowest risk, and enjoy the most liquidity (Lachman, 1990). Because of these advantageous attributes, such properties might be priced in the 5%–7% capitalization rate range for *premier* assets (Lachman, 1990). By contrast, the non-investment grade properties would be at the opposite end of such quality specifications.

A simplistic implication of scale is that institutional real estate investing implies the highest quality of property and individual investing implies the lowest quality. In fact, the differences are not at all so clear cut, consistent, or conclusive. An investment manifesting extraordinary financial attributes may by other standards of quality assessment appear to be highly deficient. Many of the so-called institutional grade real estate properties are major high-rise office buildings, prospectively attractive from a distance as pictured in the investors' annual report or the investment managers' promotional literature. But whether such properties are attractive as financial investments is another question. Although there is the premise that larger scale properties enjoy operating advantages over smaller scale ones, various factors suggest this may not be the case.

Property scale

Economic theory holds that scale allows economies of operation, leading to lower costs and therefore higher profits, but whether the economic principle of scale economies applies to real estate is debatable. Surveys of property management economics, specifically those for apartment buildings by the Institute of Real Estate Management, for office buildings by the Building Owners and Managers Association, and for shopping centers by the Urban Land Institute, indicate some diseconomies of scale in that bigger properties have higher expenses per foot and as a percentage of revenue. Reasons for this include the greater oversight attention by the smaller manager, the coordination costs involving multiple layers of reporting for larger staffs and bigger properties, the greater compliance burdens with full-time employees on larger properties as opposed to part-time employees on smaller properties (Reed, 1992). Additionally, a larger size property with more employees and layers of reporting implies greater distance between the decision maker and the tenant, a distancing of relationship that violates the "close to customer" management principle articulated in Peters' and Waterman's *In Search of Excellence* (Peters and Waterman, 1982).

Legal aspects of investor status

Investor status has significant legal implications generally, but especially for larger investors that by circumstance and scale must employ agents and employees to implement their investment strategies. The legal environment is strongly biased in favor of the smaller scale real estate participant. Exemptions to many laws, particularly those having to do with rent control, are available to owners of smaller properties, particularly four units or less and owner-occupied. Certainly, the larger property and its owner are more attractive litigation targets, if for no other reason than there are substantial assets available that can be sought as a source to pay damages. Environmental complicance standards are much more lenient for a single-family house than for a multi-family or commercial building (Kuntz).

Whereas the larger investor typically has employees, the smaller scale investor can avoid them, an organizational approach that has major legal advantages. Dealing with management tasks directly allows more control and thereby limits legal exposure over employee conduct. As a case in point, the Federal Housing Administration imposes a heavy fine if an employee utters a politically incorrect word (Reed, 1992). By operating as a family firm, the smaller investor gains exemption from such employment regulations as child labor laws and dangerous work condition rules. Employee litigation exposure embraces an array of issues, including workers' compensation, hiring and termination, and personal injury, as well as OSHA compliance requirements (Reed, personal conversation, 1992).

The smaller scale investor enjoys significant financing advantages. The terms and eligibility for financing single family housing are generally more advantageous than for commercial properties, especially in the current conditions of restricted capital access. The FIREEA legislation favors mortgages on apartment buildings no larger than 36 units, while FMMA will not finance mortgages on properties with more than four units (Reed, 1992). The Small Business Administration will provide real estate loans for users of property but not for investors (Reed, personal conversation, 1992).

The enforcement of capital markets regulations is more rigorous and restrictive than for larger scale investors. Although the authority and regulation of the Securities and Exchange Commission apply to all offerings of a security, public registration is mandatory only for offerings that do not qualify for an intrastate or private placement exemption, which latter exemption is available for smaller size offerings and those restricted to the most sophisticated investors (Roulac, 1976). Other agencies that regulate access to the capital markets include the National Association of Securities Dealers, the Federal Reserve Bank, the Internal Revenue Service, and corporate securities departments and real estate departments. Pension funds are subject to the regulation of the Employment Retirement and Income Security Act of 1974 (Roulac, 1976). While financial institutions were for many years regulated in a less than stringent manner, in recent years regulation of commercial banks, savings banks, and life insurance companies has increased dramatically in its scope, specificity, and restrictiveness.

By contrast, the majority of individual investors operate in a largely unregulated financial environment, providing significant competitive advantages over those larger investors that are subject to regulation. While there are some large pools of unregulated capital, the investors of which enjoy significant competitive advantages, such unregulated investors tend to be in the minority. The restrictions imposed by regulation include timing of gaining access to capital, what types of propeties can be purchased, what conditions must be met *prior* to properties being purchased, what information must be disclosed about the properties that are purchased, and significant ongoing financial reporting and compliance requirements.

A particularly significant point of legal differentiation in investor status has to do with tax treatment. Investor status determines how efficiently investors can use certain features of the tax laws that govern real estate investing (Reed, 1983). Depending upon the tax laws that apply at a particular time, either tax-paying or tax-exempt investors enjoy a competitive advantage. In a favorable and accommodating tax environment, tax-paying investors may enjoy *higher actual after tax returns* than tax-exempt investors. Indeed, approximately 10% of the after-tax return of individuals investing in real estate limited partnerships in the 1970s was attributable to tax shelter (Roulac and Stephen, 1985). Tax-exempt investors who do not pay taxes are thus at a competitive disadvantage in such a tax environment, since they realize a *lower return* because of their tax-exempt status than they would if they were tax-paying!

Significantly, a higher tax bracket can be a competitive advantage in real estate investing, allowing the high tax bracket investor to realize a higher return than a low tax bracket investor (Roulac, 1974). As tax rules change, the advantage of one investor status relative to another changes as well.

While the tax attributes favoring a particular type of investor can be captured through financial engineering, that tactic necessarily involves transaction costs and raises agency issues, which still result in the particular tax-favored class of investors enjoying a competitive advantage over the class of tax-disadvantaged investors.

Investor attributes and attitudes

Consideration of investor attributes reveals some surprising parallels and divergences between individual and institutional real estate investing. As highlighted in Table 1, which provides a comparison of such investor attributes as scale, tax status, sophistication, personal involvement, dominant motive, regulatory influence, role of personal use, and accountability, some factors apply only to individuals or institutions, while other attributes have very different implications. Significant strategic implications concerning which types of properties and strategies are appropriate for individual and institutional investors result from the differences in individual and institutional approaches to certain key attributes (Oestreich and Williamson, 1990).

Consideration of scale suggests that while large institutional investors have many reasons to embrace the most sophisticated investment practices, the evidence is that sophistication levels of the largest institutions and smallest institutional investors may both be exceeded by the levels of sophistication of medium-size investors. A recent survey of institutional investors active in making participating mortgages, a form of investment requiring consideration of both credit risk associated with the traditional mortgage and the factors that influence equity performance, found that while the majority employ more sophisticated investment decision-making methodologies, a few of the very largest and smallest investors favored less sophisticated investment decision-making procedures (Roulac and Friedman, 1993). Interestingly, all but a few of the very largest and smallest investors employed sophisticated decision-making methodologies, consistent with what the literature on investment decision making uniformly advocated should be utilized (Roulac and Friedman, 1993).

Because of the substantial size and dominance of such large organizations in the markets, business opportunities tend to flow readily to them implying that they may be less aggressive than medium and smaller organizations that must compete for new business. Thus, large scale

Table 1. Investor Attributes.

	INVESTOR CLASSIFICATION		
ATTRIBUTE	*Individual*	*Institutional*	*STRATEGIC IMPLICATION*
Scale	Small	Large	Institutions enjoy power/economy advantages re management tasks and professional services. Individuals may pursue strategies that are inappropriate or uneconomical for institutions, and can often react more quickly to changing market conditions.
Tax Status	Taxable	Often Tax-exempt	Different tax environments favor one investor classification over another.
Sophistication	Varies	Unbalanced	Often naive decision-makers dominate institutional investing. Opportunities to exploit and risk exposure resulting from unsophisticated practice characterize both institutional and individual investing.
Personal Involvement	Direct: hands-on	Indirect: work through agents and intermediaries	Face-to-face tenant interactions can cause burnout. Institutional investors are largely insulated from tenants.
Dominant Motives	Speculation	Prudent investing	Long term orientation often lacking as frequent short-term reporting emphasis often dominates institutional concerns.
Regulatory Influence	Not applicable	Regulatory compliance and public reporting	Individuals are more flexible in terms of which types of properties they might consider.
Role of Personal Use	Possible for personal housing	Possible for offices	Individuals may use personal housing need to promote investment objectives whereas institutions less frequently consider such a strategy.
Accountability	To self/family members	To third parties	For many institutions consequences of bad result vastly exceed those of good result.

can breed a certain insularity and aloofness from competitive market circumstances; such inward focus and the resulting implications for managerial style are by no means unique to institutional real estate investment (Peters and Waterman, 1982).

Consideration of basic investor attitudes, as well as their attributes, is central to understanding how investors approach their real estate involvements. Investor attitudes can be considered a form of cultural classification for individual and institutional investors. Among the significant cultural factors included in investor attitudes, as described in Table 2, are time horizon (both theory and actual conduct), risk tolerance (both theory and application), style, focus and emphasis, external orientation, sophistication, role of strategy versus luck, investment discipline, and property image and status.

The decision-making style, substantial scale, and long-term orientation of institutional investors may in fact place them at a competitive disadvantage in markets characterized by dynamism and discontinuity. Although the discipline of prudence and long-term orientation favor exploiting opportunities not readily considered by those investors who are more oriented to the short term, and are thus often viewed as advantages for institutional investors, in fluid markets these attributes may be less advantageous. Just as management theorists argue that large business enterprises are at a major disadvantage relative to smaller companies (Peters, 1992), so also can this concept of organizational scale advantages be applied to real estate investing strategies. Arguing that smaller investors enjoy many advantages, Reed has described this phenomenon as "the mom-and-popization of real estate" (Reed, 1992).

While institutions can employ the power advantages of superior decision models, databases, and professional advisors more economically than individuals, their inherent behavioral patterns can mitigate these advantages. These behavioral patterns cause them concurrently to neglect the efficient application of such decision-making advantages and to compromise the quality and timeliness of their decisions because of bureaucratic inertia and less than competent decision making (Roulac, 1992). In an investing environment where nimbleness, flexibility, and decisiveness are critical, institutions that are ponderous, rigid, and slow are at a competitive disadvantage.

In an era of accelerating change, investing strategies featuring long-term commitments to substantial properties may be less rewarding than those emphasizing smaller scale properties and shorter time horizons. Economic forces that threaten the viability of the substantial properties favored by institutional investors are inherently less threatening to individuals who do not consider such properties. In this regard individual investors generally enjoy significant competitive advantages over institutions in an investment battle that Reed likens to PT boats and fighter planes autmaneuvering huge oil tankers and dirigibles (Reed, personal conversation, 1992). Extending the military analogy, Reed has described "Ranger Real Estate Investing" as featuring higher skills, quicker action and more aggressive strategies (Reed, 1989), which can successfully be pursued by small individuals but not large institutions.

Beyond the implications of economic dynamism and the inherent deteriorating reliability of forecasts as the time horizon is extended, the risk consequences of the longtime horizon orientation favored by institutions are compromised by the mathematics of present value. As a longer time horizon involves greater uncertainty, investors expect a proportionately higher return to compensate for more risk. But higher return requirements translate into greater discounting of future financial events, meaning ever larger future payments are needed to justify the investment. The mathematics of present value can imply daunting if not improbably heroic assumptions about future economic conditions and financial performance associated with long-term investments.

The dynamism in the economy generally and the estate markets, specifically the office market in such major cities as Dallas, Los Angeles, and New York, raises questions about the reliability of most assumptions about future economic conditions and property performance. Concerning time horizon, Reed (1988) asserts:

> There is no such thing as a long-term investment. When you go long term, your ability to either predict or control the relevant variables drops rapidly to zero. Long-term "investments" are really speculations. Most assumptions you make about two years hence or later are "garbage in."...A real estate "investment" which relies on third year or later returns is really a crap shoot...But the crap shoot aspect of real estate investing—while not totally eliminatable—can be reduced to an acceptable level by...short-duration, high margin techniques."

Notably, such specialized techniques are more effectively pursued by individual rather than institutional investors.

Information access and economics

The differences between individuals and institutions concerning their access to and the economics of information are profound. Specifically, independent expertise has bery different roles for individuals than institutions. Independent expertise is seldom used by individual investors.

Table 2. Investor Attributes.

	INVESTOR CLASSIFICATION		
ATTRIBUTE	*Individual*	*Institutional*	*STRATEGIC IMPLICATION*
Time Horizon:			
(1) Theory	Intermediate term	Long Term	Institutions can consider certain strategies and properties that are inappropriate for individuals.
(2) Conduct	Intermediate term	Short term	Institutions' conduct often denies the strategic advantage of their long term orientation.
Risk Tolerance:			
(1) Theory	Low	High.	Institutions are more conservative with others' money than they would be with their own, whereas individuals dealing with own money are much more motivated to get it right.
(2) Application	High	Low:Risk averse	In practice individuals may pursue more aggressive strategies than warranted by their circumstances while institutions can tend to be much more cautious than is appropriate for their resources and long term orientation.
Style	Entrepreneur: aggressively seek to create value	Custodian: preserve assets and collect rent	Less aggressive management can result from some individuals emphasizing nonfinancial values as well as institutional complacency.

Focus and Emphasis	Aggressive deal-making	Prudent adherences to fiduciary process	Divergence of emphasis can created conflict when emphasis is inappropriate to setting.
External Orientation	Varies	Varies: often insular	Sensitivity to implications of external forces can be inversely related to scale.
Role of Strategy vs. Luck	Many investors are very successful because of luck	Strategy, analysis and management more dominant than luck	While all types of investors may be successful more in spite of rather than because of their strategies, this pattern tends to be more prevalent with individuals.
Investment Discipline	Few employ	Often lacking	Pervasive lack of discipline both increases risk and creates opportunities.
Property Image and Status	Ranges from *pride of ownership* and exlusivity	May emphasize status and photogenic properties	Because many institutions avoid properties that do not measure up to the image they want to portray, many individuals will own properties that institutions will not own.

Although independent expertise is more frequently used by institutions, decisions are often dominated by non-specialists, i.e., boards of trustees, who are neither trained nor experienced in business, finance, investing, real estate or real estate investing.

The different investor groups have divergent priorities in terms of where they get information and how they evaluate markets. Individual investors tend to get local market information from newspapers and real estate brokers, while institutional investors tend to look to research reports prepared by investment managers, not just by the managers they have retained, but often by managers seeking their business, as well as consultants and research organizations, whose services may be retained on either an ongoing or ad hoc basis for specific assignments.

Individuals tend to rely on newsletters and motivational seminars for information. Institutional investors tend to place more emphasis on consultants and lawyers, conferences, and professional information sources. The content of seminars they attend also reflect very different emphases. The content of seminars and conferences aimed at individuals consists largely of emotional/motivational strategies for financial independence, emphasizing especially fear of dependency in old age, in contrast to the emphasis on substantive issues and product promotions that dominate meetings oriented to institutional investors.

Significantly, presenters at both individual and institutional meetings have a not-so-hidden selling agenda, but differ in what they are selling. Those pitching to individual investors are selling a package of information products in the form of books, audio and video tapes, and further educational courses. The institutional presenters, by contrast, are selling professional agency services, seeking to gain an exclusive or near exclusive contractual relationship to represent the institutional investor in implementing their real estate investment involvements. Whereas the financial magnitude of the sale to the individual investor is in the few hundred dollar range, the value of contracts for institutional investment management services are often in the multiple hundreds of thousands or even millions of dollars.

Beyond passive versus active strategies

Considering an investor's appropriate strategy solely from the perspective of individual versus institutional classification is insufficient, since whether the investor is passive or active can exert a major influence on their investing strategy. As shown in Table 3, individuals who are passive in

Table 3. Dominant Investing Strategies for Active and Passive Investors

	INVESTING STYLE	
INVESTOR CLASSIFICATION	*PASSIVE*	*ACTIVE*
Individual	Real estate securities	Direct ownership of single family and small income properties (primarily residential)
Institutional	Real estate securities Retain investment manager	Direct ownership of all property types

their investing style pursue very different strategies than those who are active, with the former electing indirect securities involvements and the latter direct ownership of real estate. Similarly, the range of considerations that institutions might address is much narrower for those who pursue investing in a passive manner than for those who are active (Norwell, 1991).

Significantly, the motives of institutional investors can diverge dramatically from the managers they retain to implement their investment programs. Institutional investors place great priority on the process, emphasizing the imperative that the critical steps to prudent investing be adhered to through a deliberate, structured, and controlled procedure of investment policy specification, strategy articulation, manager selection, acquisition due diligence, portfolio monitoring, and performance measurement. Institutional investors' priority on adhering to the process can become an objective unto itself, oftentimes being even more important than the investment returns actually realized. In any event, such investors are much more oriented to realizing a targeted investment return, derivative of a specified objective associated with the financial policy determined by the liability side of the balance sheet, than to maximizing return on investment. Certainly, such institutional investors are risk-adverse and are *not* willing to accept any downside exposure in trade for substantial upside potential.

The managers retained by such conservative, risk-averse, process-committed institutional investors, by contrast, usually have a very different emphasis and set of priorities. Such managers are deal-driven and oriented to emphasizing the special opportunities represented by a particular acquisition rather than step-by-step process compliance. These managers are oriented to selling numbers for a particular transaction and to presenting a representation of past performance in the most advantageous light as a means to attract more capital to do deals. Whereas institutional investors can view the process and the process outputs as ends, with the real estate transaction being the means to the ends, the managers they retain view paying some lip service attention to the process as a necessary and unavoidable means to *their* ends, which is *doing deals*. That manager and institutional investor orientations diverge is not surprising. Although ther is a growing recognition of the importance of looking at an aggregate portfolio (a top down approach) rather than just a transaction (Firstenberg et al., 1988), many investment managers are inherently oriented to the specific deal at the expense of the whole.

Beyond consideration of whether investors operate with passive or active investing styles, it is important to consider whether they address their decisions in an implicit or explicit manner and whether their decision resource reliance is internal or external. The alternative decision resources and styles employed by individuals and institutional investors have major strategic implications concerning how such investors elect to implement their real estate involvements, as highlighted in Figure 2.

Since the election of a passive versus active investing style plays a pivotal role for both individual and institutional investors, issues of agency rela-

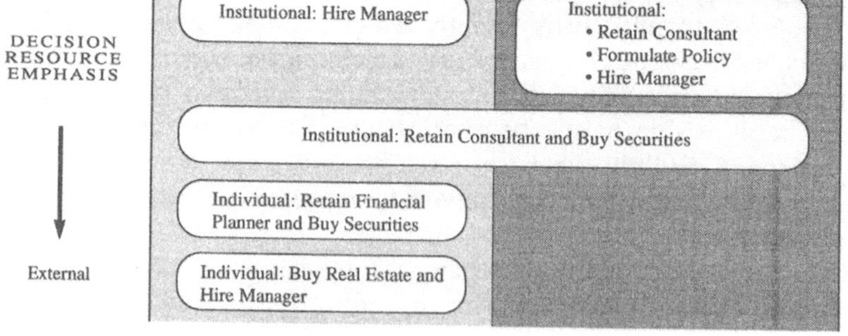

Figure 2. Strategic Implications of Alternative Decision Resources and Styles

tionships through management contracts and securitization loom large (Pratt and Zeckhauser, 1985). While securitization arrangements allow individual investors to enjoy prospectively the benefits of the power and economy of scale of the large institutional investor, crucial to the efficacy of such arrangements are economic and congruency concerns. Economic concerns embrace the cost-benefit relationship of the value of management services, while congruency concerns incorporate whether the investment manager acts in ways that promote the investors' interests. External consulting and financial planning decision resources can complement and facilitate the investors' decisions concerning these economic and congruence concerns. Nevertheless, market structures, institutional arrangements, supply shortages of competent professionals, and behavioral considerations conspire to compromise the quality of agency relationships for investment management services and therefore the performance that is delivered as a result of those services (Roulac and Webb, 1992).

Conclusion

Although the differences between individual and institutional investors are profound, the behavioral factors that influence the rationality of their decision-making processes and the legal differentiation resulting from their status loom larger than do implications of power and economy of scale. Access issues cut both ways, favoring the larger investor in some instances and the smaller in other. Securitization can transform scale, and financial engineering can effectively achieve an arbitrage of tax status. Crucial challenges common to individual and institutional investors alike are devising agency relationships for management representation and securitization that are both cost effective and promote goal congruency.

References

Allen, Robert G. *Nothing Down*. New York: Simon & Schuster, 1980.

Ellis, Charles. "The Loser's Game." *Financial Analysis Journal* (July/August 1975), 19–26.

Fama, E. "Efficient Capital Markets: A Review of Theory and Empirical Work." *The Journal of Finance* (May 1970), 383–417.

Firstenberg, Paul M., Stephen A. Ross, and Randall C. Zisler. "Real Estate: The Whole Story." *The Journal of Portfolio Management* (Spring 1988), 34–53.

Friedman, Jack. Personal conversation with the author, December 1992.

Gordon, Jeffrey N. and Lewis A. Kornhauser. "Efficient Markets, Costly Information, and Securities Research." *New York University of Law Review* (November 1985), 761–849.

Haroldsen, Mark Oliver. *How To Wake Up the Financial Genius Inside You*. Salt Lake City: Mark O. Haroldsen, 1976.

Herrnstein, Richard J. and James E. Mazur. "Making Up Our Minds—A New Model of Economic Behavior." *The Sciences* (November/December 1987), 40.

Jaffe, Austin J. and C.F. Sirmans. "The Theory and Evidence on Real Estate Financial Decisions: A Review of the Issues." *AREUEA Journal* 12:3 (1984), 378–400.

Jaffe, Austin J. and C.F. Sirmans. *Fundamentals of Real Estate Investment*. Englewood Cliffs: Prentice-Hall, 1989.

Kuntz, Glen and John Hupp. *Environmental Due Diligence*. Washington, DC: Bureau of National Affairs.

Lachman, M. Leanne. "The Future Real Estate Landscape." *Pension World* (January 1990), 26–28.

Lowery, Albert. *How You Can Become Financially Independent by Investing in Real Estate*. (New York: Simon & Schuster, 1977).

Makay, Charles. *Memories of Extraordinary Popular Delusions*. London: Richard Bentley, 1841.

Markese, John D. *Letter to Investors*. American Association of Individual Investors, 1992.

Markowitz, Harry M. "Individual vs. Institutional Investing." *Financial Services* Review 1:1 (1991), 1–8.

Markowitz, Harry M. "Portfolio Selection." *The Journal of Finance* (1952), 77–88.

Nickerson, William. *How I Turned One Thousand Dollars Into Five Million in Real Estate*. New York: Simon & Schuster, 1980.

Norwell, William. "The Real Estate Decision Process." *Journal of Property Management* (March/April 1991), 51.

Oestreich, Nathaniel and James E. Williamson. "Investment Interest in Real Estate: What Every Real Estate Professional Should Know." *Real Estate Accounting and Taxation* (Fall 1990), 45–52.

Peters, Thomas J. *Liberation Management: Necessary Disorganization for the Nanosecond Nineties*. New York: Alfred A. Knopf, 1992.

Peters, Thomas J. *Thriving on Chaos—A Handbook of Management Revolution*. New York: Alfred A. Knopf, 1987.

Peters, Thomas J. and Robert H. Waterman, Jr. *In Search of Excellence: Lessons From America's Best-Run Companies*. New York: Harper and Row, 1982.

Phyrr, Stephen A., James R. Cooper, Larry E. Wofford, Steven D. Kapplin, and Paul D. Lapides. *Real Estate Investment—Strategy, Analysis, Decisions*. New York: John Wiley & Sons, 1989.

Porter, Michael E. *Competitive Advantage—Creating and Sustaining Superior Performance*. New York: Free Press, 1985.

Pratt, John W. and Richard J. Zeckhauser (eds.). *Principles and Agents: The*

Structure of Business. Boston: Harvard University Press, 1985.
Reed, John T. "Long-Term Investment is a Contradiction in Terms." *Real Estate Investors' Monthly* (November 1988), 171.
Reed, John T. *How to Buy Real Estate for at Least 20% Below Market Value* Danville, CA: Reed Publishing, 1993.
Reed, John T. "Tax-Efficiency in Real Estate Investing—How Much Is Good for You?" *Real Estate Investing Letter* (June 1983), 5.
Reed, John T. "The Real Estate B.S. Artist Detection Checklist." John T. Reed's *The Real Estate Investors' Monthly* (January 1990), 281.
Reed, John T. "Ranger Real Estate Investing." John T. Reed's *The Real Estate Investors' Monthly* (February 1989), 195.
Reed, John T. "The Mom- and Popization of Real Estate." John T. Reed's *The Real Estate Investors' Monthly* (October 1992), 550.
Reed, John T. *How to Manage Residential Property for Maximum Cash Flow and Resale Value*, 3rd ed. Danville, CA: John T. Reed, 1991.
Reed, John T. Personal conversation with the author, December 1992.
Retkwa, Rosalyn. "Well-Funded Institution Investors are Demanding More From Their Real Estate." *National Real Estate Investor* (September 1990), 74.
Roulac, Stephen E. and Jack Friedman. "Participating Mortgates: Decision Criteria and Role in Commercial Real Estate Finance." Paper presented to American Real Estate Society Meetings, April, 1993.
Roulac, Stephen E. and James R. Webb. "The Market for Incompetence: The Implications of Unsophisticated Real Estate Decision Makers." Paper presented to American Real Estate Society Meetings, April, 1992.
Roulac, Stephen E. "Games the Stock Market Didn't Teach You." *Real Estate Investing* 36–42. Monograph published by the Institute of Chartered Financial Analysts and Dow Jones–Irwin, 1985.
Roulac, Stephen E. *Modern Real Estate Investment: An Institutional Approach* San Francisco: Property Press, 1976a.
Roulac, Stephen E. "Pension Investments in Real Estate: Diversification Goal?" *New York Law Journal* (September 17, 1976b), 29.
Roulac, Stephen E. *Real Estate Syndication Digest*, 1972: Principles and Applications. San Francisco: Real Estate Syndication Digest, Inc., 1972.
Roulac, Stephen E. "REF Special Report: Real Estate Securitization: Prologue and Prospects." *Real Estate Finance* 5 (Spring 1988), 15–14.
Roulac, Stephen E. "The Influence of Capital Market Theory on Real Estate Returns and the Value of Economic Analysis." *The Real Estate Appraiser and Analyst* (November/December 1978), 62.
Roulac, Stephen E. and Douglas E. Sobolik. "Real Estate Tax Reform: Historic Perspectives and Economic Implication." *Real Estate Finance* (Summer 1985), 13–24.
Roulac, Stephen E. "Economics of the Housing Investment Decision." *The Appraisal Journal* (July 1974), 358–371.
Tinic, S. "The Economics of Liquidity Services." *Quarterly Journal of Economics*

(February 1972), 67–86.
Train, John. "Lessons of the Masters." *Harvard Magazine* (May/June 1982), 12–14.
Touche Ross & Co. *Study on Tax Considerations and Milti-Family Housing Investments*. Washington, DC: U.S. Department of Housing and Urban Development, U.S. Government Printing Office, 1972.
Welles, Chris. *The Last Days of the Club*. New York: E.P. Dutton, 1975.

4 SUPERIOR REAL ESTATE INVESTMENT PERFORMANCE: ENIGMA OR ILLUSION? A CRITICAL REVIEW OF THE LITERATURE

Crocker H. Liu, Terry V. Grissom and David J. Hartzell

Introduction

The purpose of this paper is to critique the existing empirical evidence on the investment performance of real estate relative to alternative asset categories. The key issue which guides this review of the investment performance literature is whether abnormal real estate returns are merely an illusion which arises from the shortcomings associated with various real estate performance studies or are the result of an omission of more fundamental factors. We suggest that any superior return is a short-run phenomenon, because, according to capital market theory, all assets should exhibit similar risk and return characteristics in the long run. If real estate continues to possess superior performance in the long run, then this implies that fundamental factors have been omitted from the real estate pricing model. Moreover, we will propose that a world in which the capital asset pricing model holds might be compatible with the existing evidence, because most of the prior studies have focused on *total* risk rather than on systematic risk.[1] Consequently, all assets can plot on the security market line in equilibrium, given a CAPM world, regardless of whether one asset (portfolio) such as real estate dominates another asset (protfolio) such as stocks from a mean-variance perspective.

The remainder of this paper proceeds as follows. The first section summarizes the research to date on the investment performance of real estate. The studies surveyed include those which focus on direct investment in real estate as well as securities with real estate as an underlying asset. The next section describes the factors which might create the illusion of superior real estate returns but which are unaccounted for in the return measures of the articles surveyed. The final section summarizes and concludes the study.

The performance of real estate relative to other assets

The findings of most real estate performance studies are not comparable with one another, because some studies focus on evaluating the return or risk and return on one property type relative to common stocks, while other studies compare diversified real estate portfolios to common stocks or many investment alternatives. The various studies also use different return and risk measures to evaluate investment performance, since real estate data are frequently incomplete, with the sales price per period usually unknown due to thin trading. Typical return measures used include the internal rate of return, the cap rate, and the holding period return, while the usual risk measures examined include the standard deviation, the beta associated with the cap rate, and the holding period return.

The Wendt and Wong (1965) study is representative of research using the internal rate of return criterion to evaluate one type of real estate relative to common stock. This criterion is not adjusted for risk. Return performance of 20 FHA Section 608 apartments from the San Francisco Bay Area are compared to 76 randomly chosen industrial stocks from the COMPUSTAT tapes. The study finds that real estate outperforms common stock as a result of leverage and tax shelter effects. However, no superior real estate returns are found to exist when leverage and tax shelter are held constant.

Several shortcomings limit the validity of the performance implications arising from this study. The return measure used not only excludes risk but also assumes an implicit reinvestment rate. The conclusions also have limited generalization, since only one property type in one geographical location is examined. Special financing and tax benefits associated with FHA Section 608 properties also limit the results. Another limitation of this study is that the selling price of an apartment is assumed to equal eight times gross rent in the year of sale. Several purchase prices are also imputed using either an 8% cap rate or the loan to value ratio.

The studies of Coyne, Goulet, and Piconni (1980), Kaplan (1985), and Robichek, Cohn, and Pringle (1972), in contrast to Wendt and Wong (1965), use risk-adjusted holding period returns rather than the internal rate of return.[2] Like Wendt and Wong however, these studies examine one property type relative to one or more alternative investments.

Coyne, Goulet, and Picconi (1980) demonstrate that residential real estate exhibits higher risk-adjusted returns relative to stocks and bonds. Both leveraged and unleveraged returns are examined over the period from 1969 to 1975. Bonds, existing real estate, and new real estate are found to have similar unleveraged risk-adjusted returns, while stocks, in comparison, exhibit lower returns. However, the introduction of leverage results in lower risk-adjusted returns to stocks and bonds, with both existing and new residential real estate risk-adjusted returns invariant to leverage. Another finding of this study is that residential real estate is an important diversification tool, since both new and existing residential real estate have a low or inverse correlation with stocks and bonds.

Both Robichek, Cohn, and Pringle (1972) and Kaplan (1985) find that farmland is also an effective portfolio diversification tool. Robichek, Cohn, and Pringle (1972) illustrate how 12 investment alternatives other than stocks and bonds can influence the construction of efficient portfolios. Farmland is the real estate alternative considered, with USDA data used to compute farm returns. Total returns earned on agricultural property are found to exceed the returns on all financial assets considered except for the S&P industrials. However, farm real estate exhibits the highest average return per unit of total risk. The study also finds farm real estate returns are not significantly correlated with other investment media. Kaplan also discovers that farm real estate offers returns which are comparable to stock returns but less volatile.

The three preceding studies are consistent with the real estate performance studies based on the internal rate of return. Real estate still outperforms other investments, even after the return measure is corrected and risk is explicitly considered. *Total* risk, rather than systematic risk, is considered, since the standard deviation is used for these studies. However, the implications of these studies are limited, since only one property type is investigated. Study results are also limited for the Robichek et al. (1972), and Kaplan (1985) studies, because the USDA farm values used in both studies not only contain lagged adjustment periods but also include opinions of values in addition to actual prices. The portfolio implications of Kaplan (1985) are also tenuous, given that the means, variances, and covariances are not statistically meaningful. This phenomenon arises, since the number of time series observations is less than the number of parameters. None of the studies attempt to investigate why real estate outperforms alternative investment media.

Friedman (1971) and Webb and Sirmans (1980) also demonstrate that real estate not only offers diversification opportunities but, in addition, affords superior investment performance relative to other assets. The findings are more representative of real estate investment performance, since more than one property type is considered. The Friedman study differs from the Webb and Sirmans study with respect to both the return measure and the portfolio formation process employed.

Friedman (1971) modifies the quadratic programming decision process of modern portfolio theory to address the integer problem associated with real estate. This integer problem arises since real estate is indivisible. A sample of 50 properties diversified with respect to geographical orientation and property type is used together with a random sample of 50 NYSE stocks. Annual holding period returns and variances are calculated for the years 1963 to 1968. Real estate portfolios are found to dominate stock portfolios with respect to a mean-variance criterion when each asset class is evaluated separately. This result holds both before and after taxes. Another finding is that a mixed-asset portfolio reduces portfolio risk, since real estate returns covary inversely to common stocks.

In contrast to Friedman, Webb and Sirmans (1980) compute real estate yields with cap rates. Thirteen different types of real estate are examined in addition to common stocks, bonds, and U.S. Treasury bills from 1951 to 1976. The authors find that rates of return for different property types exceed returns on other financial media with lower risk. Another finding of the study is that leverage results in higher return and risk for all real estate considered. The study also indicates that heterogeneous risk and return characteristics are associated with different property types.

Several deficiencies temper the implications of the Friedman (1971) and the Webb and Sirmans (1980) studies. The data that Friedman uses contain only the initial 1963 market value and the sales price at the end of 1968. Interpolation of intermediate changes in market values is therefore required to calculate annual holding period returns, which in turn understates the total varibility in return. Systematic real estate risk is also understated, given that the real estate index used consists of the Boeckh construction cost indices combined with the *American Appraisal Association Index*. Construction cost indices overstate prices on existing real estate, since no depreciation is considered. In contrast, appraisals smooth returns, and therefore understate variability. Webb and Sirmans, on the other hand, do not interpolate market values. However, their use of cap rates understates the true equity return, since the property value is assumed to decline to the present value of equity. No appreciation component is explicitly considered, since the cap rate is analogous to a dividend yield for stocks. This suggests that the standard deviation of the cap rate understates total real estate risk to the extent that appreciation rather than income has historically accounted for most of the variability in total return.

Deficiencies with direct real estate investment data have prompted some authors to investigate real estate securities. Real estate securities considered include real estate investment trusts (REITs) and commingled real estate funds (CREFs). Controversy exists as to whether REITs have earned superior risk-adjusted returns relative to stocks. In contrast, risk-adjusted CREF returns are found to dominate stock returns. Smith and Shulman (1976) and Burns and Epley (1982) have both investigated REITS, while Miles and McCue (1984a) have evaluated CREFs.

Smith and Shulman (1976) compare the return performance for nine equity REITs relative to 15 closed-end investment companies. The geometric mean return and the intercept, the beta, and the R^2 from the single index model are used to compare the two types of investment vehicles with the S&P *Composite Index* chosen as the market proxy. The major finding is that equity REITs and closed-end investment companies exhibit similar investment performance. Neither type of investment dominates over all subperiods examined. Another finding is that investing in an equity REIT is not useful for portfolio diversification.

In contrast to Smith and Shulman (1976), Burns and Epley (1982) find that investing in real estate equities can increase portfolio returns. The main issue addressed is whether an efficient frontier consisting of real estate and stocks dominates the efficient frontier for a single asset type. The main finding is that a mixed-asset frontier dominates single-asset efficient frontiers with respect to mean-variance. Real estate returns dominate stock returns at the middle and lower risk-return levels. Stocks exhibit higher risk-risk-adjusted returns however, as one moves along the efficient frontier.

Different methodologies are partly responsible for the contradictory findings of Smith and Shulman (1976) relative to Burns and Epley (1982). Smith and Shulman use individual risk-adjusted performance measures. No correlations are computed for equity REITs relative to closed-end investment companies, therefore, their conclusion that no incremental benefit arises from real estate is questionable. Another questionable aspect of the Smith and Shulman study is that the same data are used to estimate the parameters and test the model. Although the Burns and Epley study does not suffer from the preceding methodological flaws, neither study addresses whether REITs are reliable proxies for direct real estate investment. No real estate performance insights obtain if REITs represent inadequate surrogates.

Mengden and Hartzell (1986) find preliminary evidence that REITs do not adequately represent real estate. Quarterly real estate returns computed with the PRISA fund of Prudential are compared to the S&P 500 and the Salomon Brothers equity REIT (EREIT) index. The major finding is that EREITs are hybrid securities with the price appreciation component positively related to general stock market movements, and the REIT dividend component positively correlated with real estate cash flows. This suggests that equity REIT shares might not be substitutes for direct real estate investment. However, a deficiency of this and all other studies which use CREF data is that the CREF returns are based on appraised values which understate the return variability. Another study limitation is that the extent to which REIT returns arise from capital market risk, and real estate market risk is not investigated.

Miles and McCue (1984a) empirically evaluate the impact of property type, region, and lease structure on CREF commercial real estate portfolio diversification. A proprietary CREF data base is analyzed over the 1973 to 1981 period with quarterly holding period returns computed relative to these three dimensions. The main finding is that commercial real estate diversification across both geographic regions and property types appears to be advantageous. Returns from various geographic regions and property types not only exhibit low correlations with stock and bond returns but also dominate stock from a risk-adjusted return perspective. Miles and McCue also find that systematic risk comprises only 10 to 15% of the total real estate risk. These results are tentative however, since the lease parameters are not held constant. The use of appraised values in lieu of market prices also affects the results, although Miles and McCue argue that minimal bias occurs, since the aggregation of appraisals does result in a fund price.

The existing literature reviewed thus far indicates that real estate exhibits equal or higher returns, with lower risk relative to common stocks and other assets. Real estate returns are also inversely related or not correlated to common stocks and bonds. This suggests that real estate is beneficial for portfolio diversification even if one accepts the argument that the risk and return for real estate is similar to stocks in the long run. REIT studies provide the only exception to this general consensus. However, shortcomings of various studies not only limit the applicability of results but also make comparison among studies difficult. These shortcomings include but are not limited to (1) noncomparable time periods; (2) incorrect return measures; (3) unreliable or insufficient data; (4) singular variance-covariance matrices of returns and questionable parameter estimates arising from more assets than time periods; (5) unrepresentative data such as data for a single property type or single geographical region; and (6) an assumed sales price, assumed appreciation growth rate, or appraised values in computing rates of return.

Zerbst and Cambon (1984) attempt to rectify some of these study deficiencies to facilitate comparison among real estate performance studies. Their main objective is to obtain conclusions about the performance of real estate relative to other asset classes. Only studies using either the IRR or holding period returns are reviewed, with all studies deflated to a real return perspective. Zerbst and Cambon find that except for REIT stocks, real estate outperforms stocks and bonds on both an unadjusted and risk-adjusted basis. This result is consistent with past empirical studies.

The illusion of superior risk-adjusted real estate returns

Several authors suggest that superior real estate investment performance is an illusion.[3] "Abnormal" real estate returns should not arise, since arbitrage is expected to equalize investment alternatives. Reasons that these and other authors cite for superior real estate returns include:

- Inadequate theory and deficient valuation models,
- Omitted asset markets and misspecification of risk,
- Market imperfections such as thin trading, information/transaction costs, and divisibility,
- Market segmentation arising from clientele effects, and
- Inflation risk.

However, little real estate research exists with respect to the influence of each factor on property returns. Following is an examination of each of these factors with respect to the performance and pricing of real estate.

Inadequate Theory and Deficient Valuation Paradigms. Capital market theory presumes that all assets should possess similar risk-adjusted returns in equilibrium. Two alternative asset pricing models are associated with capital market theory. The capital asset pricing model (CAPM) of Sharpe (1964), Lintner (1965), and Mossin (1966) represents one equilibrium model. The CAPM describes the expected return on an asset as a function of its covariation with return on the market portfolio. This covariation is known as systematic risk. Investors are only compensated for bearing market risk in a CAPM world, since nonmarket risk is diversifiable. Every asset in a CAPM equilibrium is priced so that its risk-adjusted return falls exactly on the security market line.

The arbitrage pricing model (APT) provides an alternative explanation of the behavior of returns. Ross (1976) developed the APT to circumvent the restrictive CAPM assumption that the market portfolio is observable. For the APT to hold, all individuals believe that returns on assets are generated by a k-factor linear model. This assumption is not required in a CAPM world. However, no presumption is made ex ante in the APT that one of the factors is the "market," although the factors are unknown a priori. In contrast to the APT, the CAPM requires not only that the market portfolio exist, but also that this portfolio be mean-variance efficient. All assets fall on a security hyperplane, given that a no arbitrage equilibrium exists.

Draper and Findlay (1982) question the appropriateness of the capital market theory and the CAPM for real estate, since the CAPM assumptions are violated, given the nature of the asset and the market within which real estate trades. They point out, however, that the CAPM is robust to unique property characteristics, since these attributes are amenable to mapping into risk-return space. Other market imperfections such as information, transaction costs, and indivisibility are regarded as short-term phenomena, since no entry restrictions exist for financial intermediaries to perform arbitrage. The appropriateness of the APT to real estate, on the other hand, is questioned, given the newness of the technique and the factor identification problem. Draper and Smith therefore advocate using either the hedonic pricing model (HPM) or the Hoag model for real estate.

Although Draper and Findlay question whether the CAPM is suitable for real estate, given the model's assumptions, their study does not empirically investigate whether the CAPM adequately predicts real estate returns. The empirical investigation of the CAPM with respect to real estate is necessary, since Friedman (1971) points out that violation of model assumptions is insufficient to invalidate a theory. Friedman advocates that the final test of a model is how well the model describes reality. The superior real estate performance studies reviewed might be compatible with a CAPM world, since these studies use *total* risk rather than systematic risk. All assets plot on the security market line in equilibrium regardless of whether these assets lie on the mean-variance efficient frontier. Except for the study by Liu, Grissom, and Hartzell (1990), which is discussed in a subsequent section of this paper, no real estate study to date has relaxed the CAPM model assumptions to determine the resulting impact on real estate prices. Although Friedman (1971) and Findlay, et al. (1979) incorporate some of the unique real estate characteristics into the MPT, neither study derives a theoretical real estate pricing paradigm from their modified MPT models.

The hedonic pricing model (HPM) which Draper and Findlay advocate relates the price of a property to its physical, legal, and environmental attributes. Nothing in the HPM theoretical framework prohibits risk as a characteristic, although risk is not considered, since consumption theory rather than investment theory underlies the HPM. This consumption theory posits that consumers derive utility from the characteristics associated with a good rather than the good itself. Therefore, a demand and supply curve is assumed to exist for each attribute, with hedonic prices representing the marginal equilibrium price for each attribute.

Two functional forms of the HPM exist. The linear functional form is associated with Lancaster (1966), while the nonlinear form is associated with Rosen (1974).[4] Both versions of the HPM focus solely on the local real estate market within which a property trades, with no interaction among asset markets considered in the price formation process. Another deficiency of the hedonic theory is that neither the attributes nor the functional form is known a priori. Which attributes are priced therefore is a function of which characteristics are chosen. The functional form chosen has serious implications with respect to market segmentation. These consequences are subsequently discussed.

Hoag (1980) proposes a multifactor model for income-producing real estate that captures the "spirit" of the HPM. The model incorporates financial characteristics in addition to physical characteristics and recognizes both macromarket and micromarket influences on real estate. In contrast, the traditional HPM recognizes only micromarket factors. Using a sample of 463 industrial properties, Hoag finds that industrial real estate exhibits risk and return characteristics which are comparable to common stock. This suggests that the superior risk-adjusted real estate return phenomenon is partly attributable to the smoothing tendencies of appraisals.[5] However, this study is consistent with other studies in finding that industrial real estate returns exhibit low correlations with stock returns.

The contrary findings of Hoag relative to other real estate studies arise in part from two factors. The Hoag model essentially simulates continuous trading for commercial real estate, which in turn increases the variability in prices. No liquidity premium is consequently required for a Hoag or HPM type of model. Another factor which biases the results in favor of similar risk-adjusted real estate and stock returns is the different levels of diversification used in the comparison process. The investment performance of a specific type of real estate—industrial properties—is compared to a well diversified stock porfolio (S&P 500). This comparison is similar to evaluating one stock industry group such as gold stocks relative to the S&P 500. A more appropriate comparison is to use either a real estate portfolio diversified across property types and economic bases against the S&P 500 or to compare dthe industrial real estate funds to different stock industry groups on an individual basis. Comparison of a well diversified real estate fund with a stock fund might support existing empirical evidence.

Hoag does not substantiate that estimates from his model differ significantly from appraisals, although he alludes to the understatement of risk as the result of appraisal smoothing. The appraised price is related to the sales price, since the appraiser either has prior knowledge of the transaction price or the transaction price is executed with a knowledge of the appraisal. Another limitation of the Hoag study is that only one property type is analyzed over a relatively short period, with the same data used to develop and test the model.

Another theory which reflects the spirit of the hedonic pricing theory is the new equilibrium theory (NET) which Ibbotson. Diermeier, and Siegel (1984) propose to recognize both the risk and nonrisk characteristics in pricing assets. Risk characteristics include market risk, unanticipated inflation risk, real interest rate risk, and risk from a lack of diversification. Taxes and marketability costs, i.e., information costs, search and transaction costs, and divisibility costs are among the nonrisk factors cited. Clientele effects are also recognized in the NET framework, although no mention is made as to whether clientele effects result in an asset pricing premium. The NET theory is assumed to hold regardless of whether perfect markets (arbitrage) or imperfect markets (arbitrage) exist. No one is assumed to hold the market portfolio in a NET world, although all investors hold diversified portfolios.

The lack of a closed form quantitative model limits the usefulness of NET, although the theory is conceptually appealing. This limitation makes it difficult to empirically investigate the extent to which arbitrage opportunities arise from market imperfections. Another weakness of NET and also a drawback of the HPM and the Hoag model is that the portfolio formation process is not addressed, given market imperfections. The NET theory also does not address the question of why NET model development cannot proceed from relaxing the CAPM assumptions to account for market imperfections.

Omitted Real Estate Asset Markets. Mayers (1972) and Roll (1977) both demonstrate that all assets fall on the security market line when the market proxy is correctly specified. Correct specification of the market portfolio implies that asset markets other than stocks and bonds, such as real estate, are explicitly recognized. A decomposition of the true market portfolio into component asset submarkets is therefore necessary to understand the nature of the omitted asset problem. Mathematically, the traditional Sharpe–Lintner–Mossin CAPM is

$$E(\tilde{R}_j - r_f) = \lambda M \operatorname{cov}(\tilde{R}_j, \tilde{R}_m), \tag{3}$$

where M is the aggregate market value of all assets, and λ is the risk-aversion factor. But the dollar return on the market portfolio is decomposable as

$$M\tilde{R}_m = \sum_{i=1}^{p} M_i \tilde{R}_{m_i}, \tag{4}$$

where i represents the ith asset market. Substitution of (4) into (3) yields

$$E(\tilde{R}_j - r_f) = \lambda \left\{ \sum_{i=1}^{p} M_i \operatorname{cov}(\tilde{R}_j, \tilde{R}_{m_i}) \right\}. \tag{5}$$

If M_s is defined as the aggregate market value of a security market proxy such as the S&P 500, then (5) is alternatively expressed as

$$E(\tilde{R}_j - r_f) = \lambda M_s \operatorname{cov}(\tilde{R}_j, R_{m_s}) + \{\lambda \sum_{i \neq s} M_i \operatorname{cov}(\tilde{R}_j, \tilde{R}_{m_i})\}, \tag{6}$$

where the term in brackets {.} represents the return from the omitted asset markets. If the covariance of the return on asset j with the return on the ith asset submarket is zero, where i does not represent the security submarket S, i.e.,

$$\operatorname{cov}(\tilde{R}_j, \tilde{R}_{mi}) = 0 \qquad \forall_i, \ i \neq s \ j = 1, \ldots, N, \tag{7}$$

then (6) degenerates to

$$E(\tilde{R}_j - r_f) = \lambda \ M_s \operatorname{cov}(\tilde{R}_j, \tilde{R}_{mS}). \tag{8}$$

The key issue therefore is not whether the true market portfolio is required, as Roll (1977) contends, but whether the term in brackets is significantly different from zero for the jth asset class.

Both Fama and Schwert (1977a) and Stambaugh (1982) empirically demonstrate that omitted asset markets do not pose a problem in estimating common stock returns. However, neither study investigates whether the omitted real estate asset market is important with respect to real estate returns. Another related issue not addressd in either study is whether the S&P 500 adequately represents the real estate market. Real estate is not totally omitted, since the S&P 500 includes real estate related components such as homebuilding, financials, and building materials.

Miles and Rice (1978) show that omitted real estate markets do affect real estate returns. Miles and Rice (1978) construct a new market proxy, which consists of stocks, farm real estate, and human capital, to test the CAPM; they find that higher betas result for farm returns when the new market index is used relative to the S&P 500. However, the study does not investigate whether abnormal risk-adjusted returns exist for real estate after accounting for systematic real estate market risk. Liu et al. (1990) extend the Miles and Rice (1978) study by examining if superior risk-adjusted real estate returns exist after incorporating omitted real estate markets. More specifically, the study considers whether the composition of the market portfolio leads to different inferences on real estate performance. As a point of departure, the study investigates if the omitted asset phenomenon results in a biased measurement of investment performance. The study finds that ranking investment performance is not a meaningless exercise, even if measurement bias exists. Another study finding is that different inferences on real estate investment performance do not necessarily result, given variations in the composition of the market proxy. Liu et al. also find that both the omitted asset phenomenon and smoothing bias account in part for superior real estate investment performance.

Market Imperfections: Transaction and Information Costs, Taxes, and Illiquidity. Ibbotson and Siegel (1984) find evidence that "abnormal" real estate returns occur even after various types of real estate are included in the market portfolio. The authors therefore argue that nonmarket risks are priced. These market imperfections include high transaction and information costs, taxes, and illiquidity. However, no attempt is made to determine which nonmarket risk factor has a premium associated with it. Although the real estate literature recognizes that these imperfections distinguish real estate from other assets, few real estate studies rigorously investigate the relationship of these imperfections to return. Only the relationship of taxes and illiquidity to real estate returns exists in the real estate literature.

The combined impact of taxes and leverage do not adequately account for superior real estate returns. Wendt and Wong (1965) find that the return on apartments relative to common stock is almost identical when cash flows are adjusted for taxes and financing. Certain limitations cited earlier, however, limit the interpretation of the study's conclusions. The study conclusions are further limited, since the contribution of leverage is not separated from tax shelter. Ricks (1969) rectifies this deficiency of Wendt and Wong through an investigation of the independent and joint impact of leverage and taxes on real estate IRRs. However, no attempt is made to compare returns for different property types to common stock. Ricks finds that financing raises the return, while taxes lower the return, with the positive leverage effect tending to offset the negative tax effect in general. However several deficiencies inherent in the Wendt and Wong study also temper the conclusions of Ricks. Ricks imputes certain parameter values for the equity investor and assumes that no change occurs in either operating income or price over time. Returns are therefore hypothetical. Other limitations of the study are that the IRR is used as the measure of return and that risk is not explicitly considered.

Webb and Sirmans (1980) also find that leverage partly accounts for higher rates of return to different property types. In contrast to Ricks (1969) and Wendt and Wong (1965) however, risk is explicitly considered with cap rates used in lieu of IRR as the measure of return. Higher risk-adjusted real estate returns are found to exist regardless of the leverage effect. Unfortunately, the tax aspect is not considered.

The real estate literature also recognizes that higher real estate returns and lower risk could arise from illiquidity. Illiquidity is reflected in one of several ways, including an allowance for thin trading, the use of appraisals, and the use of either the HPM or the Hoag model. The Friedman (1970) study exemplifies the first alternative. An allowance for thin real estate markets is incorporated in the analysis through a 15% decrease in the real estate sales price, with no justification given as to why 15% is chosen. In contrast to Friedman, most real estate performance studies reviewed use appraisals in lieu of market prices to obviate the need for a liquidity premium. Roulac and King (1977, p. 63) rationalize the use of appraised values as surrogates for prices as follows:

> Many assert that stock prices are "facts", whereas real estate appraisal values are opinions, largely because a transaction at that price could confidently be executed for the former but not the latter. Others would dispute this on two grounds, the effects of large block trades on prices and...the presumed illiquidity in the real estate markets. When properly priced, an investment property transaction can be properly executed, just as a stock order at a price above the market may not be executed.

The implicit assumption which underlies this argument is that no systematic appraisal bias exists. This assumption is tenuous when individual properties are analyzed, although the law of large numbers might eliminate appraisal bias for aggregated data.

Cole, Guilkey, and Miles (1986) compare sales prices to appraised values on a mean absolute differences basis and find preliminary evidence that is consistent with the contention of Roulac and King (1977). The major finding is that no significant appraisal bias exists after major outliers are removed although a large confidence interval exists around any appraisal. Appraisal bias is thus a concern with respect to individual properties. The study unfortunately does not investigate whether this bias still exists when appraised values are aggregated into property types or regions.

Hoag (1980) questions the validity of appraisals in dealing with thin trading, given his finding that real estate risk is comparable to stock risk when continuous real estate trading is simulated. However, the study does not investigate the bias from an appraisal model relative to the Hoag model. The models differ in that the appraisal process adjusts prices of comparable properties to the subject property, while the Hoag model constructs a representative property from comparables and then adjusts the subject property to this representative property.

None of the three alternative real estate methods for dealing with illiquidity directly adjusts systematic or total risk. The methods thus contrast methods proposed in the finance literature for dealing with thin trading bias. Scholes and Williams (S−W) (1977) and Dimson (1978) both propose techniques for estimating systematic risk of infrequently traded assets which essentially increase beta for thin trading and therefore increase the return. A downward bias in systematic risk thus occurs for infrequently traded assets. Systematic risk is not examined in real estate with respect to illiquidity, given the lack of adequate time series real estate market returns until recently and questions about the appropriateness of the CAPM to real estate.

Market Segmentation. Another type of market imperfection which might account for superior risk-adjusted returns on real estate relative to stocks is the clientele effect. Clientele effects arise either as the result of different sets of investors known as clienteles associated with different components of return—income versus capital appreciation—or different types of asset markets. Each clientele group represents a market segment. The existence of clienteles is a consequence of self-imposed barriers, legal and institutional constraints, geographical impediments, or a combination of these factors.

Liu, Grissom, and Hartzell (1990) theoretically investigate the impact of dividend clienteles on real estate returns, given that illiquidity exists. Intuitively, the authors argue that illiquidity represents a proportionate cost on the resale but not on the income component of return. An "illiquidity tax" is therefore associated with real estate capital appreciation but not the cap rate. This asymmetrical cost situation is the reverse of the tax-induced dividend effect in the finance literature, since a higher tax is associated with dividends relative to capital gains. Thus, the consequences of illiquidity for real estate returns in a no-tax or tax-neutral world should inversely mirror the consequence of tax-induced clienteles in finance. As expected, the study finds that illiquidity causes real investors to bid up the price of real estate the higher the expected income yield. Moreover, illiquidity is found to reduce the extent to which investors hold real estate in their portfolios. Given the ambitious nature of the study, the authors leave much room for further refinements and extensions including looking at illiquidity from a multiperiod context, assuming that a stochastic risk-free rate exists. This might yield further insights into optimal hedging strategies involving the use of real estate in mixed asset portfolios.

The key issue in Liu, Grissom, and Hartzell (1990) of whether dividend clienteles affect returns is distinct from the issue of whether investor clienteles exist. The real estate literature notes that different investor clienteles are associated with different real estate market tiers. The first tier consists of institutional investors investing in income properties. Individual investors trading in single family residential homes represent the second tier. However, these two tiers are not mutually exclusive, because some clientele participation across tiers is present. Both Webb (1984) and Miles and McCue (1982) find that institutional investors favor income-producing properties. No equity interests in single family homes exist, although mortgages on homes are a part of institutional portfolios. Miles and McCue (1982, p. 187) therefore recognize that a super risk premium might arise for certain property types:

> Recent institutional interest has focused in office and retail properties to the exclusion for the most part of residential. Residential properties. . . are perceived as more risky for institutional investors. . . Consequently, one would expect the relative yields of office and retail properties to be lower relative to residential properties due to the large market impact of institutional buyers.

No attempt is made however to test this proposition.

The existence of a segmentation between the commercial real estate market and the single family home market is puzzling. No reason is given why institutional investors cannot purchase large blocks of residences, since this is analogous to purchasing an apartment complex. Insititutional investor avoidance or unwillingness to take an equity position in homes might arise from pressures relating to their fiduciary responsibilities.

Specifically, the type of revenue-earning assets acquired should approximately match expected institutional liabilities incurred or contractual obligations. Homes provide little if any income, with most of the return associated with resale. This resale component is less certain and is also subject to illiquidity, which implies that institutional investors might experience difficulties in timing the resale to coincide with contractual obligations. Diermeier, Freundlich, and Schlarbaum (1985) posit that institutional investors do not take equity positions in single family residences given the lack of a direct, profitable vehicle to currently purchase single family homes in large quantities for institutional portfolios and the substitutability issue of consumption for investment. Bosch (1986) demonstrates, however, that the consumption decision is separable from the investment decision if a real estate rental market exists, since individuals can adjust their consumption flows. Bosch shows that the optimal portfolio of residential real estate is independent of consumption. Everyone holds the same portfolio of financial and real estate assets, given that a rental market exists. The equilibrium price of residential real estate is derived, conditional on an efficient rent market.

The real estate literature is more developed with respect to segmentation within the commercial real estate market or the housing market, with more literature available on the latter than the former. Market segmentation is presumed to arise, given that buyers typically restrict their search process to centain neighborhoods due to monetary considerations and concerns dealing with the quality of amenities. A hedonic model is typically used to investigate segmentation, with stratification evidenced if prices associated with housing attributes vary for identical properties located in different geographic areas.

In one of the few studies on commercial market segmentation, Grissom, Hartzell, and Liu (1987) investigate whether a segmented market exists for industrial real estate with respect to risk and return characteristics using the APT framework. The authors find that regional markets exist for industrial real estate, because different risk attributes influence property returns in various industrial submarkets even if the same pricing paradigm holds. In addition to this, the study finds that the number of priced risk factors differs across regions, with some risk factors systematic across two or more regions, while other risk factors are found to be systematic only within a given region. Further, some of the risk factors priced are unique to a given region, while ubiquitous risk factors are not compensated for in all regions. A limitation of the study is that appraised values which understate the factor loadings, are used. In addition the use of factor analysis in estimating the APT parameters has been questionned on the grounds that there is no unique factor solution. Therefore, a researcher can obtain whichever set of factors he is looking for by continuing to rotate the "axes." Consequently, a more modern test of the APT applied to real estate, using the technology in McElroy and Burmeister (1988), in which the unknown random factors of factor analysis are replaced with observed macroeconomic variables, might provide additional insights, as well as verification of the phenomena that Grissom et al. observed. A question which arises from the findings of Grissom et al. is why segmentation should exist if institutional investors are not restricted as to type of property and areas of the country in which they can invest.

The real estate literature is more developed with respect to housing market segmentation, with the empirical studies consistently finding evidence in support of housing market segmentation. The implicit assumption underlying each of these studies is that the HPM is portable across submarkets so that identical attributes are priced in each neighborhood. Controversy exists however over whether more precise value estimates arise through focusing solely on the micromarket within which a property trades. Richardson and Thalheimer (1982), Schnare and Struyk (1976), and Sonstalie and Portney (1980) find that estimating separate pricing equations for each submarket does not increase the predictive power of intra-SMSA variations in housing prices. In contrast, both Goodman (1978, 1981) and Dale-Johnson (1982) find evidence that market segmentation improves valuation estimates.

A limitation of all the preceding HPM studies is that the functional form is not known a priori. This poses a problem, since the HPM functional form determines whether segmentation exists. A nonlinear HPM is a sufficient condition for market segmentation. In contrast, theoretically market segmentation should not occur if a linear HPM is used. Another deficiency with these studies is that the housing submarkets are unknown ex ante. Therefore, different studies use different attributes to stratify markets, with segmentation variables that consumers perceive to exhibit inelastic supply, inelastic demand, or both usually chosen. Stratification schemes are therefore arbitrary. No study investigates why super price premiums should occur if buyers have access to all submarkets.

A key question which arises if segmented property markets or property and capital markets are present is whether super risk premiums exist. Liu et al. (1980) investigate the interrelationship of stock and real estate clienteles, focusing on the extent to which real estate securitization has integrated these market structures. The existence of super risk premiums would suggest that more securitization is needed to complete the markets.

This leads to the related question as to how to repackage real estate attributes to arbitrage away any premium if no investment barriers exist. The authors find evidence that the commercial real estate market is segmented from the stock market. However, the primary cause of segmentation varies and is a function of the market proxy chosen and of whether appraised values or imputed sales prices are used. Indirect barriers are found to represent the prime segmentation catalyst when appraised values are employed. In contrast, inconclusive evidence exists as to whether segmentation is the result of indirect barriers or legal constraints when imputed sales prices are evaluated. This is not surprising, given that a problem with the study is that imputed sales prices are measured with error, and therefore the power of the tests is weakened.

Inflation Risk. The real estate literature recognizes that a premium for inflation could also account for the superior risk-adjusted returns associated with real estate relative to stocks and bonds. However, although most studies show that real estate returns possess an inflation premium, controversy exists as to whether real estate hedges against both anticipated and unanticipated inflation.

Merton (1973) theoretically demonstrates that differences among expected returns on assets can exceed variations in systematic market risk, given a multiperiod context, if the risk-free rate is not constant over time. This is due to the fact that investors are not only exposed to systematic market risk, but are also exposed to risk from unfavorable shifts in the opportunity set. Consequently, differentials in asset returns can occur due to the fact that different assets do not provide equivalent hedges against intertemporal changes in the portfolio opportunity set.

Fama and Schwert (1977b) use the Merton CAPM to evaluate the ability of several alternative asset classes to hedge against inflation. Residential real estate is found to hedge against both expected and unanticipated inflation, while common stocks do not hedge against either type of inflation. This finding is consistent with the theory in Merton (1973), namely, that different assets do not provide equivalent inflation hedges. Several problems, however, limit the study findings. First, the home purchase price component of the CPI is used as the real estate proxy, which might overstate the degree to which real estate provides an inflation hedge, since the CPI is used as the measure of inflation. Another limitation which Fama and Schwert recognize is that only capital gains are associated with their real estate series. The series is also limited to only FHA insured residences, which currently account for only 7% of all home sales according to the Bureau of Labor Statistics. Further, only lower priced homes are represented in the FHA data, given the existence of legal constraints on the price ceilings of loans.

In contrast to Fama and Schwert (1977b), Miles and McCue (1984a) find that real estate hedges against anticipated but not unanticipated inflation when individual, commercial real estate returns from a large CREF are examined. However, the returns that the authors use are based on appraised values and as such are subject to smoothing. Smoothing tends to exert an upward bias on the correlation of the rate of inflation to quarterly real estate returns. Another problem with the study is that inflation continuously trends upward over the time period chosen. Potential bias also exists since an ex post commercial paper rate which incorporates default risk rather than bids on Treasury Bills is used as a proxy for anticipated inflation.

Brueggeman, Chen, and Thibodeau (1984) rectify the deficiency with the anticipated inflation proxy present in Miles and McCue (1984a). Overall returns on two CREFs are used rather than property-specific CREF data. The study results are consistent with Miles and McCue in that commercial real estate hedges against anticipated but not unexpected inflation. Another study finding is that commercial real estate outperforms corporate bonds, even after inflation risk and omitted real estate markets are accounted for. Like the Miles and McCue study, however, a limitation of the study is that appraised values are used, which Liu et al. (1989) argue could increase the likelihood of superior returns for real estate in the form of positive Jensen alphas.

In contrast to other real estate inflation studies, Fogler, Granito, and Smith (1985) find inconclusive evidence as to whether inflation is priced. Two hypotheses are proposed to account for the superior risk-adjusted returns of real estate relative to other assets. Both hypotheses presume real estate returns are positively related to unanticipated inflation. The random event hypothesis posits that a change in the perceived sensitivity of returns to unanticipated inflation does not result in a structural change to expected returns. In contrast, the hedge demand hypothesis postulates that inflation risk is priced. Although some support is found for the hedge demand hypothesis, the power associated with the empirical tests is weak. The study also suffers from the same deficiencies inherent in the Fama and Schwert (1977b) study, since the home purchase price component of the CPI is used as the real estate proxy, which might bias the results in favor of the hedge demand hypothesis. The interesting conjecture which Fogler et al. make, but do not test, given data limitations, is that an inflation premium may exist only in certain time periods, depending on whether real estate is in vogue. They contend that if investing in real estate is fashionable, and a period of rising inflation exists, then inflation is priced. However, no inflation premium will arise if investing in real estate is not considered faddish, even though an inflationary economic environment exists.

Hartzell, Hekman, and Miles (1987) revaluate the findings of Miles and McCue (1984a), focusing on the response of various real estate return classifications to inflation. These classifications include returns according to property type, property size, and the economic growth of SMSAs, in addition to overall real estate returns. Returns are computed from the Miles and McCue (1984a) database over a larger time period, to recognize both inflation and disinflation environments, with bids on T-bills used in lieu of the commercial paper rate to derive anticipated inflation. In contrast to Miles and McCue (1984a), the study finds that both anticipated and unanticipated inflation are priced with respect to commercial real estate. This result also holds for industrial and office property types, in addition to larger properties. In contrast, retail properties do not adequately hedge against either anticipated or unanticipated inflation. Nor is the inflation hedging advantage found from grouping properties into portfolios representing differential SMSA growth rates. Once again, a limitation of the study is that appraised values are employed in lieu of market prices.

Summary and conclusions

Empirical evidence suggests that "abnormal" returns exist for real estate. Such evidence is purported to represent an enigma, since arbitrage should equalize investment alternatives. Controversy arises as to whether this conundrum is attributable to shortcomings of various real estate performance studies or to more fundamental factors. The current study argues that, from the perspective of economic theory, superior real estate performance arises from an omission of certain fundamental factors, including (1) inadequate theory and deficient valuation models, (2) omitted asset markets and misspecification of risk, (3) market imperfections such as thin trading, information/transaction costs, and divisibility, (4) market segmentation arising from clientele effects, and (5) inflation risk. However, little theoretical or empirical real estate research exists concerning whether additional return premiums are associated with these factors. Most literature on the preceding factors deals with financial assets. Extant real estate literature suggests omitted real estate markets and inflation risk both result in additional premiums, but do not totally account for abnormal returns. Some evidence also exists that illiquidity might explain superior real estate performance.

The current study suggests that a CAPM world is compatible with the real estate performance studies reviewed, since the studies focus on total risk rather than systematic risk. Therefore, all assets could still plot on the security market line in equilibrium, given a CAPM world, regardless of whether one asset (portfolio) dominates another asset (portfolio) from a mean-variance perspective.

Notes

1. Even those studies which have used systematic risk in demonstrating that real estate outperforms stock might be compatible with the CAPM, because these studies are based on appraised data which Giliberto (1988) has shown leads to a positive return bias for real estate.

2. Although real estate performance is investigated, the primary purpose of these studies is to demonstrate the incremental contribution that real estate makes to either a stock or stock and bond efficient portfolio.

3. These authors include Draper and Findlay (1982), Hoag (1980), Jaffe and Sirmans (1984), Miles and McCue (1984), Roulac (1976) and Zerbst and Cambon (1984), among others.

4. Lancaster develops a demand oriented theory from a household production perspective. The spirit of the Lancaster work is that consumers play a dual role of producers. Goods are purchased as inputs into the housing production function of a consumer for ultimate characteristics. Lancaster assumes that a linear consumption technology exists which is additive and homogeneous of degree one. A linear specification of the hedonic price function thus results. The nonliner functional form of Rosen (1974), in contrast to a Lancastrian world, is based on a market orientation with buyers and sellers explicitly recognized.

5. Giliberto (1988) offers theoretical support for this finding by demonstrating that a positive return bias will always exist if appraisal errors are serially independent.

References

Bosch, J.C. "Portfolio Choices, Consumption, and Prices in a Market with Durable Assets." *Journal of Financial Research* 9:3 (1986), 239–250.

Brennan, Michael J. "Taxes, Market Valuation, and Corporate Financial Policy." *National Tax Journal* 23:4 (1970), 417–428.

Brueggeman, William, Andrew Chen, and Thomas Thibodeau. "Real Estate Investment Funds: Performance and Portfolio Considerations." *AREUEA Journal* 12:3 (1984), 333–354.

Burns, William, and Donald Epley. "The Performance of Portfolios of REITS and Stocks." *Journal of Portfolio Management* 8:3 (1982), 37–42.

Cole, Rebel, David Guilkey, and Mike Miles. "Toward an Assessment of the Reliability of Commercial Appraisals." *Appraisal Journal* 54:3 (1986), 422–432.

Coyne, Thomas J., Waldemar M., Goulet, and Mario J., Picconi. "Residential Real Estate Versus Financial Assets." *Journal of Portfolio Management* 7:1 (1980), 20–24.

Dale-Johnson, David. "An Alternative Approach to Housing Market Segmentation Using Hedonic Price Data." *Journal of Urban Economics* 11:3 (1982), 311–332.

Diermeier, Jeffrey J., J. Kurt Freundlich, and Gary G. Schlarbaum. "The Role of Real Estate in a Multi-Asset Portfolio." In: Tom Sale (ed.), *Real Estate Investing*. New York: Dow Jones, Irwin, 1985.

Dimson, Elroy. "Risk Measurement When Shares are Subject to Infrequent Trading." *Journal of Financial Economics* 7:2 (1979), 197–226.

Draper, Dennis W. and M. Chapman Findlay III. "Capital Asset Pricing and Real Estate Valuation." *AREUEA Journal* 10:2 (1982), 152–183.

Fama, Eugene F. and G. William Schwert. "Asset Returns and Inflation." *Journal of Financial Economics* 5:2 (1977), 115–146.

Fama, Eugene F. and G. William Schwert. "Human Capital and Capital Market Equilibrium." *Journal of Financial Economics* 4:1 (1977), 95–125.

Findlay, M. Chapman III, Carl W. Hamilton, Stephen D. Messner, and Jonathan S. Yormark. "Optimal Real Estate Portfolios." *AREUEA Journal* 7:2 (1979), 298–317.

Fogler, H. Russell, Michael R. Granito, and Laurence R. Smith. "A Theoretical Analysis of Real Estate Returns." *Journal of Finance* 40:3 (1985), 711–719.

Friedman, Harris C. "Real Estate Investment and Portfolio Theory." *Journal of Financial and Quantitative Analysis* 6:2 (1971), 861–874.

Giliberto, S. Michael. "A Note on the Use of Appraisal Data in Indexes of Performance Measurement." *AREUEA Journal* 16:1 (1988), 77–83.

Goodman, Allen C. "Submarkets within Urban Areas: Definitions and Evidence." *Journal of Regional Science* 21:2 (1981), 175–185.

Goodman, Allen C. "Hedonic Prices, Price Indices, and Housing Markets." *Journal Urban Economics* 5:4 (1978), 471–484.

Grissom, Terry V., David Hartzell, and Crocker H. Liu. "An Approach to Industrial Real Estate Market Segmentation and Valuation Using the Arbitrage Pricing Paradigm." *AREUEA Journal* 15:3 (1987), 199–219.

Hartzell, David, John Hekman, and Mike Miles. "Real Estate Returns and Inflation." *AREUEA Journal* 15:1 (1987), 617–637.

Hoag, James W. "Towards Indices of Real Estate Value and Return." *Journal of Finance* 35:2 (1980), 569–580.

Ibbotson, Roger G. and Laurence B. Siegel. "Real Estate Returns: A Comparison with Other Investments." *AREUEA Journal* 12:3 (1984), 219–242.

Ibbotson, Roger G., Jeffrey J. Diermeier, and Laurence B. Siegel. "The Demand for Capital Market Returns: A New Equilibrium Theory." *Financial Analysts Journal* 40:1 (1984), 22–33.

Jaffe, Austin J. and C.F. Sirmans. "The Theory and Evidence on Real Estate Financial Decisions: A Review of the Issues." *AREUEA Journal* 12:3 (1984), 378–400.

Kaplan, Howard M. "Farmland as a Portfolio Investment." *Journal of Portfolio Management* 11:2 (1985), 73–78.

Kelleher, Dennis G. "How Real Estate Stacks Up to the S&P500." *Real Estate Review* 6:2 (1976), 60–65.

Lancaster, K.J. "A New Approach to Consumer Theory." *Journal of Political Economy* 74:2 (1966), 132–157.

Lintner, John. "Security Prices, Risk, and Maximal Gains from Diversification." *Jounal of Finance* (1965) 587–615.

Liu, Crocker H., David J. Hartzell, Terry V. Grissom, and Wylie Grieg. "Alternative Rationales for Superior Real Estate Investment Performance: An Empirical Reinterpretation of Prior Research." Working Paper, New York University, 1990.

Liu, Crocker H., David J. Hartzell, Terry V. Grissom, and Wylie Grieg. "The Composition of the Market Portfolio and Real Estate Investment Performance." *AREUEA Journal* 18:1 (1990), 49–75.

Liu, Crocker H. Terry V. Grissom, and David J. Hartzell. "The Impact of Market Imperfections on Real Estate Returns and Optimal Investor Portfolios." *AREUEA Journal* (forthcoming).

Liu, Crocker H. David J. Hartzell, Wylie Grieg, and Terry V. Grissom. "The Integration of the Real Estate Market and the Stock Market: Some Preliminary Evidence." *Journal of Real Estate Finance and Economics* 3:3 (1990), 261–282.

McElroy, Marjorie B. and Edwin Burmeister. "Arbitrage Pricing Theory as a Restricted Nonlinear Multivariate Regression Model." *Journal of Business and Economic Statistics* 6:1 (1988), 29–42.

Mengden, Anne E. and David Hartzell. "Real Estate Investment Trusts: Are They Stocks or Real Estate?" Salomon Brothers Inc., August 27, 1986.

Merton, Robert C. "An Intertemporal Capital Asset Pricing Model." *Econometrica*, 41:5 (1973), 867–887.

Miles, Mike and Arthur Esty. "How Well Do Commingled Real Estate Funds Perform?" *Journal of Portfolio Management* 8:2 (1982), 62–68.

Miles, Mike and Michael Rice. "Toward a More Complete Investigation of the Correlation of Real Estate Investment Yield to the Rate Evidenced in the Money and Capital Markets: The Individual Investor's Perspective." *The Real Estate Appraiser and Analyst* 44:6 (1978), 8–19.

Miles, Mike and Tom McCue. "Commercial Real Estate Returns." *AREUEA Journal* 12:3 (1984), 355–377.

Miles, Mike and Tom McCue. "Diversification in the Real Estate Portfolio." *Journal of Financial Research* 7:1 (1984), 57–68.

Mossin, Jan. "Equilibrium in a Capital Asset Market." *Econometrica* 34:4 (1966) 786–83.

Richardson, David H. and Richard Thalheimer. "On the Use of Grouping Methods in the Analysis of Residential Housing Markets." *Regional Science and Urban Economics* 12: (1982) 285–304.

Ricks, Bruce R. "Imputed Equity Returns on Real Estate Financed with Life Insurance Company Loans." *Journal of Finance* 24:5 (1969), 921–937.

Robichek, Alexander A., Richard A. Cohn, and John J. Pringle. "Returns on Alternative Investment Media and Implications for Portfolio Construction." *Journal of Business* 45:3 (1972), 427–443.

Roll, Richard. "A Critique of the Asset Pricing Theory's Tests." *Journal of Financial Economics* 4:2 (1977), 129–176.

Rosen, Sherwin. "Hedonic Prices and Implicit Markets: Product Differentiation in Pure Competition. *Journal of Political Economy* 82:1 (1974), 34–55.

Ross, Stephen. "The Arbitrage Theory of Capital Asset Pricing." *Journal of Economic Theory* 13:3 (1976), 341–360.

Roulac, Stephen E. "Can Real Estate Returns Outperform Common Stocks." *Journal of Portfolio Management* 2:2 (1976), 26–43.

Roulac, Stephen E. and Donald A. King, Jr. "Institutional Strategies for Real Estate Investment." *Journal of Portfolio Management* 3:4 (1977), 58–65.

Sack, Paul. "Management of Real Estate Portfolio." In: Sumner Levine (ed.), *The Investment Manager's Handbook.* New York: Dow-Jones, Irwin. 1980.

Schnare, Ann B. and Raymond J. Struyk. "Segmentation in Urban Housing Markets." *Journal of Urban Economics* 3:2 (1976), 146–166.

Scholes, Myron and Joseph Williams. "Estimating Betas from Nonsynchronous Data." *Journal of Financial Economics* 5:3 (1977), 309–327.

Sharpe, William F. "Capital Asset Prices: A Theory of Market Equilibrium Under Conditions of Risk." *Journal of Finance* 19:3 (1964), 425–42 .

Smith, Keith V. and David Shulman. "The Performance of Equity Real Estate Investment Trusts." *Financial Analysts Journal* 32:5 (1976), 61–66.

Sonstelie, Jon C. and Paul R. Portney. "Gross Rents and Market Values: Testing the Implications of Tiebout's Hypothesis." *Journal of Urban Economics* 7:1 (1980), 102–118.

Stambaugh, Robert F. "On the Exclusion of Assets from Tests of the Two Parameter Model: A Sensitivity Analysis." *Journal of Financial Economics* 10:3 (1982), 237–268.

Webb, James R. "Real Estate Investment Acquisition Rules for Life Insurance Companies and Pension Funds: A Survey." *AREUEA Journal* 12:4 (1984), 495–520.

Webb, James, R. and C.F. Sirmans. "Yields and Risk Measures for Real Estate, 1966–1977." *Journal of Portfolio Management* 7:1 (1980), 14–19.

Wendt, Paul F. and Sui N. Wong. "Investment Performance: Common Stocks vs. Apartment Houses." *Journal of Finance*, 20:4 (1965), 633–646.

Zerbst, Robert H. and Barbara H. Cambon. "Real Estate: Historical Returns and Risk." *Journal of Portfolio Management* 10:3 (1984), 5–20.

5 THE EFFECT OF UNBUNDLING ASSET RETURNS ON RESTRICTED MIXED-ASSET PORTFOLIOS

James R. Webb and Jack H. Rubens*

Introduction

Research on mixed-asset portfolios has attracted increased attention in recent years (Brueggeman *et al.*, 1984; Friedman, 1971; Hartzell and Webb, 1988; Webb *et al.*, 1988; Webb and Rubens 1986, 1988). A mixed-asset portfolio is simply a portfolio that contains different types of assets, both financial (such as bonds and equities) and real (such as real estate). Many institutional investors (for example, life insurance companies, pension funds, and bank trust departments) cannot invest in all types of assets, due to various state and federal laws, as well as ERISA. Hence, their portfolios are "restricted."

To a large extent, the composition of these restricted mixed-asset portfolios for financial institutions depends upon rates-of-return and the concomitant risk measures over time, in relation to other assets. However, the sensitivity of the composition of these portfolios is generally unknown, since rates-of-return from just one source are generally used

* Deceased.

for these types of studies (Ibbotson and Siegel, 1984; Ibbotson and Associates, 1992). In addition, asset returns for all previous studies have been "bundled." That is, returns due to income and appreciation (total return in a no-taxes and no-leverage environment) from a single asset class were added together.

The purpose of this study is to address these issues. A restricted portfolio is constructed which includes four financial assets and three types of real estate. Specifically, the assets which are included are large capitalization common stocks, small capitalization common stocks, corporate and government bonds, residential real estate, business real estate, and farmland. Using rate-of-return estimates from two different sources Ibbotson and Siegel, 1984; Loarie (*Finnegan's Financial Green Sheet*), for residential real estate, business real estate, and farmland, the optimal portfolio is derived, using each data set separately for four different portfolios. The optimal portfolios to be estimated are the four financial assets only, the three types of real estate only, the financial assets with only business/commercial real estate (typical institutional portfolio), and all financial assets with all three types of real estate. In addition, all return series will be unbundled into the income and appreciation components for use in the optimal portfolio algorithm. Finally, all optimal portfolios are estimated using both Ibbotson data and Loarie's (Finnegan's) data. Results of the four sets of optimal portfolio composition derivations are then compared and contrasted to ascertain the sensitivity of the optimal portfolios to different estimates of returns for residential real estate, business real estate, and farmland, as well as to the unbundling of the asset returns.

The next section contains the literature review. The section which follows that review explains the research design and methodology. A discussion of the results is presented in the subsequent section. The final section contains the conclusions.

Literature review

Beginning with the Markowitz (1952) mean/variance portfolio formulation over four decades ago, a veritable revolution has taken place in investment research, theory and practice. Unfortunately, this research has been very narrowly based thus far. Until recently, portfolio research has centered almost exclusively on bonds and common stocks. This has been primarily due to the readily available data for determining dividends, interest payments, and price changes, and, therefore, returns on stocks and bonds. Such practical considerations, while often necessary in the short run, do not represent the reality of the average investor's portfolio, and probably not the average financial institution's portfolio. Therefore, these portfolio studies must be reformulated in the longer run in order to approximate actual market behavior. The notable exceptions are few but include Brueggeman, Chen, and Thibodeau (1984), Friedman (1991), Hartzell and Webb (1988), Webb, Curcio, and Rubens (1988) and Webb and Rubens (1986, 1988).

Finally, after many years of virtually no data on real estate returns, some data series are gradually becoming available. Two of these—Ibbotson and Siegel (1984) and Loarie (Finnegan's Green Sheet) were mentioned in the introduction and have been used in some of the previous studies cited (for example Webb *et al.*, 1986; Webb and Rubens, 1988). However, all previous studies used bundled-asset returns. That is, the returns (and variances) from income and appreciation were combined before using them.

Research design

Eight portfolios are constructed from before-tax returns and their concomitant risk measures. All returns are unbundled into income returns and appreciation returns.[1]

The specific assets used in this study include large capitalization common stocks (S&P 500), small capitalization common stock, long-term U.S. government bonds, high-rated long-term corporate bonds, residential real estate, business/commercial real estate, and farmland. Two different sources of returns for the three types of real estate are used. They are:

1. Ibbotson and Siegel (1984), as well as updates obtained through personal communication from Ibbotson Associates in Chicago, Illinois. These return data will be designated "I&S."
2. *Finnegan's Financial Green Sheet Rate-of-Return*. These return data will be designated "Green."

As detailed in Ibbotson and Siegel (1984), the I&S farmland appreciation and income data are from the USDA annual surveys. Residential appreciation is based upon annual changes in the home purchase component of the CPI. Income is from a series developed by Sprinkel and Genetski (1977). Business income and appreciation returns are from a commingled real estate fund managed by the First National Bank of Chicago. The

Green data is proprietary and has been used in a previous study (Webb and Rubens, 1988).

Geltner (1989) and Gilberto (1989) show a positive bias in holding-period returns due to appraisal errors, although Geltner concludes that the holding-return bias is offset by the arithmetic-mean-return bias in the opposite direction. However, Gau and Wang (1990) use appraisal data from a CREF to show that the effect of this bias is minimal and unlikely to significantly effect return indices.

In order to examine the effects of different sources of real estate returns and the unbundling of real estate risks and returns on efficiently diversified mean-variance, mixed-asset portfolios, the return and variances for each of the specific investments must be obtained or estimated. The source for the financial asset returns is Ibbotson and Associates (1992). The period of 1960 through 1986 will be analyzed. This is, of course, historical information and, as such, may or may not represent the ex ante expectations of investors. Since sensitivity of alternative rate-of-return estimates and risks for real estate and the effect of unbundling are being examined, it should suffice here.

The specific portfolios to be estimated are as follows:

Portfolio one: Financial Assets only. This includes eight return series. They are income returns and appreciation returns for long-term U.S. government bonds, long-term high-rated corporate bonds, large capitalization stocks (S&P 500), and small capitalization stocks. A uses "I&S" real estate data in the market index. B uses "Green" real estate data in the market index.

Portfolio Two: Real Estate only. This includes six return series. They are income returns and appreciation returns for residential real estate, business/commercial real estate, and farmland. A uses "I&S" real estate data. B uses "Green" real estate data.

Portfolio Three: Same as Portfolio One with only Business/Commercial Real Estate added (income returns and appreciation returns). This is the type of real estate which most portfolio managers would consider. A uses "I&S" real estate data. B uses "Green" real estate data.

Portfolio Four: Combines Portfolio One and Two (all financial assets and all three types of real estate). A uses "I&S" real estate data. B uses "Green" real estate data.

Table 1 contains the mean annual returns and standard deviation of the returns for all seven assets and both real estate data sources used in this study. All return series have been unbundled into income and appreciation. While the division into income and appreciation was reported for the Ibbotson and Siegel (1984) real estate data, it was not reported for the Finnegan's Green Sheet real estate data. Therefore, the division of the Finnegan's Green Sheet rates-of-return for real estate were assumed to be proportional to the division used for the Ibbotson and Siegel (1984) real estate data. Income and appreciation returns were reported by Ibbotson and Associates (1992) for all the financial assets.

For mixed-asset portfolios to be beneficial, the different asset returns must not be perfectly correlated. The lower the inter-investment correlations, the more beneficial is diversification across asset types and income streams. That is, the lower the inter-investment correlations, the greater the risk reduction of the portfolio. The potential risk reduction due to diversification across asset types can quickly be estimated by observing a correlation matrix of the various assets. The correlation matrix for all assets and data sources used in this study is shown in Table 2.

Table 1. Historical returns on investment media: 1960–1986

Investment type	*Mean (%)*	*Standard deviation (%)*
Government bonds—Income	7.62	3.09
Government bonds—Appreciation	−0.84	10.48
Corporate Bonds—Income	8.33	3.60
Corporate Bonds—Appreciation	−0.91	10.74
Common stock income—Income	4.02	0.92
Common stock—Apreciation	6.72	16.15
Small stock—Income	2.28	0.11
Small stock—Appreciation	16.04	27.65
Residential real estate (I&S)—Income	3.54	0.52
Residential real estate (I&S)—Appreciation	4.90	4.12
Residential real estate (Green)—Income	2.61	1.62
Residential real estate (Green)—Appreciation	3.98	4.65
Business real estate (I&S)—Income	5.49	2.30
Business real estate (I&S)—Appreciation	2.95	3.37
Business real estate (Green)—Income	3.96	2.22
Business real estate (Green)—Appreciation	2.25	2.89
Farmland (I&S)—Income	4.01	2.11
Farmland (I&S)—Appreciation	5.72	9.19
Farmland (Green)—Income	3.78	5.42
Farmland (Green)—Appreciation	2.39	15.26

Table 2. Inter-investment correlation coefficients: 1960–1986

	GOVT BONDS INCOME	*GOVT BONDS APPRE*	*CORP BONDS INCOME*	*CORP BONDS APPRE*	*COMM STOCK INCOME*	*COMM STOCK APPRE*	*SMALL STOCK INCOME*	*SMALL STOCK APPRE*	*RESID (I&S): INCOME*	*RESID (I&S): APPRE*	*BUSIN (I&S): INCOME*	*BUSIN (I&S): APPRE*	*FARM (I&S): INCOME*	*FARM (I&S): APPRE*	*RESID GREEN INCOME*	*RESID GREEN APPRE*	*BUSIN GREEN INCOME*	*BUSIN GREEN APPRE*	*FARM GREEN INCOME*	*FARM GREEN APPRE*
GOVT BONDS: INCOME	1.00																			
GOVT BONDS: APPRE	−0.07 (0.73)	1.00																		
CORP BONDS: INCOME	0.81 (0.00)	0.04 (0.86)	1.00																	
CORP BONDS: APPRE	−0.08 (0.70)	−0.97 (0.00)	0.06 (0.77,	1.00																
COMMON STOCKS: INCOME	0.78 (0.00)	.0020.07 (0.74)	0.61 (0.00)	−1.10 (0.64)	1.00															
COMMON STOCKS: APPRE	0.14 (0.47)	0.13 (0.51)	0.28 (0.16)	0.21 (0.29)	−0.00 (0.99)	1.00														
SMALL STOCKS: INCOME	0.05 (0.80)	0.38 (0.05)	−0.02 (0.93)	0.37 (0.06)	0.14 (0.49)	−0.03 (0.86)	1.00													
SMALL STOCKS: APPRE	0.15 (0.47)	−0.17 (0.39)	−0.21 (0.28)	−0.10 (0.63)	0.15 (0.46)	0.74 (0.00)	−0.05 (0.80)	1.00												
RESIDEN (I&S): INCOME	−0.30 (0.12)	0.16 (0.42)	−0.23 (0.25)	0.18 (0.37)	−0.33 (0.09)	0.07 (0.72)	−0.12 (0.54)	−0.05 (0.79)	1.00											
RESIDEN	0.48	−0.23	0.24	−0.22	0.43	0.09	0.14	0.20	−0.72	1.00										

(I&S): APPRE	(0.01)	(0.24)	(0.23)	(0.28)	(0.02)	(0.66)	(0.49)	(0.32)	(0.01)											
BUSIN	0.82	−0.02	0.75	0.02	0.81	0.30	0.15	0.40	−0.39	0.40	1.00									
(I&S): INCOMI	(0.01)	(0.94)	(0.00)	(0.94)	(0.00)	(0.13)	(0.44)	(0.04)	(0.04)	(0.04)										
BUSIN	0.34	−0.41	0.19	−0.39	0.14	−0.12	−0.24	−0.06	−0.10	0.33	−0.03	1.00								
(I&S): APPRE	(0.08)	(0.04)	(0.33)	(0.05)	(0.48)	(0.55)	(0.22)	(0.77)	(0.64)	(0.09)	(0.90									
FAREM	−0.10	0.26	−0.23	0.20	−0.33	−0.20	0.02	−0.48	0.01	−0.01	−0.39	−0.08	1.00							
(I&S): INCOME	(0.63)	(0.19)	(0.24)	(0.33)	(0.10)	(0.31)	(0.93)	(0.01)	(0.96)	(0.97)	(0.04)	(0.70)								
FARM	−0.13	−0.34	−0.15	−0.37	−0.08	−0.08	−0.02	0.18	0.61	0.46	−0.03	0.17	0.11	1.00						
(I&S): APPRE	(0.50)	(0.08)	(0.47)	(0.06)	(0.70)	(0.69)	(0.93)	(0.38)	(0.00)	(0.02)	(0.90)	(0.41)	(0.57)							
RESIDEN	0.25	−0.39	−0.01	−0.45	0.12	−0.38	−0.10	−0.23	−0.13	−0.01	0.12	0.24	0.24	0.27	1.00					
(GREEN): INCOME	(0.21)	(0.05)	(0.94)	(0.02)	(0.56)	(0.06)	(0.60)	(0.24)	(0.52)	(0.94)	(0.54)	(0.22)	(0.22)	(0.17)						
RESIDEN	0.44	−0.37	−0.20	−0.39	0.41	−0.13	0.12	0.04	−0.71	0.82	0.34	0.44	0.02	0.60	0.46	1.00				
(GREEN): APPRE	(0.02)	(0.06)	(0.33)	(0.05)	(0.03)	(0.53)	(0.54)	(0.85)	(0.00)	(0.00)	(0.08)	(0.02)	(0.91)	(0.00)	(0.02)					
BUSIN	0.04	−0.41	−0.02	−0.39	0.20	−0.08	0.03	0.23	−0.54	0.39	0.22	−0.17	−0.31	0.48	0.15	0.52	1.00			
(GREEN): INCOME	(0.85)	(0.03)	(0.92)	(0.04)	(0.33)	(0.69)	(0.86)	(0.25)	(0.00)	(0.04)	(0.26)	(0.39)	(0.12)	(0.01)	(0.45)	(0.01)				
BUSIN	0.09	−0.42	−0.12	−0.40	−0.08	−0.27	−0.05	−0.18	−0.16	0.42	−0.26	0.86	0.10	0.30	0.21	0.50	−0.00	1.00		
(GREEN): APPRE	(0.67)	(0.03)	(0.55)	(0.04)	(0.70)	(0.18)	(0.79)	(0.36)	(0.42)	(0.03)	(0.18)	(0.00)	(0.62)	(0.12)	(0.29)	(0.01)	(0.99)			
FARM	0.14	0.27	0.03	0.23	0.02	0.09	0.37	0.10	−0.34	0.34	0.15	−0.29	0.45	0.30	0.09	0.26	−0.00	−0.11	1.00	
(GREEN): INCOME	(0.48)	(0.16)	(0.90)	(0.24)	(0.92)	(0.67)	(0.36)	(0.60)	(0.08)	(0.08)	(0.47)	(0.14)	(0.02)	(0.13)	(0.66)	(0.19)	(0.98)	(0.57)		
FARM	−0.01	−0.42	0.01	−0.44	−0.03	−0.00	−0.28	0.28	−0.49	0.46	0.07	0.16	0.02	0.88	0.22	0.54	0.48	0.23	0.30	1.00
(GREEN): APPRE	(0.99)	(0.03)	(0.94)	(0.02)	(0.90)	(0.98)	(0.16)	(0.15)	(0.01)	(0.02)	(0.73)	(0.43)	(0.93)	(0.00)	(0.26)	(0.00)	(0.01)	(0.24)	(0.12)	

Note: The numbers in parentheses are significance levels for the rejection of the null hypothesis of zero rank correlation.

Before proceeding, it is necessary to specify the portfolio investment problem. When there is a risk-free asset paying the risk-free interest rate of R_f, the portfolio investment problem can be reduced to the maximization of the slope θ, i.e.,

$$Max\ \theta = (\bar{R}_p - R_f)/\sigma_p$$
$$\text{subject to } x_i = 1, \tag{1}$$

where R_p and σ_p refer to the expected rate-of-return on the portfolio and its standard deviation, respectively, while x_i refers to the fraction of wealth allocated to asset i. There are restrictions on short-selling. (See Figure 1.)

Next the market index was constructed, which includes the seven assets used in this study plus T-Bills, so that beta, nonsystematic risk, desirability index, cutoff rate, and other calculations could be made. The market index was constructed as shown in Table 3 which is approxi-

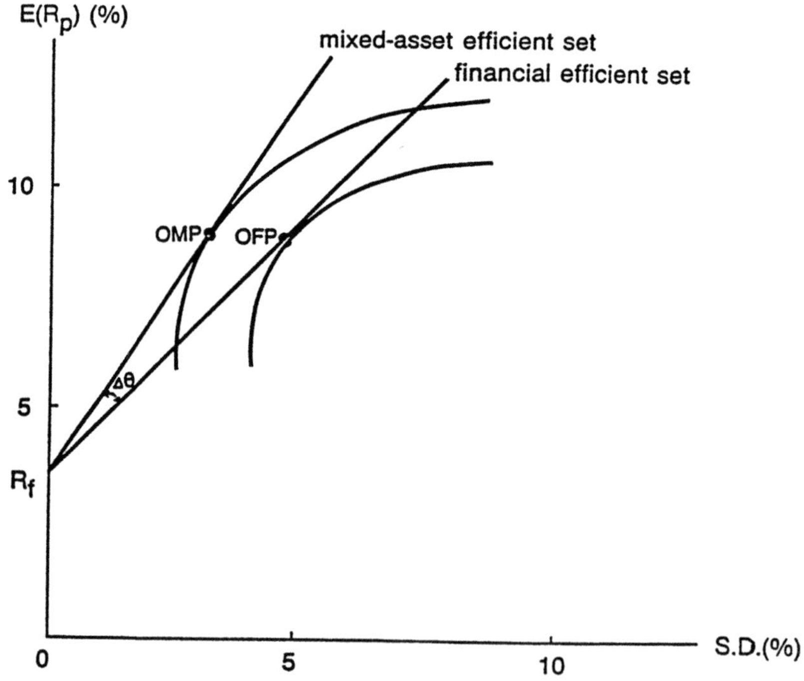

Figure 1: Gains in Mean-Variance Efficiency From Mixed-Asset Diversification.

Table 3. Construction of the Market Index

Asset class	*Weighting*
Treasury bills	5.0%
Government bonds	2.0%
Corporate bonds	5.0%
S&P 500 stocks	16.0%
Small cap common stocks	8.0%
Residential real estate	47.0%
Business real estate	8.0%
Farmland	9.0%

Based upon wealth figures from Ibbotson and Siegel (1979) and Ibbotson, Siegel, and Love (1985).

mately the content suggested by Ibbotson and Siegel (1979) and Ibbotson, Siegel, and Love (1985). Using the process enumerated by Elton and Gruber (1987) and Elton, Gruber, and Padberg (1976), the optimal portfolio is then calculated. This process assumes use of the single-index model. Elton, Gruber, and Padberg have shown that once the single-index model is assumed, the "desirability" of an asset, from the viewpoint of selecting the optimal portfolio, can be readily measured by the asset's "excess return to beta" ratio:

$$(R_j - R_f)/B_j \tag{2}$$

where $B_i = \text{Cov}(R_j, I_m)/\text{Var}(I_m)$. They have further shown that asset i will be included in the optimal portfolio if and only if the asset's desirability index exceeds a certain cutoff rate.

The desirability index (Dl) is defined as the asset's excess return to beta and is calculated as follows:

$$Dl = (R_j - R_f)/B_i \tag{3}$$

where

R_j = the rate of return on asset i

R_f = the risk-free rate

B_i = beta, a constant specific to asset i.

Only assets whose desirability index exceeds the cutoff rate will be included in the optimal portfolio. Since this technique relies upon the estimation of beta for a constructed market index, all of the assumptions and associated problems discussed by Roll (1977) should be remembered when reviewing the results.

Results

A summary of the relationship of the unbundled asset returns to the market index is contained in Table 4 for "I&S" data and Table 5 for Finnegan's "Green" Sheet data. Large capitalization common stock appreciation and small capitalization common stock appreciation are highly related to the market index in a positive direction for both data sources. Long-term U.S. government bond appreciation, long-term corporate bond appreciation, and farmland appreciation are significantly negatively related to the market index when the Green data is used.

Table 6 displays the results of the optimal portfolio estimates for the "I&S" data, while Table 7 displays the same results for the "Green" data. The "financial assets only" portfolios (1, A and B) are virtually identical, as would be expected. Only the real estate data was changed in the index portion, while the returns for all financial assets were exactly the same. The results for the "real estate only" portfolios (2, A and B) are slightly different for the two data sets. Both have very little residential real estate appreciation; a substantial amount (55% or 86%) of business real estate income; a significant amount (37% or 13%) of farmland income; and no residential real estate income, business real estate appreciation, or farmland appreciation.

Table 4. Relationship of assets to new market index: 1960–1986
I&S Data

Investment type	R^2	B_i
Government bonds—Income	0.06	0.20
Government bonds—Appreciation	0.01	−0.03
Corporate bonds—Income	0.10	0.30
Corporate bonds—Appreciation	0.00	−0.01
Common stock income—Income	0.12	0.09
Common stock—Appreciation	0.66	3.49
Small stock—Income	0.00	−0.01
Small stock—Appreciation	0.80	6.57
Residential real estate (I&S)—Income	0.07	−0.04
Residential real estate (I&S)—Appreciation	0.19	0.48
Business real estate (I&S)—Income	0.25	0.31
Business real estate (I&S)—Appreciation	0.01	0.08
Farmland (I&S)—Income	0.15	−0.21
Farmland (I&S)—Appreciation	0.03	0.44

Table 5. Relationship of assets to new market index: 1960–1986
Green Sheet Data

Investment type	R^2	B_i
Government bonds — Income	0.04	0.17
Government bonds — Appreciation	0.09	−0.90
Corporate bonds — Income	0.05	0.23
Corporate bonds — Appreciation	0.05	−0.64
Common stock income — Income	0.11	0.09
Common stock — Appreciation	0.48	3.14
Small stock — Income	0.00	−0.01
Small stock — Appreciation	0.74	6.68
Residential real estate (Green) — Income	0.01	−0.05
Residential real estate (Green) — Appreciation	0.14	0.49
Business real estate (Green) — Income	0.22	0.29
Business real estate (Green) — Appreciation	0.01	−0.06
Farmland (Green) — Income	0.00	−0.09
Farmland (Green) — Appreciation	0.05	−0.98

Table 6. Optimal portfolio composition
I&S Data

Investment type	*Financial assets (FA) only*	*Real estate (RE) only*	*FA & business RE*	*FA & RE*
Government bonds — Income	27%	N/E	27%	25%
Government bonds — Appreciation	—	N/E	—	—
Corporate bonds — Income	23%	N/E	23%	21%
Corporate bonds — Appreciation	—	N/E	—	—
Common stock — Income	50%	N/E	50%	50%
Common stock — Appreciation	—	N/E	—	—
Small stock — Income	—	N/E	—	—
Small stock — Appreciation	—	N/E	—	—
Residential real estate — Income	N/E	—	N/E	—
Residential real estate — Appreciation	N/E	1%	N/E	2%
Business real estate — Income	N/E	86%	—	—
Business real estate — Appreciation	N/E	—	—	—
Farmland — Income	N/E	13%	N/E	1%
Farmland — Appreciation	N/E	—	N/E	—

Note: N/E = not entered.

Table 7. Optimal portfolio composition
Green Sheet Data

Investment type	*Financial assets (FA) only*	*Real estate (RE) only*	*FA & business RE*	*FA & RE*
Government bonds—Income	28%	N/E	25%	18%
Government bonds—Appreciation	—	N/E	—	—
Corporate bonds—Income	23%	N/E	21%	15%
Corporate bonds—Appreciation	—	N/E	—	—
Common stock—Income	49%	N/E	39%	35%
Common stock—Appreciation	—	N/E	—	—
Small stock—Income	—	N/E	—	—
Small stock—Appreciation	—	N/E	—	—
Residential real estate—Income	N/E	—	N/E	—
Residential real estate—Appreciation	N/E	8%	N/E	2%
Business real estate—Income	N/E	55%	15%	16%
Business real estate—Appreciation	N/E	—	—	—
Farmland—Income	N/E	37%	N/E	14%
Farmland—Appreciation	N/E	—	N/E	—

Note: N/E = not entered

Some variation between the optimal portfolios for the two real estate data sets is manifested in the "all financial assets plus business real estate" portfolios (3, A and B). Only business real estate income enters (only for I&S data (15%) and mostly as a substitute for common stock income). Long-term U.S. government bond income (25% and 27%) and long-term corporate bond income (21% and 23%) entered the optimal portfolios. Small capitalization stock income and appreciation from all of the assets used for this portfolio never entered the portfolio.

Finally, the portfolios with all financial assets and all three types of real estate (4, A and B) show the most variation. Residential real estate appreciation is the only appreciation for any asset in either data set which enters the optimal portfolio and only in a minor way (2%). Small capitalization stock income and residential real estate income never enter the optimal portfolio for either data set. Real estate of some form comprises 32% of the optimal portfolio, with I&S data, but only 3%, with the Green data.

Table 8 contains the optimal portfolio characteristics for all four portfolios for both data sets. The theta is maximized for both data sets by the portfolio with "financial assets and all three types of real estate." However, theta is only significantly different from that for the "financial assets only" portfolio for the I&S data set.

Table 8. Optimal portfolio characteristics: 1960–1986

Green Sheet Data

Portfolio type	*Mean return* (R_p)	*Standard deviation* (σ_p)	θ
Financial assets only	6.02%	1.97%	2.90
Real Estate only	3.90%	2.17%	0.67
Financial assets and Business real estate	5.82%	1.77%	2.99
Financial assets and real estate	5.27%	1.40%	3.02

I&S Data

Portfolio type	*Mean return* (R_p)	*Standard deviation* (σ_p)	θ
Financial assets only	5.98%	1.95%	2.89
Real Estate only	5.25%	1.89%	2.20
Financial assets and Business real estate	5.98%	1.95%	2.89
Financial assets and real estate	5.81%	1.79%	2.96

Conclusions

The unbundling of the asset returns into the income component and the appreciation component reveals large differences in risk for the two income streams for any given asset. Examining standard deviation from Table 1 reveals that the standard deviation for residential real estate appreciation is eight to 62 times as great as for residential real estate income, while the return for residential real estate appreciation is only 1.4 to 1.5 times as great as residential real estate income. For business real estate, the returns from appreciation are less than those for income, yet the variance of business real estate appreciation returns is 1.3 and 1.45 times the variance for business real estate income returns. Farmland displays similar characteristics, as do the financial assets. Clearly the unbundling of asset returns is needed in order to clearly visualize the risk and return characteristics of capital asset returns.

While previous mixed-asset portfolio studies result in very large allocations of real estate to the optimal portfolio, such was not the case for this study. The maximum allocation in this study was 32%, which is less than the estimated proportion of real estate in the U.S. wealth portfolio (Ibbotson *et al.*, 1985). Perhaps portfolio managers have found synthetic means to approximate the return and risk characteristics of the real estate demonstrated in this study by unbundling asset returns, and, therefore, they do not need to actually invest in real estate. Obviously, more research is needed on this topic.

Notes

1. Although financial instruments are not yet available to perform this unbundling for portfolio managers, the possibility is not far off. Witness the growth in recent years of stripped government bonds, whhich do exactly this by selling the reversion to one person and the income stream to another.

References

Brueggeman, W.B., A.H. Chen, and T.G. Thibodeau. "Real Estate Investment Funds: Performance and Portfolio Consideration." *AREUEA Journal* (Fall 1984), 333–354.

Elton, E. and M.J. Gruber. *Modern Portfolio Theory and Investment Analysis*, 3rd ed. New York: John Wiley & Sons, 1987.

Elton, E.J., M.J. Gruber, and M.W. Padberg. "Simple Criteria for Optimal Portfolio Selection." *Journal of Finance* 31 (December 1976).

Friedman, H.C. "Real Estate Investment and Portfolio Theory." *Journal of Financial and Quantitative Analysis* (March 1971), 861–874.

Gau, G. and K. Wang. "A Further Examination of Appraisal Data and the Potential Bias in Real Estate Return Indexes." *AREUEA Journal* (Spring 1990), 40–48.

Geltner, D. "Bias, in Appraisal Based Returns." *AREUEA Journal* (Fall 1989), 338–353.

Gilberto, S. "A Note on the Use of Appraisal Data in Indexes of Performance Measurement." *AREUEA Journal* (Spring 1989), 77–83.

Hartzell, D. and J.R. Webb. "The Allocation of Equity Real Estate Investments in Real Estate Portfolios." Mimeo, 1988.

Ibbotson, R.G. and L.B. Siegel. "The United States Market Wealth Portfolio." *Journal of Portfolio Management* (Fall 1979), 82–92.

Ibbotson, R.G. and L.B. Siegel. "Real Estate Returns: A Comparison With Other Investment." *AREUEA Journal* (Fall 1984), 219–242.

Ibbotson, R.G., L.B. Siegel, and K. Love. "World Wealth: Market Values and Returns." *Journal of Portfolio Management* (Fall 1985).

Ibbotson and Associates. *1992 Yearbook*. Ibbotson Associates: Chicago, 1992.

Kapplin, S.D. "Institutional Real Estate Portfolios." In: S.A. Phyrr and J.R. Cooper, *Real Estate Investment: Strategy, Analysis, Decisions*. Boston; Warren, Gorham, and Lamont, 1982, pp. 665–697.

Loarie, R.F. "Farm Real Estate Rates of Return." *Finnegan's Financial Green Sheets Rates-of-Return* 87:1. "Residential Real Estate Rates-of-Return." Same Journal 87:2. "Commercial Real Estate Rates-of-Return." Same Journal 87:3. 1337 Huntington Drive, Mundelein, IL 60060.

Markowitz, H.M. "Portfolio Selection. *Journal of Finance* (March 1952), 77–91.

Roll, R. "A Critique of the Asset Pricing Theory's Tests, Part I: One Past and Potential Testability of the Theory." *Journal of Financial Economics* (March 1977), 129–176.

Sprinkel, B. and R. Genetski. *Winning with Money: A Guide for Your Future*. Homewood, IL: Dow-Jones-Irwin, 1977.

Webb, J.R., R.J. Curcio, and J.H. Rubens. "Diversification Gains From Including Real Estate In Mixed-Asset Portfolios." *Decision Sciences* (Spring 1988), 434–452.

Webb, J.R. and J.H. Rubens. "Portfolio Considerations in the Valuation of Real Estate." *AREUEA Journal* (Fall 1986), 466–495.

Webb, J.R. and J.H. Rubens. "Effects of Alternative Return Estimates on Restricted Mixed-Asset Portfolios." *AREUEA Journal* (Summer 1988), 123–137.

6 REAL ESTATE PORTFOLIO DIVERSIFICATION BY SOURCES OF RETURN

JOHN E. WILLIAMS

Introduction

The primary objective of diversification is to assemble an investment portfolio that contains a minimum level of risk relative to the expected return of the portfolio ("Minimum Variance Portfolio"). Investors such as REITS, pension funds, insurance companies, etc. diversity their real estate portfolios through selecting different property types (apartments, office buildings, etc.) and/or acquiring properties from different geographical locations.

The above approach toward achieving a minimum variance real estate portfolio is logically sound, since variation in geographic appreciation/depreciation rates in real estate can be easily observed. In addition, investigations by Miles and Rice (1978), Miller (1978), and others, have shown that different types of real estate contain different levels of investment risk. Kapplin (1976), Roulac (1978), and Young (1977) have adopted a framework from "capital market theory" that can be utilized to evaluate the risk contained in real estate projects and portfolios.

Markowitz's (1952) was the first study to approach portfolio analysis through quantifying risk and return. The most important contribution from Markowitz's research to the finance literature was the mathematical proof which demonstrated that portfolio risk is determined through the covariance of the assets in the portfolio rather than by the amount of risk contained in the individual assets comprising the portfolio.

Sharpe (1963) simplified the data requirements of the Markowitz model by proposing a single index model. Sharpe's index model substituted the covariance of each security in a portfolio with a common market index.

Black and Scholes (1976) completed a study in which the findings contained implications concerning the risk/return tradeoff of stock portfolios composed of securities with high and low dividend payout ratios. Since corporate earnings that are not paid out in the form of dividends increase the value of shares outstanding (capital gains), a parallel relationship exists between dividends and capital gains of a corporation, and the operating and reversion cash flows accruing to real estate projects.

Research results from studies by Valachi (1978) and Zerbst (1980) indicate that there is an "aggregate bias" in evaluating the risk and return associated with real estate projects. According to Valachi this "aggregate bias" is evident in that real eastate investors are (or should be) concerned with the components of return on real estate projects, as well as the overall return, and therefore should partition the estimates of return for a potential project into the operating, tax shelter, and reversion cash flows. The implication is that different investors are interested in different cash flow patterns. Moreover, Zerbst states that a more precise measurement of the risk contained in a real estate project can be obtained through partitioning the total return.

Research hypothesis

The major objective of this paper is to investigate the real estate portfolio effects (risk/return tradeoff) of including projects with different cash flow patterns (operating and reversion) in the portfolio. The basic research question is whether investors can attain or approach a "minimum variance" real estate portfolio through diversifying by cash flow patterns.

The investment return to a real estate project can be divided into the general components of operating and reversion cash flows (Valachi, 1978). An analysis of the total risk/return tradeoffs from combining projects in a portfolio wherein the percentages of total return flowing to the operating and reversion components of return are correlated is important information for constructing a diversified real estate portfolio. This type of analysis is even more important given that there is very little market information available describing the risk (such as "betas" and "sigmas") contained in real estate investments; however, since real estate investors usually attempt to estimate the expected cash flows from a potential project, an understanding of the risk/return implications of the cash flow patterns of the projects included in their portfolios can improve diversification.

The hypothesis of this study is that real estate portfolios assembled to emphasize both operating and reversion cash flows perform better (risk/return) than those portfolios that are constructed with no consideration given to the cash flow patterns of the projects included in that portfolio. In other words, the greater the relative balance of return (percentage) from operating and reversion, the more diversified the portfolio, and thus the better the portfolio performance.

Methodology

The research hypothesis was tested through statistical simulation. Market data were collected from a pension fund (managed by a major insurance company) on ten recently acquired real estated projects (existing properties). It was important to focus on recently acquired projects in order to simulate the ex ante probabilistic expectations of the overall rate of return and certain stochastic variables. These data inputs were supplied by the manager of the projects, who assumed an ownership cycle of ten years for each of the projects.

The Real Estate Simulation program ("GSUWMS3") that was utilized to complete the computer runs treated the following variables as stochastic: (1) occupancy rate; (2) rental income; (3) growth rate of rental income; (4) operating expenses; (5) growth rate of operating expense ratio; and (6) growth rate of property value. The Monte Carlo Technique and the "rectangular approximation method" (Martin, 1978) were employed to develop the probability distributions from the subjective probabilistic inputs supplied by the data source.

The internal rate of return (IRR) was calculated for both the operating and reversion components of return, and used to calculate the level of cash flow concentration (CFCL), which is based on the percentage of each source of return to the total portfolio return (4).

The partitioned (operating and reversion) returns for each of the ten projects were input to a portfolio program, which was used to calculate 45 different portfolios consisting of eight projects each (3). Miles and McCue (1984) found that the reduction in portfolio risk is very small after the eighth project is added to the portfolio. The Portfolio program ("REALPORT"; GSU) contained five major subroutines, including algorithms to calculate covariance, total portfolio risk, expected portfolio return, and Sharpe's portfolio performance index.

The equations listed below calculate values for the following variables: portfolio risk (1); portfolio performance index (2); the number of eight project portfolios that can be formed from ten projects (3); and level of cash flow concentration (4).

As shown below, the calculation of total portfolio risk includes the individual asset's risk (which contains some non-diversifiable systematic risk), as well as the covariance between assets.

$$\text{Portfolio risk} = \blacktriangledown_Z = \sqrt{W_X^2\blacktriangledown_X^2 + W_Y^2\blacktriangledown_Y^2 + 2W_XW_Y\,{}'_{XY}\,\blacktriangledown_X\blacktriangledown_Y}, \quad (1)$$

where

W = individual asset's value percentage of the total value of assets in the portfolio

$\blacktriangledown$ = risk of the individual asset

${}'_{XY}$ = correlation of returns between assets included in the portfolio.

Sharpe's portfolio performance index

$$S_t = \frac{R_t - r^*}{\blacktriangledown_t} \quad (2)$$

where

S_t = the Sharpe Index

R_t = the average return on portfolio t

r^* = the riskless rate of interest

$\blacktriangledown_t$ = the risk (standard deviation) of portfolio t.

Number of portfolios

$$nCr = \binom{n}{r} = r!\,\frac{n!}{(n-r)!} = 10C8 = \binom{10}{8} = \frac{10!}{8!\,(10-8)!} = \underline{45} \quad (3)$$

where

nCr is the number (n) of combinations (C) of n different objects (real estate projects), taken r (eight) at a time.

Level of cash flow concentration

$$\mathrm{CFCL} = \left|\sum_{i=1}^{n} \frac{R_i}{T_i} x_i\right| - 1/C + \left|\sum_{i=1}^{n} \frac{O_i}{T_i} x_i\right| - 1/C \tag{4}$$

where

n is equal to the number of projects
T_i is equal to the total return to the project
R_i is the percentage of total return from reversion source
O_i is the percentage of total return from operating cash flow
x_i is the percentage of portfolio invested in the project
C is equal to the number of components of return being considered.

The less balanced the cash flow concentration, the larger the value of CFCL from (4); this relationship holds because an equally balanced portfolio is represented by an equal percentage of return from each source (operating and reversion).

For instance, if a hypothetical portfolio consists of investments in three projects, with two sources of return (reversion and operating), the level of cash flow concentration is calculated as follows (4):

	Column 1		*Column 3*	*Column 4*
	% of Port.	*IRR*	*Reversion Return/IRR*	*Operating Return/IRR*
Project #1	.4	.20	.06/.20 = .3	.14/.2 = .7
Project #2	.3	.25	.025/.25 = .1	.225/.25 = .9
Project #3	.3	.22	.176/.22 = .8	.044/.22 = .2
Total return	Σ(col 1 × col 3) = .39		Σ(col 1 × col 4) = .61	
	|.39 − .5| = .11	+	|.61 − .5| = .11	
		CFCL = .22		

Hypothesis test

To test the research hypothesis concerning the relationship between portfolio performance and cash flow patterns, a regression analysis was undertaken using the 45 computed portfolio performance indices (2) as the dependent variable (y), and the CFCL (4) as the independent variable

(x), to determine whether the level of cash flow concentration (CFCL) could predict the portfolio performance index (PPI).

To further examine the research hypothesis, returns from the projects were used as inputs in a Markowitz protfolio model to generate an "efficient frontier" consisting of the 45 portfolios. As noted above, each portfolio consisted of eight projects.

The level of cash flow concentration of the portfolios along the efficient frontier was compared to the portfolios "off" the efficient frontier. It was expected that a lower level of cash flow concentration (more balanced) would be found among those portfolios on the efficient frontier, since the dependent variable (PPI) should increase as the independent variable (CFCL) decreases.

In order to examine the relative strength of this naive approach, a regression analysis of the PPI (dependent variable) by a "true" (Markowitz: based on correlation of returns) diversification index (DI) was undertaken.

To construct a diversification index, a correlation coefficient between the projects included in the portfolio was calculated for each component of return. This procedure was necessary because the level of cash flow concentration (CFCL) was calculated by components of return. Calculation of the diversification index (DI) is shown below in (5).

Diversification index

$$\mathrm{DI} = \left[\left(\sum_{i=1}^{N} \frac{R_i}{T_i}\right) - 1/C\,('_{ri})\right] + \left[\left(\sum_{i=1}^{N} \frac{O_i}{T_i}\right) - 1/C\,('_{oi})\right], \qquad (5)$$

where

N is equal to the number of projects
T_i is equal to the total return to the project
R_i is the percentage of total return from reversion source
O_i is the percentage of total return from operating cash flow

C is equal to the number of components of return being considered ($C=2$ for this research)

$'_{ri}$ and $'_{oi}$ are the portfolio's correlation coefficients for reversion and operating returns respectively; and

$$'_{ri} = \sum_{i=1}^{N}\sum_{j=1}^{N} {'_{rij}}; \quad '_{oi} = \sum_{i=1}^{N}\sum_{j=1}^{N} {'_{oij}},$$

where

N = the number of projects included in the portfolio (8)

i = project i and j = project j
$'_{rij}$ = correlation coefficient between projects i and j operating returns
$'_{oij}$ = correlation coefficient between projects i and j reversion returns.

Results

This section contains the following exhibits and related discussions: Table 1, calculation of partitioned internal rate of return for each project; Table 2, variable values for the 45 portfolios consisting of eight projects each; Table 3, a regression analysis of PPI (dependent variable) on CFCL; Table 4, a regression analysis of PPI (dependent variable on DI); and Table 5, calculation of DI portfolios on the efficient frontier.

Output from the portfolio program used to generate the variable values for each of the forty-five (45) eight-project portfolios is shown in Table 2. The variable values generated were: (1) portfolio return; (2) portfolio risk; (3) Sharpe's performance index; and (4) diversification index. The variable values for Sharpe's performance index and the level of cash flow concentration were input to the regression model to test the research hypothesis.

The first regression run tested the linear relationship between portfolio performance (PPI) and the diversification index (DI) that was devised to determine the extent of true (Markowitz) diversification. The form of the model tested is shown below (6).

Table 1. Partitioning IRR by Components of Return

	Internal rate of return (IRR)	*Operating return*	*Reversion return*	*Operating % of total return*	*Reversion % of total return*
Project #1	.1174	.0739	.0434	.63	.37
Project #2	.1685	.1129	.0556	.67	.33
Project #3	.1367	.0848	.0519	.62	.38
Project #4	.1255	.0690	.0565	.55	.45
Project #5	.1010	.0616	.0394	.61	.39
Project #6	.1767	.1484	.0283	.74	.26
Project #7	.1366	.0847	.0519	.62	.38
Project #8	.1306	.0771	.0535	.59	.41
Project #9	.1429	.0843	.0586	.59	.41
Project #10	.1500	.1050	.0450	.70	.30

Table 2. Variable Values for 45 Eight-Project Portfolios

Portfolio Number	*Portfolio return*	*Portfolio risk*	*PPI*	*CFCL*	*DI*
1	13.66	2.73	4.96	.2600	−.3231
2	13.82	2.64	5.19	.2600	−.0811
3	13.91	3.16	4.36	.2875	.3785
4	13.74	2.47	5.51	.2525	−.3139
5	13.8	2.64	5.19	.2800	−.3077
6	13.98	2.54	5.45	.2800	−.2080
7	13.24	2.61	5.02	.2225	−.1705
8	13.33	2.70	4.88	.2500	−.2791
9	13.48	2.62	5.09	.2500	−.2138
10	13.41	2.34	5.68	.2425	−.2810
11	14.19	2.66	5.28	.2550	−.2602
12	14.28	3.08	4.59	.2825	.1198
13	14.43	3.07	4.66	.2828	.4758
14	14.35	2.43	5.86	.2750	−.4419
15	13.85	2.56	5.35	.2450	−.3136
16	13.88	2.62	5.25	.2700	−.3272
17	13.97	3.03	4.56	.2975	−.0308
18	14.12	3.02	4.64	.2975	.3728
19	14.05	2.36	5.89	.2900	−.4644
20	13.55	2.46	5.46	.2600	−.4239
21	14.49	3.02	4.76	.2925	−.0080
22	13.74	2.70	5.03	.2525	−.1257
23	13.83	3.20	4.28	.2800	.3650
24	13.97	3.18	4.36	.2800	.7006
25	13.91	2.52	5.47	.2725	−.1655
26	13.41	2.58	5.15	.2425	−.1811
27	14.35	3.16	4.5	.2750	.2966
28	14.05	3.11	4.47	.2900	.2570
29	13.34	2.54	5.19	.2400	−.4056
30	13.43	2.64	5.04	.2675	−.5439
31	13.58	2.53	5.32	.2675	−.5020
32	13.51	2.23	6.00	.2600	−.5259
33	13.01	2.40	5.36	.2300	−.4441
34	13.95	2.67	5.17	.2625	−.5281
35	13.65	2.60	5.19	.2775	−.6338
36	13.51	2.70	4.95	.2600	−.3907
37	13.98	2.59	5.34	.2475	−.3868
38	14.07	2.73	5.10	.2750	−.4881
39	14.22	2.66	5.30	.2750	−.4018
40	14.15	2.29	6.13	.2675	−.5214

41	13.65	2.45	5.52	.2375	−.4379
42	14.59	2.74	5.27	.2700	−.4964
43	14.29	2.70	5.24	.2850	−.5733
44	14.15	2.82	4.98	.2675	−.3071
45	13.75	2.58	5.27	.2550	−.6855

$$\text{PPI} = a + \beta(\text{DI}) + e. \tag{6}$$

The null hypothesis which stated no relationship ($\beta = 0$) between the PPI (dependent variable) and the diversification index (DI) was rejected at both the 95 and 99 fractile levels for $V1 = 1$ and $V2 = 43$ degrees of

Table 3. Multiple Regression and Correlation Analysis
PPI on DI

VARIABLE I	β(I)	BETA(I)	XBAR(I)	S(I)
1	4.91014	N.D.	5.1439	.428263
2	−2.00985	−.746871	−.116309	.159145

INDEX OF DETERMINATION (R^2) = .558304
CORRELATION COEFFICIENT (R) = .747197

C O R E L A T I O N   M A T I X

1	−.746873
−.746873	1

A N A L Y S I S   O F   V A R I A N C E

SOURCE	SS	DF	MS	F
REGRESSION	4.60791	1	4.60791	54.352
ERROR	3.6455	43	.847791E−01	
TOTAL	8.25342	44		

STANDARD DEVIATION OF ERROR ITEM .291168

VARIABLE	COEFFICIENT	STD ERROR	*t*-STATISTIC	95% CONFIDENCE LIMITS(+,−)
2	−2.009985	.272738	−7.36917	.550031
D.F.				

freedom; critical values were 4.07 and 7.27 respectively. Also, the t-statistic (−7.37) was significant at the 95 (critical value = 2.021) and 99 (critical value = 2.704) fractile levels.

The second regression run has the following form:

$$\text{PPI} = a + (\beta)\ \text{CFCL} + e. \tag{7}$$

The dependent variable is the portfolio performance index (PPI) and the independent variable is the level of cash flow concentration (CFCL)

A negative relationship ($\beta = -.3703$) was found between the portfolio performance index (dependent variable) and the level of cash flow concentration. The negative sign is consistent with the research expectations. The index of determination ($R^2 = .138163$) is significant (F-ratio = 6.89) at the 95 (critical value = 2.021), but not at the 99 fractile level (critical value = 2.704) for 43 degrees of freedom.

The null hypothesis which states that there are no portfolio benefits to be gained from constructing portfolios based on cash flow sources is therefore rejected.

Table 4. Multiple Regression and Correlation Analysis
PPI on CFCL

VARIABLE I	β(I)	BETA(I)	XBAR(I)	S(I)
1	7.50111	N.D.	5.1439	.428263
2	−8.86172	−.370331	−.265999	.0178971

INDEX OF DETERMINATION (R^2) = .138163
CORRELATION MATRIX (R) = .371702

ANALYSIS OF VARIANCE

SOURCE	SS	DF	MS	F
REGRESSION	1.14031	1	1.14031	6.8934
ERROR	7.1131	43	.165421	
TOTAL	8.25342	44		

STANDARD DEVIATION OF ERROR ITEM .40672

VARIABLE	COEFFICIENT	STD ERROR	t-STATISTIC	95% CONFIDENCE LIMITS(+,−)
2	−8.86172	3.38916	−2.61472	6.83492

Verification of diversification index

To verify the Diversification Index, project returns for each of the 45 portfolios were input in a Markowitz model to generate an efficient frontier as shown in Figure 1. The diversification index of the portfolios along the efficient frontier was compared to the remaining portfolios. A "difference of means" test was employed to the test following hypothesis:

$$H_0\colon \mu_1 - \mu_2 = 0;$$
$$H_A\colon \mu_1 - \mu_2 > 0.$$

As expected, the mean DI (−.445) of portfolios occupying the efficient frontier was significantly less (computed = 2.99; critical value = 2.42) than the mean DI (−.20) of the portfolios "off" the efficient frontier at the 99 percent confidence level.

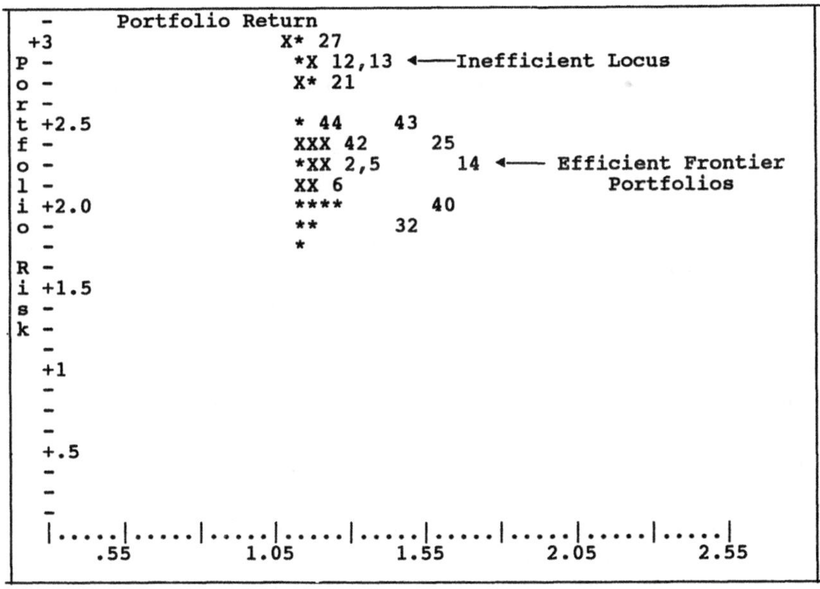

Figure 1. Efficient frontier.

*Portfolios "off" the efficient frontier occupying the same position as the adjacent numbered portfolio.
[X]Multiple portfolios "off" the efficient frontier occupying the same position.
Note: The above designations (X & *) are controlled by the program.

Notwithstanding the fact that the average DI of portfolios occupying the efficient frontier is lower than the average DI of portfolios "off" the efficient frontier, several portfolios "off" the efficient frontier have a lower DI than those "on" the efficient frontier. In other words, while the DI is a good predictor ($R^2 = .55$) of portfolio performance, it is not an absolute predictor. This disparity may be explained by the fact that the DI is based on the simple correlation of returns to the portfolio, whereas the efficient frontier predicts the minimum varianced portfolios that resulted from plotting the portfolio's return against total portfolio risk. Total portfolio risk includes systematic and unsystematic risk. Portfolio diversification only reduces unsystematic risk.

Conclusions

The primary intent of the research was to determine if naive diversification based on cash flow patterns could improve the portfolio performance of real estates projects in the E-V (expected return/risk) framework.

A regression test generated a negative correlation between the portfolio performance index and the level of cash flow concentration (CFCL). The t-statistic representing the beta of the independent variable (CFCL) was significant at the 95 fractile level. The regression equation was also significant (F-test) at the 95 fractile level. An R^2 of .138 revealed that approximately fourteen percent of the variation in return per unit of risk (PPI) can be explained by the level of cash flow concentration. Stated succinctly, the less dependent a real estate portfolio is on a particular component (operating or reversion) of return to achieve the overall expected return, the more efficient (E-V) the portfolio.

Further verification compared the strength of the relationship between PPI and CFCL, to that of the PPI and a "true" diversification index (DI) that was based on the correlation of returns between projects. Not surprisingly, the results of this comparison indicated the association of PPI on DI to be more statistically significant ($F = 54.4$) and a considerably better predictor ($R^2 = .56$) of portfolio performance. In addition, as expected the mean DI of the efficient frontier portfolios was less than the mean DI of the remaining portfolios.

The results of this study indicate that along with other naive approaches (property type, geographical, etc.), diversification by cash flow patterns can also improve the performance of real estate portfolios. Further tests of existing (non-simulated) data should confirm the findings of this research.

References

Black, Fisher and Scholes, Myron. "The Effects of Dividend Yield and Dividend Policy on Common Stock Prices and Returns." In Meyers, Stewart C. (ed.) *Modern Developments in Financial Management*. New York: Praeger, 1976, pp. 95–117.

Fischer, . . and . . Jordan. *Security Analysis and Portfolio Management*. Place of publication: publisher, year, p. 501.

Kapplin, Stephen D. "Financial Theory and the Valuation of Real Estate under Conditions of Risk." *The Real Estate Appraiser* (September/October 1976), 28–37.

Markowitz, Harry M. "Portfolio Selection." *Journal of Finance* 1 (March 1952), 77.

Martin, William B., Jr. "A Risk Analysis Rate-of-Return Model for Evaluating Income Producing Real Estate Investment." *The Appraiser Journal* (July 1978), 424–442.

Miles, Mike and Tom McCue. "Diversification in the Real Estate Portfolio." *The Journal of Financial Research* (Spring 1984), 57–67.

Miles, Mike and Michael Rice. "Toward a More Complete Investigation of the Correlation of Real Estate Investment Yield to the Rate Evidenced in the Money and Capital Markets: The Individual Investor's Perspective." *The Real Estate Appraiser and Analyst* (November/December 1978), 8–19.

Miller, Stanley F. "Correlation of Real Estate Investment Yield to the Rate Evidenced in the Money and Capital Markets." *The Real Estate Appraiser and Analyst* (November/December 1978), 20–31.

Roulac, Stephen E. "Influence of Capital Market Theory on the Real Estate Return and the Value of Economic Analysis." *The Real Estate Appraiser* (November/December 1978), 62–71.

Sharpe, William F. "A Simplified Model for Portfolio Analysis." *Management Science* 9 (January 1963), 277–293.

Valachi, Donald J. "Three Faces of IRR." *Real Estate Review* (Fall, 1978), 74–78.

Young, Michael S. "Evaluating the Risk of Investment Real Estate." *The Real Estate Appraiser* (September/October 1977), 39–45.

Zerbst, Robert H. "Evaluating Risk by Partitioning the Internal Rate of Return." *Real Estate Review* (Winter 1980), 80–84.

7 AN EMPIRICAL ANALYSIS OF EFFICIENT REAL PROPERTY LIQUIDITY PREMIUMS

David N. Leggett

Introduction

The efficient valuation of real property is no different from the valuation of any other asset except that its relative illiquidity adds to the cost of being wrong. Some thirty years ago, it was postulated that investors are risk-averse and that they make decisions about risky assets on the basis of mean-variance efficiency (see Markowitz, 1959). That is, investors prefer higher returns for higher levels of perceived risk. This disposition toward risk aversity does not vanish with the efficient analysis of real property investments. Even those who subscribe to the more subjective methods of determining the acceptability of a project recognize the need for greater returns as compensation for "more risky" projects.

The first section briefly reviews prior research in the evaluation of real property returns relative to mean-variance efficiency. The following section develops the hypothesis that, in addition to mean-variance efficiency, risk-averse investors consider investment liquidity as a factor in utility maximization, and that the resulting premium for the relative illiquidity of real property markets is measurable. The next section contains a discussion of the data used to test the hypothesis, and the final section reports the results of the empirical evaluation.

A Review of Prior Research

Building on the utility maximizing risk-return threshold developed by Ratcliff and Schwab (1970), Pyhrr (1973), and Wofford and Gitman (1978), Miles and Estey (1979) developed a model that evaluates relevant after-tax cash flows from real property investments subject to an appropriate risk-adjusted discount rate in the context of capital asset pricing theory. Their work complements earlier contributions in its recognition that the risk-return efficiencies associated with real property investments cannot be determined outside the parameters defining the risk-return equilibrium for all assets available to investors at any static point in time.

Further defining the relationship between the returns on real property and the returns on financial assets, Ford (1988) posits that the returns on long-term real estate projects are a function of the unique risks inherent in real property equity investments and a long-term risk-free rate that matches the expected holding period of the assets. This concept is both intuitively appealing and empirically consistent with the one-period model as defined by Sharpe (1964). It provides further insight into the differences between the markets for financial assets, where one period would be measured as a day, a week, a month, or a year, and the markets for real property equity investments, where one period may be measured in terms of several years. Ford concludes that if the risk premium changes, the required returns on real estate should adjust as a result of changes in the financial markets.

This relationship is supported by several more recent studies. Liu, Hartzell, Greig, and Grissom (1990) develop a model which evaluates the existence of market segmentation. Their work finds support for the hypothesis that segmentation between the commercial real property market and the stock market exists, and that it is the "result of indirect barriers such as the cost, amount and quality of information for real estate rather than legal constraints." Evans (1990), in his extension of the market efficiency studies of Darrat and Glascock (1989), found that there is a strong association between real property capitalization rates and stock market price/earnings ratios, and that both adjust over time to the changes in monetary market conditions and other economic conditions.

Consistent with these and other contributions, this work presents a model that seeks to identify and measure the connection between the risk-return efficiencies of financial assets and the required expectations from real property equity investments.

The Relationship Between Real Property Equity Investments and Financial Assets

In the contect of an efficient required rate of return as defined by Sharpe, the expected return on an equity investment in real property can be defined as:

$$y_i = R_F + \beta_{i,M} (R_M - R_F) + \epsilon_i, \quad (1)$$

where

- R_F is the cost of risk-free funds with a maturity equal to the equity holding period;
- $\beta_{i,M}$ is the unique systematic-risk factor for the equity investment i, relative to a Markowitz efficient portfolio M;
- R_M is the expected return on a Markowitz efficient portfolio M; and
- ϵ_i is an undefined error term which should be random and should, for all assets taken together, sum to zero.[1]

One of the keys to this formulation is the relationship between the variation of returns on real property investments compared to the returns on the other assets which make up an investor's opportunity set. Zerbst and Cambon (1984) have analyzed several studies that evaluate the returns on long-term real property equity investments relative to returns from financial assets. These studies report that the ex post returns on real property equity investments dominate the returns on financial asset equity investments, while at the same time exhibiting less return volatility. They also report that "every study that examined the correlation among asset classes reported a negative correlation between real estate and common stock returns." These findings are supported by more recent studies. Both Ibbotson, Siegel, and Love (1985) and Conroy, Miles, and Wurtzebach (1986) report evidence that the degree of correlation between returns on all types of real property and the returns on financial assets is either low or in some instances negative. Liu, Hartzell, Greig, and Grissom, who evaluate real property relative to a very broad market proxy, report "that the correlation between the rate of return on either commercial real estate market proxy and the overall market portfolio is not statistically significant from zero."

The risk-return relationship identified by Ross and Zisler (1991) raises some probing questions about the comparability of the data which is necessary to evaluate the risk-return performance of real property markets relative to financial asset markets. Their work concludes that, as measured by total standard deviation, "real estate risk, in the 9 percent to 13 percent range, is much closer to that of stocks (S&P 500) and bonds than previously thought," and that an index of equity weighted REIT portfolios that trade in the continuous auction markets "follows the stock market quite closely," but that the correlation between real property assets which do not have access to continuous markets is quite low. They also provide evidence that it is misleading to compare financial assets with real property assets, whose returns may be dependent in part upon potentially biased appraisals.

This work supported the earlier work by Giliberto (1990), which directly examined the relationship between equity REITs and the real estate returns measured by the *Russell-NCREIF Property Index*.[2] Abstracting out financial market volatility on equity REITs and appraisal-based smoothing on the Russell-NCREIF Property Index, Giliberto's analysis develops return residuals which show a strong positive correlation. His analysis concludes that investors can gain exposure to real property return attributes through investment in equity REITs, but that these liquid return attributes are subject to the costs associated with financial market volatility.

In efficient risk-return space, these findings imply that if the market is pricing the financial assets properly, or at least seeking a static equilibrium, then there are excess returns associated with real property equity investments. Ceteris paribus, this should cause investment dollars to move out of financial assets and into real property assets.

Consistent with the work done by both Liu, Hartzell, Greig, and Grissom (1990), and Ross and Zisler (1991), we assert that there are two major attributes of financial markets that are not available to investors in real property equity investments. The first is the existence of organized markets for financial assets where buyers and sellers meet to clear transactions. These continuous markets provide investors with a high degree of liquidity along with relatively low transaction costs. Second, financial asset markets operate so as to disseminate information throughout the market in a manner that enables investors to evaluate the expectations of investment opportunities in an efficient and relatively inexpensive manner.[3]

We hypothesize that the absence of these attributes in real property markets is manifest as a "liquidity differential" that should have a measurable and systematic-risk sensitive cost. If this hypothesis is correct, this cost contributes to the apparent risk-return equilibrium differential that exists between financial asset markets and real property markets, and the random error term in (1) must include an identifiable premium for this liquidity differential. Hence, it follows that the error factor is not random, and cannot be expected to satisfy the requirement that it sum to zero for all assets taken together.[4] Therefore, ϵ_i should be respecified as:

$$\epsilon_i = \delta_p \beta_{i,RE} + \epsilon'_i, \tag{2}$$

where δ_p is a measurable premium added by investors in real property equity investments to compensate for the differential in the liquidity of financial asset investments relative to real property equity investments. $\beta_{i,RE}$ is an asset specific systematic-risk measurement that is relative only to the segmented real estate market. ϵ'_i becomes the newly specified residual, maintaining the expectation attributes normally associated with a random error term.

Data Compilation and Analysis of Real versus Nominal Returns

To analyze and test our hypothesis, we compiled the observed quarterly returns from the *Prudential Property Investment Separate Account* (PRISA)[5] and the *CRSP New York and American Combined Index Value: With Dividends* (CIV) for the period beginning with the quarter ending December 31, 1970 through the quarter ending December 31, 1988. The correlation between the total returns on the portfolio of equity financial asset investments and returns on the portfolio of real property equity investments is graphed in Figure 1(a).

The quarterly returns on the PRISA portfolio are appraisal-based; an analysis of the data shows a high degree of first-order autocorrelation (0.608), with a highly significant Durbin–Watson D statistic of 0.758 with 68 degrees of freedom. Further analysis shows that more than 50% of a periodic return could be explained by the return in the prior quarter. This evidence is consistent with Ross and Zisler's (1991) finding that a material portion of the variation in the quarterly returns on appraisal-based real property portfolios can be explained by previous quarters' returns.

To expose the "true" relationship between the periodic PRISA returns and eliminate the effect of the trend, we differentiate the returns following the model developed by Ross and Zisler. An analysis of the residuals shows that the appraisal bias measured by the first order autocorrelation is thereby eliminated, and the associated Durbin-Watson *D*-statistic of 3.055 clearly supports this conclusion. Adding these residuals to the appraisal-based periodic returns adjusts the volatility of the returns to provide the foundation for a better estimate of the risk of the real property portfolio.

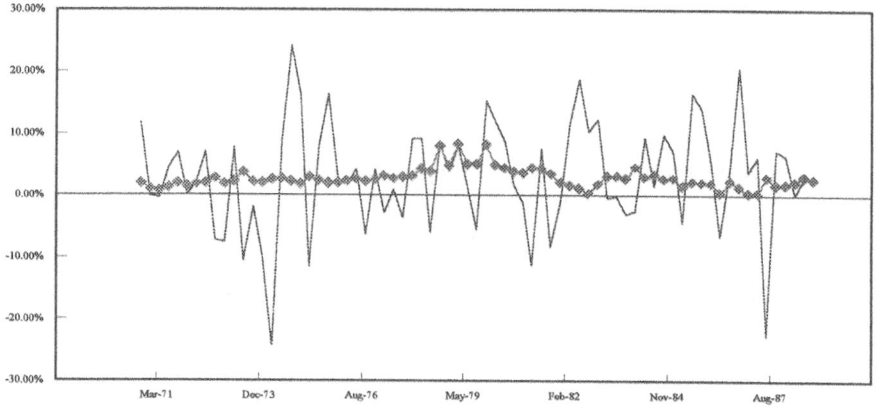

Figure 1(a). Quarterly Returns December 1970 to December 1988

..... New York and American Combined Index Value (CIV)
...◇... The Prudential Property Investment Separate Account (PRISA)
Source: CRSP and The Prudential

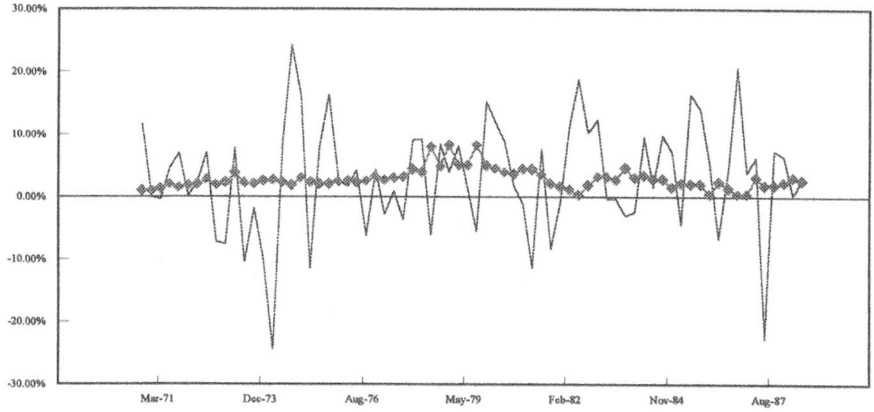

Figure 1(b). Adjusted Quarterly Returns December 1970 to December 1988

..... New York and American Combined Index Value (CIV)
...◇... PRISA (adjusted for first-order autocorrelation)
Source: CRSP and author's calculations

The total returns and variances that result from this adjustment are shown in Table 1 and in Figure 1(b). We use these total returns to test our null hypothesis that investors in real property equity investments do not require a measurable liquidity premium over financial assets; i.e., H_o: $\delta_P = 0$.

Consistent with the much broader results reported by both Zerbst and Cambon (1984), and Liu, Hartzell, Greig, and Grissom (1990), there is evidence that the degree of correlation between returns on real property equity investments and financial assets is quite low, and possibly negative. If this is in fact the case, it follows that, abstracting out any liquidity or segmentation effect, the required returns on real property equity investments should be well below historically observed returns. In the context of the efficient portfolio structure defined by Markowitz, the opportunity for a diversification benefit therefore exists.

The Existence of a Liquidity Premium

To isolate any systematic differential in the pricing of risk-return relationships in real property valuation relative to financial assets, we use unleveraged portfolio returns rather than individual asset returns. Consistent with Sharpe's (1964) security market line, individual real property assets should be priced relative to an efficient "market" portfolio of all assets.

To measure the relationship between the portfolio of unleveraged real property equity investments and financial assets, we define M as being proxied by the CIV; and since

$$\sum_{n=1}^{\infty} (w_i \beta_{i,M}) = \beta_{P,M}, \tag{3}$$

where $\beta_{P,M}$ is the systematic risk factor of a portfolio of real property equity investments relative to M, we evaluate the portfolio of real property equity investments according to:

$$y_P = R_F + \beta_{P,M} (R_M - R_F) + \delta_P + \epsilon'_P, \tag{4}$$

where R_F is more specifically correlated with the returns on a portfolio of three- to five-year treasury notes,[6] and $\delta_P = 0$.

The results of this evaluation of expected returns on an efficient portfolio of real property investments relative to the returns on financial assets are reported in Table 2. Due to the portfolio benefit provided by real property

Table 1. Summary of Periodic Returns and Correlation between PRISA and CIV

	PRISA	Quarterly returns RESIDUAL	TOTAL	Quarterly returns CIV
03/31/71–06/30/75				
Mean	2.1111%	0.0572%	2.1683%	1.5309%
High	3.8100%	1.5100%	5.3200%	24.2136%
Low	0.8900%	1.6100%	0.0000%	−24.3802%
Standard Deviation	0.7223%	0.7624%	1.3048%	11.1825%
z statistic—total quarterly returns				11.0355%
09/30/75–12/31/79				
Mean	3.7839%	0.1156%	3.8995%	2.6558%
High	8.3400%	4.0800%	12.1100%	16.3398%
Low	1.9900%	−3.2500%	1.6100%	−11.5633%
Standard Deviation	1.8959%	1.7130%	3.0559%	6.8842%
z statistic—total quarterly returns				−18.2059%
03/31/80–06/30/84				
Mean	3.4128%	−0.1161%	3.2967%	3.5836%
High	8.2700%	3.1800%	11.4500%	18.7917%
Low	0.3300%	−3.3000%	−0.4800%	−11.4405%
Standard Deviation	1.7768%	1.4193%	2.6224%	8.6850%
z statistic—total quarterly returns				−35.3533%
09/30/84–12/31/88				
Mean	2.0011%	0.0217%	1.9794%	4.5294%
High	3.3800%	2.6500%	5.6800%	20.6237%
Low	0.3800%	−1.5700%	−1.1500%	−22.7557%
Standard Deviation	0.9167%	1.0641%	1.7390%	9.5386%
z statistic—total quarterly returns				−17.0033%
12/31/70–12/31/88				
Mean	2.8272%	0.0088%	2.8360%	3.0749%
High	8.3400%	4.0800%	12.1100%	24.2136%
Low	0.3300%	−3.3000%	−1.1500%	−24.3802%
Standard Deviation	1.5934%	1.2935%	2.4220%	9.0766%
z statistic—total quarterly returns				−14.8788%

Table 2. Efficient Real Return Expectations CIV

	Covariance	*Beta*	*Expected 3-5 year risk-free**	*Expected market returns***	*Expected real property returns*
Annualized quarterly returns	−0.0186%	−0.02287702	8.8322%	12.8787%	8.7396%
Annualized one-year returns	−0.0434%	−0.01161293	8.9633%	12.2341%	8.9253%
Annualized three-year returns	0.0307%	0.03493387	9.1879%	11.7483%	9.2774%
Annualized five-year returns	0.0203%	0.04572155	9.3912%	12.3470%	9.5263%

* Derived from a least squared analysis of expost U.S. Treasury returns.
** Taken from the sample distribution CIV.

Table 3. Expected Real Returns and Mean Liquidity Premium On Efficient Real Property Investment Portfolios

	CAPM Expected Return	*Observed Periodic Return*	*Mean liquidity premium*	*Liquidity premium Standard deviation*	*95% Confidence interval*
Annualized quarterly returns	8.7396%	11.6172%	2.8776%	6.5614%	1.3513% −4.4038%
Annualized one-year returns	8.9253%	11.7828%	2.8575%	6.1285%	1.4009% −4.3141%
Annualized three-year returns	9.2774%	12.6398%	3.3624%	5.1104%	2.0693% −4.6555%
Annualized five-year returns	9.5263%	13.2231%	3.6968%	3.8660%	2.6460% −4.7476%

assets, the analysis implies that, abstracting out the effect of any liquidity or segmentation premium, investors should be willing to accept rates of return on real property investments that are approximately equal to the rate investors require on risk-free investments of comparable maturity.

The fact that investors apparently are not willing to accept these lower expected returns is consistent with all of the prior studies, which report that investors appear to expect returns on real property equity investments that are higher than the risk-comparable returns on financial equity investments. In Table 3, we show the relationship between the expected returns derived from equation (4) and the expost PRISA returns. These results, which are further supported by an evaluation of real property investment returns relative to the broader wealth indices compiled by Ibbotson et al. (1985),[7] indicate that the additional return requirements in response to the lack of liquidity and continuity in real property markets are highly predictable.

It is the existence of an efficient frontier, which Markowitz defines as the locus of all efficient combinations of assets, that provides the most dramatic support for the hypothesis of an efficient liquidity premium. Table 4(a) reports the standard deviation and expected return for twelve possible portfolio combinations of common stocks, equity real property investments (unadjusted for any liquidity premium effect) and intermediate-term government debt obligations. As Figure 2(a) shows, the portfolio expectations are uncorrelated (the computed r of 0.5646 is not significant at the 95% level), and do not therefore meet the definition of an efficient frontier.

A liquidity premium adjustment to the efficient returns required by real property investors eliminates these mean-variance inefficiencies. Table 4(b) reports the standard deviation and liquidity premium-adjusted returns for the same twelve possible portfolio combinations. The results, shown in Figure 2(b), are consistent with a highly efficient mean-variance relationship, with a statistically significant r of 0.8482. The one portfolio outlier in this distribution is the PRISA portfolio. This would seemingly confirm that holding a portfolio of only real property investments, even if it is well diversified, is not as efficient in a risk-return utility context as holding a portfolio balanced with financial assets.

Conclusions

We find evidence of an empirically definable relationship between the efficient expectations for returns on real property investments and financial

Table 4(a). Sample Distribution of Potentially Efficient Portfolio Composition Unadjusted For Liquidity Premium Effect

			Weight		
	Standard deviation	*Return*	*CIV*	*PRISA*	*RF*
Portfolio 1	6.6698%	12.3470%	100.00%	0.00%	0.00%
Portfolio 2	3.8660%	13.2231%	0.00%	100.00%	0.00%
Portfolio 3	1.7091%	9.3912%	0.00%	0.00%	100.00%
Portfolio 4	3.0761%	11.6538%	33.33%	33.33%	33.33%
Portfolio 5	3.9843%	12.7850%	50.00%	50.00%	0.00%
Portfolio 6	3.5794%	10.8691%	50.00%	0.00%	50.00%
Portfolio 7	3.2968%	11.9366%	37.50%	37.50%	25.00%
Portfolio 8	4.2468%	11.7394%	60.00%	15.00%	25.00%
Portfolio 9	3.8471%	12.2103%	50.00%	35.00%	15.00%
Portfolio 10	3.6539%	12.2541%	45.00%	40.00%	15.00%
Portfolio 11	3.4898%	12.2979%	40.00%	45.00%	15.00%
Portfolio 12	3.7056%	12.4457%	45.00%	45.00%	10.00%

Table 4(b). Sample Distribution of Potentially Efficient Portfolio Composition Adjusted For Liquidity Premium Effect

			Weight		
	Standard deviation	*Return*	*CIV*	*PRISA*	*RF*
Portfolio 1	6.6698%	12.3470%	100.00%	0.00%	0.00%
Portfolio 2	3.8660%	9.5263%	0.00%	100.00%	0.00%
Portfolio 3	1.7091%	9.3912%	0.00%	0.00%	100.00%
Portfolio 4	3.0761%	10.4215%	33.33%	33.33%	33.33%
Portfolio 5	3.9843%	10.9366%	50.00%	50.00%	0.00%
Portfolio 6	3.5794%	10.8691%	50.00%	0.00%	50.00%
Portfolio 7	3.2968%	10.5503%	37.50%	37.50%	25.00%
Portfolio 8	4.2468%	11.1849%	60.00%	15.00%	25.00%
Portfolio 9	3.8471%	10.9164%	50.00%	35.00%	15.00%
Portfolio 10	3.6539%	10.7753%	45.00%	40.00%	15.00%
Portfolio 11	3.4898%	10.6343%	40.00%	45.00%	15.00%
Portfolio 12	3.7056%	10.7821%	45.00%	45.00%	10.00%

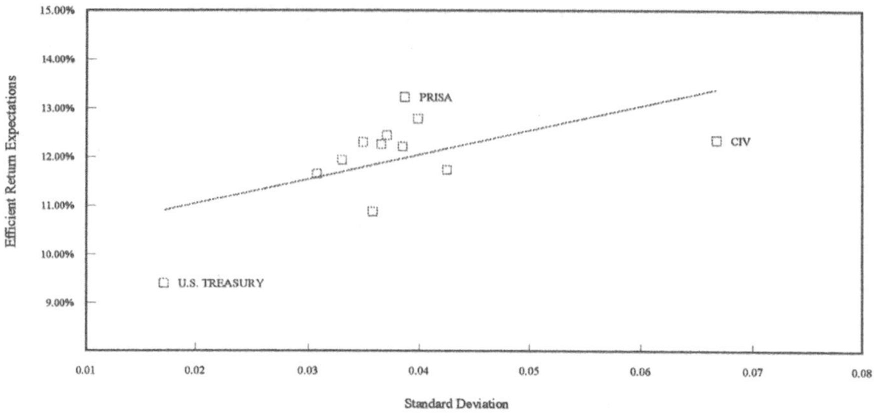

Figure 2(a). Distribution of Potentially Efficient Portfolios Unadjusted for Liquidity Premium Effect

□Unadjusted Mean-Variance Efficient Combined Asset Portfolios
......Least-Squared Regression Line
Source: Author's Table 4(a)

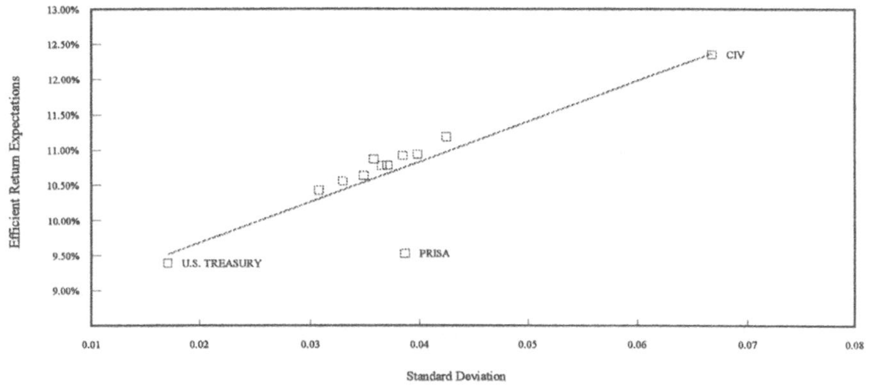

Figure 2(b). Distribution of Potentially Efficient Portfolios Adjusted for Liquidity Premium Effect

□Mean-Variance Efficient Combined Asset Portfolios
......Least-Squared Regression Line
Source: Author's Table 4(b)

assets. It appears to be a measurable relationship that probably includes a premium which is sensitive to the systematic risk parameters of individual real property portfolios. Our analysis does not therefore support the hypothesis H_o: $\delta_p = 0$, and we conclude that the evidence is consistent with the identification of a premium which compensates for the illiquidity and segmentation of real property markets.

Although the true variance of real property returns is probably comparable with the variance on common stocks, the low degree of correlation between the returns provides an opportunity to reduce portfolio risk through efficient diversification. At the same time, while the broader indices compiled by Ibbotson et al., *World Market Wealth Portfolio*, and *U.S. Market Wealth Portfolio* show high correlation to the PRISA index, the computed liquidity premium estimates support our primary conclusions.

Notes

1. While this randomly distributed error term should be normally distributed, the inefficiency of real property markets and the strong desire on the part of investors to structure transactions with non-normal risk distributions may result in an investor perception that the error term is not normally distributed. This perception by investors of a skewed distribution will lead to the conclusion that ϵ_i is negative and, therefore, a lower expected return on the equity investment is acceptable.

2. The *Russell-NCREIF Property Index* is an appraisal-based, value-weighted index consisting of more than 1,700 unleveraged real properties compiled by the Frank Russell Company and the National Council of Real Estate Investment Fiduciaries (NCREIF).

3. One of the necessary attributes of a continuous market is the efficient and inexpensive dissemination of information.

4. While studies indicate that the risk-return equilibrium differential also includes the effect of transaction costs, these costs can be distingiushed from costs associated with illiquidity in that they should be more homogeneous among real property assets and not augmented by risk differentials.

5. The investment performance of PRISA (a commingled pension fund portfolio) is published quarterly by The Prudential Real Estate Investors, a division of The Prudential. PRISA is a geographically diversified portfolio of unleveraged real property investments that, as of March 31, 1990, consisted of 147 properties worth $3.4 billion. The PRISA returns are highly correlated with the broader *Russell-NCREIF Property Index* for the fourteen year period ending June 1992. This correlation (.93478) demonstrates that PRISA is a viable index for testing the relationship between the real property markets and alternative investment opportunities.

6. The returns for the portfolio of three- to five-year U.S. Treasury Notes are compiled from data reported in the *Federal Reserve Bulletin*. For the period December 31, 1970 to March 31, 1980, a "3-5" year average portfolio return is reported. For the period June 30, 1980 to December 31, 1988, an average of the reported returns using an equal 50%

weighting on 3-year and 5-year returns is used. The use of a weighted average between the 3-year and 5-year returns as a proxy for the "3-5" year portfolio was tested for the period March 31, 1977 to March 31, 1980, with a resulting *r*-statistic of 0.999774.

7. Using our equation (4), we develop liquidity premium confidence intervals based on the *World Market Wealth Portfolio* and *U.S. Market Wealth Portfolio*, as well as for the two wealth portfolios restated to exclude the U.S. residential returns, which are highly influenced by one-to four-family housing. Our analysis of the liquidity premiums identifies a high degree of correlation (99%) between those computed using CIV and those computed using the four wealth portfolios, with statistically significant chi-square statistics of 6.607 for the *U.S. Market Wealth Portfolio* excluding U.S. residential real property, and 22.682 for the *U.S. Market Wealth Portfolio*. This supports the utilization of the subset CIV index as a proxy for U.S. market wealth. The chi-square statistics computed relative to the *World Market Wealth Portfolio* index lead us to reject the CIV index as a proxy for world wealth.

References

Conroy, B. M. Miles, and C.H. Wurtzebach. "A Practical View of Real Estate and Modern Portfolio Theory." *Industrial Development* (May/June 1986).

Darrat, A.F. and J.L. Glascock. "Real Estate Returns, Money and Fiscal Deficits: Is the Real Estate Market Efficient?" *Journal of Real Estate Finance and Economics* 2 (1989).

Evans, R.D. "A Transfer Function Analysis of Real Estate Capitalization Rates." *The Journal of Real Estate Research* 5, 3 (Fall 1990).

Ford, D.A. "Hurdle Rates and Real Estate Investment." *The Real Estate Appraiser and Analyst* (Winter 1988).

Giliberto, S.M. "Equity Real Estate Investment Trusts and Real Estate Returns." *Journal of Real Estate Research* 5, 2 (Summer 1990).

Ibbotson, R.G. L.B. Siegel, and K.S. Love. "World Wealth: Market Values and Returns." *Journal of Portfolio Management* (Fall 1985).

Liu, C.H. D.J. Hartzell, W. Greig, and T.V. Grissom. "The Integration of the Real Estate Market and the Stock Market: Some Preliminary Evidence." *Journal of Real Estate Finance and Economics* 3 (1990).

Markowitz, H. *Portfolio Selection: Efficient Diversification of Investments*. New York: John Wiley, (1959).

Miles, M.E. and A.S. Estey. "The Relevant Required Rate of Return." *The Appraisal Journal* (October 1979).

Pyhrr, S.A. "A Computer Simulation Model To Measure The Risk In Real Estate Investment." *AREUEA Journal* (June 1973).

Ross, S.A. and R.C. Zisler. "Risk and Return in Real Estate." *Journal of Real Estate Finance and Economics* 4 (1991).

Ratcliff, R.U. and B. Schwab. "Contemporary Decision Theory and Real Estate Investment." *The Appraisal Journal* (April 1970).

Sharpe, W.F. "Capital Asset Prices: A Theory of Market Equilibrium Under Conditions of Risk." *Journal of Finance* (September 1964).

Wofford, L.E. and L.J. Gitman. "Measuring a Project's Ability to Survive Adversity." *Real Estate Review* (Spring 1978).

Zerbst, R.H. and B.R. Cambon. "Real Estate: Historical Returns and Risks." *Journal of Portfolio Management* (Spring 1984).

8 FARMLAND AS AN INFLATION HEDGE

Jack H. Rubens* and James R. Webb

Introduction

As inflation declined in the late 1980s from the double-digit rates of previous years, investor concerns of rising price levels diminished. However, viewed from the longer historical perspective of post-WWI performance, inflation has been at significant levels since the late 1960s. A major concern of investors is that their wealth portfolio provide positive real rates of return. During periods of inflation, some investiments increase in value more quickly than others, while some decrease in value.

Nelson (1976), Jaffe and Mandelker (1976), and Stulz (1986), among others, have shown that common stock has served as a negative hedge against inflation in the United States. Gultekin (1983), Mandelker, and Tandon (1985), and Peel and Pope (1985) have noted such a relationship between common stocks and inflation internationally. However, few studies have investigated the inflation-hedging effectiveness of real estate. Only studies by Reilly, Marquardt, and Price (1977); Fama and Schwert (1977);

---

* Deceased.

Fogler, Granito, and Smith (1985); Hartzell, Heckman, and Miles (1987); and Irwin, Forster and Sherrick (1988) rigorously examine the inflation-hedgin ability of real estate. Only work by Reilly, et al. and Irwin et al. has farmland as its focus. Farmland would seem to be a particularly germane real asset to examine, because the rapid rise of farmland values in the 1970s, the precipitous drop in the early 1980s, and the subsequent partial recovery make possible examination of the inflation-hedging effectiveness through a full boom-and-bust cycle.

The purpose of this research study is to examine the inflation-hedging effectiveness of farmland from 1919 through 1988 by extending the work of Reilly, Marquardt, and Price (1977). This 70-year period of analysis will allow us to also observe farmland's performance in periods of both significant inflation and deflation, as well as the boom-and-bust cycles of the last two decades.

Literature review

Reilly, Marquardt, and Price (1977) use cost data for residential real estate and farmland appreciation to examine inflation-hedging effectiveness. They find that both types of real estate are effective inflation-hedging devices. Hadaway and Hadaway (1981) note a positive correlation between real assets (including farmland, residential housing, and silver) and the CPI, and a negative relationship between financial assets and inflation. Webb and Rubens (1986) also find a positive correlation between farmland and the CPI.

Kaplan (1985) examines farmland's hedging effectivenss and potential diversification gains. He notes the positive relationship between farmland and the CPI and the negative relationship between farmland and financial assets. Unfortunately, the significance of the correlation coefficients was not tested.

Irwin, Forster, and Sherrick (1988) examine farmland returns and find strong evidence of its low correlation with both actual and unexpected inflation and a significant contribution to risk reduction in mixed-asset portfolios. Following Fama and Schwert (1977), they use the Treasury bill rate as a measure of expected inflation. As discussed by Kaul (1987), the result of using such a proxy is a spurious correlation between the asset returns and the inflation rate. That is, the expected real rate of interest is not independent of the expected inflation rate.

Rubens, Bond, and Webb (1989) examine the inflation-hedging effectiveness of three types of real estate (including farmland), and four financial instruments, as both individual assets and parts of portfolios. They find that farmland is a positive hedge against the unexpected component of inflation and helps the hedging effectiveness of portfolios in which farmland is included.

Development of the model and data sources

The six-step methodology of Reilly, Marquardt, and Price [RMP] (1977) is used in this study to examine the inflation-hedging effectiveness of farmland. First, the periods with deflation, relative noninflation, and significant inflation were identified. Following RMP, inflation was defined as being significant if the annual change in the Consumer Price Index (CPI) exceeded 3%. This step is considered necessary, since only during periods of significant inflation is it important to determine whether inflation-hedging effectiveness exists. For example, in the 1980s, stock returns averaged well over 20% per annum, yet research has shown that the negative relationship between stock returns and inflation persisted. Such high nominal returns, relative to the inflation rate, made investor concerns over this relationship a moot point.

The data used are the average value per acre of farmland from the USDA's "Farm Real Estate Market Developments" and its replacement publication "Agricultural Land Values and Markets: Outlook and Situation Report." Aggregate data is available for the 48 contiguous states as well as selected individual states (Arizona, Colorado, Idaho, Illinois, Indiana, Iowa, Kansas, Michigan, Missouri, Montana, Nebraska, Nevada, New Mexico, New York, Pennsylvania, Utah, Wishconsin, and Wyoming). The hedging effectiveness of farmland is examined in the aggregate and for the individual states where data is available. For comparison purposes, changes in the S&P 500 Index are also examined. Dividends will be excluded from the analysis to make the results more comparable with the farmland returns. Furthermore, following results in Ibbotson (1989), we assume that there is relative dividend stability and that stock price changes are the source of inflation-hedging effectiveness or ineffectiveness.

Although this study is modelled after RMP, results in overlapping periods occasionally differ due to changes in the data basis or the use of more generally accepted sources of data. For example, the reporting period for the farm data was changed from March to January in the publications cited above. The January figure was used for the entire time period in this study. Also, the Ibbotson figures for CPI changes were used for the 1926–1988 period, since they have become widely accepted in academic and practitioner research. This resulted in a new period of significant inflation (1934) not identified in the RMP study. For this reason, the results here and those in RMP, while yielding comparable figures, differ slightly. However, in no case, did these differences result in differing conclusions between this study and RMP, for the few overlapping time periods contained in both studies.

Third, the nominal rates-of-return were compared with the CPI to determine if farmland is what RMP define as a traditional inflation hedge ($r' > 0$, where r' = real rate-of-return).

Fourth, thee real rates-of-return were computed for periods of significant inflation:

$$\frac{1 + \text{nominal rate of return}}{1 + \text{rate of inflation}} - 1 = \text{real rate of return.} \tag{1}$$

Following RMP, a *complete hedge against inflation* is defined as the case where the real rate-of-return is greater than the normal rate-of-return for a period of significant inflation or:

$$r' \geq k \tag{2}$$

where: r' is the real rate-of-return. This real rate is simply the normal rate of return during a period (r), adjusted for the inflation rate during period g.

k is the normal rate of return for the risk class of real estate assuming zero inflation.

In addition, we define a *partial hedge against inflation* as those cases where the investment has a nominal rate of return during a period of inflation greater than the normal rate of return ($r \geq k$ or $r' > 0$ but less than k). That is, there is at least some inflation protection.

Fifth, asset performance during periods of significant deflation was also analyzed. Finally, we examined comovements among the alternative media returns via a correlation matrix to determine if significant geographic differences in farmland rates-of-return exist.

Results

Table 1 shows the annual percentage changes in the Consumer Price Index over the time period examined (1919–1988). Note that, with the exception of 1986 (the year oil prices collapsed), the U.S. economy has faced significant inflation since the late 1960s. Also, significant deflation has not occurred since the Great Depression, and prices have only fallen

Table 1. Annual percentage change in the consumer price index: 1919–1988

Year	% *change*	*Year*	% *change*	*Year*	% *change*
1919	16.56*	1944	0.94	1969	5.07*
1920	20.53*	1945	2.38	1970	6.02*
1921	−7.28**	1946	2.83	1971	4.64*
1922	−8.63**	1947	20.02*	1972	3.50*
1923	0.69	1948	6.87*	1973	4.68*
1924	1.54	1949	1.76	1974	10.26*
1925	1.01	1950	−1.13	1975	10.28*
1926	2.99	1951	9.43*	1976	6.12*
1927	−2.62	1952	1.95	1977	6.38*
1928	−1.24	1953	1.02	1978	6.48*
1929	−0.52	1954	1.15	1979	10.22*
1930	−0.42	1955	−0.47	1980	14.69*
1931	−8.05**	1956	0.34	1981	10.55*
1932	−9.91**	1957	3.61*	1982	6.79*
1933	−10.23**	1958	3.74*	1983	3.64*
1934	5.84*	1959	0.37	1984	4.74*
1935	2.83	1960	1.49	1985	3.74*
1936	0.00	1961	1.46	1986	2.26
1937	3.80*	1962	1.14	1987	3.03*
1938	−0.88	1963	1.07	1988	3.09*
1939	−1.65	1964	1.41		
1940	0.91	1965	1.22		
1941	1.28	1966	2.75		
1942	12.91	1967	2.73		
1943	7.51	1968	3.91*		

* Indicates a period of significant inflation
** Indicates a period of significant deflation
Sources: 1919–1926, "Consumer Price Indexes for Urban Wage Earners and Clerical Workers: U.S. City Averages." *Historical Series A through I*. U.S. Bureau of Labor Statistics.
1927–1988, *Stocks, Bonds, Bills and Inflation 1989 Yearbook*. Chicago: Ibbotson Associates, 1989.

in two years since 1940. Thus, we can scrutinize hedging effectiveness against significant inflation in nine periods, but significant deflation in only two periods.

Descriptive statistics for all variables are shown in Table 2. As expected, the S&P 500 shows the highest mean, standard deviation, and coefficient of variation (CV). Mean returns for the state farmland prices exhibit little

Table 2. Average of annual percentage changes for consumer price index, S&P 500 prices and land values: 1919–1988

Variable	*Mean*	*Standard deviation*	*Coefficient of variation*	*Variable*	*Mean*	*Standard deviation*	*Coefficient of variation*
CPI	3.23	5.74	1.78	Missouri	3.59	9.66	2.69
S&P 500	8.36	23.76	2.84	Montana	3.60	10.10	2.80
Farmland	3.76	8.53	2.27	Nebraska	3.16	11.46	3.62
Arizona	3.63	11.76	3.24	Nevada	3.69	10.46	2.83
Colorado	4.12	10.10	2.45	New Mexico	4.65	11.14	2.39
Idaho	3.82	9.09	2.38	New York	4.22	6.75	1.60
Illinois	3.54	10.67	3.01	Pennsylvania	5.12	7.46	1.46
Indiana	3.81	10.35	2.72	Utah	4.07	2.58	2.58
Iowa	3.22	12.25	3.81	Wisconsin	3.35	2.60	2.60
Kansas	3.23	9.25	2.87	Wyoming	3.93	11.28	2.87
Michigan	4.00	7.95	1.99				

Sources: Stock Prices: 1919–1926, "Standard Statistical Bulletin 1930–1931 Base Book Issue." *Standard Trade and Securities Services*. Standard Statistics Company, Inc., March 1930.

1927–1988, *Stocks, Bonds, Bills and Inflation; 1989 Yearbook*. Ibbotson Associates Chicago, 1989.

1985–1988, *Agricultural Land Values and Markets, Outlook and Situation Report*. United States Department of Agricultural, various issues.

variation (ranging from a minimum of 3.22% for Iowa to a maximum of 5.12% for Pennsylvania), but widely varying standard deviations, resulting in CVs from a low of 1.46 for Pennsylvania to a high of 3.81 for Iowa.

Compounded annual nominal and real rates-of-return for the entire period are shown in Table 3. Whereas all investment types provided positive nominal rates of return, only stocks, aggregate farmland, and nine of the 18 individual state return series rendered positive real rates-of-return, as defined in equation (1). Varying results such as these also demonstrate the benefits of geographic diversification. These results, however, obfuscate one of the major tenets of this study, namely, that hedging ability is only important during periods of significant inflation or defaltion. Thus, Table 4 through 6 show results for periods of relative price instability. Table 4 contains the results for the S&P 500, as well as for aggregate and for individual state farmland, during the nine periods of significant inflation. Common stocks exhibit some hedging effectiveness in the earlier periods. However, in later periods, the S&P 500's performance against inflation is as dismal in this study as documented elsewhere. During the longest period of significant inflation (1968–1985), common stocks are the only asset which failed to provide a positive (nominal or real) return!

Aggregate farmland performed as a better inflation hedge in recent years than the S&P 500. During the periods encompassing 1950 through 1985, farmland provided a positive real rate-of-return. In the most recent

Table 3. Average annual compound rate of change for consumer price index, S&P 500 prices and land values: 1919–1988

Variable	r' *(nominal)*	r' *(real)*	*Variable*	r *(nominal)*	r *(real)*
CPI	3.11	—	Missouri	3.05	−0.06
S&P 500	5.36	2.19			
Farmland	3.35	0.23	Montana	3.10	−0.01
Arizona	3.05	−0.06	Nebraska	2.41	−0.68
Colorado	3.68	0.56	Nevada	3.07	−0.04
Idaho	3.40	0.28	New Mexico	4.15	1.01
Illinois	2.92	−0.19	New York	4.04	0.91
Indiana	3.28	0.17	Pennsylvania	4.90	1.74
Iowa	2.42	−0.67	Utah	3.42	0.30
Kansas	2.79	−0.31	Wisconsin	2.98	−0.13
Michigan	3.76	0.63	Wyoming	3.10	−0.01

Table 4. Average percent change in consumer price index, S&P 500 prices and land values during periods of significant inflation: 1919–1988

Year		*CPI*	*S&P 500 Prices*	*All Farmland*	*Ariz.*	*Color.*	*Idaho*	*Ill.*	*Indi.*	*Iowa*	*Kans.*	*Mich.*
1919–1920	r	18.55	17.32	14.20	5.56	10.06	13.10	16.08	11.91	21.54	10.29	6.73
	r′		−1.04	−3.67	−10.96	−7.16	−4.60	−2.08	−5.60	2.52	−6.97	−9.97
1934	r	5.84	83.84	3.33	−7.14	−8.33	4.00	7.69	4.17	7.69	3.33	2.22
	r′		73.70	−2.37	−12.26	−13.39	−1.74	1.75	−1.58	1.75	−2.37	−3.42
1937	r	3.80	20.10	3.13	−18.18	8.33	10.00	5.33	5.17	0.00	3.13	8.51
	r′		15.70	−0.65	−21.18	4.36	5.97	1.47	1.32	3.66	−0.65	4.54
1942–1943	r	10.21	12.50	9.01	14.29	7.42	11.49	8.75	10.95	7.33	6.51	9.37
	r′		2.08	−1.09	3.70	−2.53	1.16	−1.32	0.67	−2.61	−3.36	−0.76
1947–1948	r	13.45	−8.34	9.94	7.69	21.08	8.14	10.03	8.28	11.44	16.37	8.16
	r′		−19.21	−3.09	−5.08	6.73	−4.68	−3.01	−4.56	−1.77	2.57	−4.66
1951	r	9.43	23.76	15.38	20.00	15.63	15.71	17.24	20.44	16.77	10.61	15.15
	r′		13.10	5.44	9.66	5.67	5.74	7.14	10.06	6.71	1.08	5.23
1957–1958	r	3.68	−6.79	6.39	14.06	7.07	3.62	6.90	7.37	4.91	5.23	7.25
	r′		−10.10	2.61	10.00	3.27	−0.06	3.11	3.56	1.19	1.49	3.44
1968–1985	r	6.76	5.02	8.48	8.96	9.93	9.49	7.23	7.66	7.71	7.32	8.17
	r′		−1.63	1.61	2.06	2.97	2.56	0.44	0.84	0.89	0.52	1.32
1987–1988	r	3.47	8.92	−2.48	−3.41	0.98	−3.77	−0.95	−3.21	3.96	−1.95	−4.30
	r′		5.27	−5.75	−6.64	−2.41	−7.00	−4.27	−6.46	0.47	−5.24	−7.51
Overall	r	7.72	8.56	8.02	7.49	9.28	8.57	7.81	7.69	8.44	7.15	7.33
Average	r′		0.78	0.28	−0.21	1.45	0.79	−0.03	−0.03	0.67	−0.53	−0.36

Missouri	*Mont.*	*Nebra.*	*Nevada.*	*N.Mex.*	*N.York*	*Penn.*	*Utah*	*Wisc.*	*Wyom.*
15.66	7.63	19.23	15.48	6.25	7.31	7.51	13.90	12.84	19.54
−2.44	−9.21	0.57	−2.59	−10.38	−9.48	−9.31	−3.92	−4.82	0.84
3.13	0.00	0.00	0.00	0.00	0.00	0.00	0.00	−1.82	0.00
−2.56	−5.52	−5.52	−5.52	−5.52	−5.52	−5.52	−5.52	−7.24	−5.52
0.00	14.29	−5.88	9.09	0.00	0.00	0.00	0.00	5.45	0.00
−5.52	10.11	−9.33	5.10	−3.66	−3.66	−3.66	−3.66	1.59	−3.66
10.40	6.25	10.80	3.85	18.33	6.27	7.26	8.71	5.72	8.33
0.17	−3.59	0.54	−5.77	7.37	−3.57	−2.68	−1.36	−4.07	−1.71
6.51	14.36	15.53	2.50	12.88	8.61	9.24	9.56	9.73	12.88
−6.12	0.54	1.83	−9.65	−0.50	−4.27	−3.71	−3.43	−3.28	−0.50
17.19	23.53	13.79	15.79	20.00	6.52	14.95	11.63	11.24	15.38
7.09	12.88	3.98	5.81	9.66	−2.66	5.04	2.01	1.65	5.44
8.28	5.42	4.18	1.79	0.11	6.29	6.73	4.98	6.79	9.01
4.44	1.68	0.48	−1.82	−3.44	2.52	2.94	1.25	3.00	5.14
8.02	9.05	7.94	10.18	8.91	7.95	10.31	11.76	9.46	10.15
1.18	2.14	1.11	3.20	2.01	1.11	3.33	4.68	2.53	3.18
−2.64	−9.97	0.64	−1.25	−0.38	7.84	12.21	−5.37	−5.66	−4.62
−5.91	−12.99	−2.74	−4.56	−3.72	4.22	−8.45	−8.54	−8.82	−7.82
7.78	8.00	8.12	8.16	8.22	7.17	9.25	9.25	7.87	9.30
0.05	0.26	0.37	0.41	0.46	−0.51	1.41	1.42	0.14	1.47

period of significant inflation, however, farmland failed to provide even a positive nominal rate-of-return. Thus, recent results with respect to farmland's hedging ability are somewhat noteworthy.

As would be expected, individual state results mirror the aggregate farmland results, but interesting differences exist. In only one period of significant inflation (albeit the longest one) do all states provide positive real returns (1968–1985). Also, no state provided positive real returns during all perids of significant inflation.

Another trend seen in the aggregate farmland series is also present in the hedging performance of indicidual state returns, namely, recent results are more encouraging than earlier ones. It appears that, in recent decades, more active markets and general awareness of the effects of inflation have affected the pricing of assets by investors. As summarized in Table 5, the number of state farmland returns acting as complete hedges against inflation increased markedly in the post-WWII period. Further, individual state returns reveal that all provided positive nominal returns (and thus partial hedging effectiveness) during the years encompassing the 1942–1985 period. In contrast, S&P 500 returns were negative in two of these five periods of significant inflation.

Table 6 shows the hedging performance of common stock and farmland durring the two periods of significant deflation occuring within the 1919–1988 period. All return series reveal the poor performance of the investment media during deflationary periods. The S&P 500 results are particularly dismal. In both time periods, stock returns fell by greater amounts than the decline in prices (nearly four times the drop of the CPI during the latter period). Although the aggregate farm returns are nearly as abysmal, the decline was not as precipitous as that for stocks.

Individual state results show marginal improvements. For example, during the 1921–1922 deflation, rates of decline in farmland prices in six of the twenty states fell by a lesser amount than the general level of

Table 5. Number of states with positive real rates of increase in land values during periods of significant inflation

Year	*Number*	*Year*	*Number*
1919–20	3	1951	17
1934	2	1967–58	15
1937	8	1968–85	18
1942–43	6	1987–88	3
1947–48	4		

Table 6. Average percent change in consumer price index, S&P 500 prices and land values during periods of significant deflation: 1919–1988

Year	*CPI*	*S&P 500 Prices*	*All Farmland*	*Ariz.*	*Color.*	*Idaho*	*Ill.*	*Indi.*	*Iowa*	*Kans.*	*Mich.*
1921–22	−7.96	−8.70	−9.06	−14.34	−5.89	−11.44	−10.70	−12.97	−12.32	−5.65	0.01
1931–33	−9.40	−35.75	−15.06	−8.01	−18.03	−17.72	−15.79	−12.58	−19.14	−14.92	−12.73
Overall Average	8.82	24.93	−12.63	−10.54	−13.17	−15.21	−13.75	−12.74	−16.41	−11.21	−7.63

Missouri	*Mont.*	*Nebra.*	*Nevada.*	*N.Mex.*	*N.York*	*Penn.*	*Utah*	*Wisc.*	*Wyom.*
−10.07	−12.09	−10.12	−9.36	−11.81	−2.94	−4.78	−9.59	−2.50	−13.13
−15.46	−16.39	−14.32	−14.22	−16.99	−7.86	−10.10	−16.07	−11.37	−17.59
−13.60	−14.67	−12.64	−12.27	−14.91	−5.89	−7.97	−13.48	−7.82	−15.81

Table 7. Correlation coefficients for annual percent changes in consumer price index, S&P 500 prices and land values: 1919–1988

	CPI	*S&P 500 Prices*	*Farm-land*	*Ariz.*	*Color.*	*Idaho*	*Ill.*	*Indi.*	*Iowa*	*Kans.*	*Mich.*	*Misso.*	*Mont.*	*Nebra.*	*Nevada*	*N.Mex.*	*N.York*	*Penn.*	*Utah*	*Wisc.*	*Wyom.*
CPI	1.00																				
S&P 500	0.11	1.00																			
All Farmland	0.72	0.07	1.00																		
Ariz.	0.46	0.06	0.67	1.00																	
Color.	0.66	0.06	0.87	0.64	1.00																
Idaho	0.69	0.11	0.94	0.59	0.85	1.00															
Ill.	0.62	0.02	0.93	0.52	0.77	0.86	1.00														
Indi.	0.58	0.03	0.93	0.58	0.76	0.87	0.95	1.00													
Iowa	0.63	0.05	0.93	0.82	0.77	0.88	0.95	0.93	1.00												
Kans.	0.61	0.00	0.93	0.61	0.86	0.90	0.88	0.87	0.91	1.00											
Mich.	0.55	0.08	0.91	0.59	0.83	0.84	0.88	0.87	0.85	0.83	1.00										
Missouri	0.66	0.09	0.95	0.67	0.82	0.87	0.90	0.88	0.89	0.87	0.87	1.00									
Mont.	0.60	0.13	0.88	0.61	0.83	0.89	0.80	0.81	0.78	0.86	0.82	0.85	1.00								
Nebra.	0.62	0.06	0.89	0.63	0.79	0.82	0.81	0.81	0.87	0.91	0.79	0.84	0.78	1.00							
Nevada	0.56	0.12	0.77	0.66	0.73	0.75	0.64	0.68	0.65	0.68	0.68	0.75	0.67	0.61	1.00						
N.Mex.	0.55	0.14	0.80	0.61	0.77	0.78	0.70	0.78	0.75	0.79	0.72	0.79	0.71	0.78	0.70	1.00					
N.York	0.54	0.04	0.66	0.54	0.62	0.63	0.59	0.51	0.58	0.66	0.51	0.62	0.53	0.57	0.54	0.39	1.00				
Penn.	0.60	−0.01	0.79	0.59	0.74	0.75	0.76	0.72	0.76	0.77	0.68	0.76	0.66	0.69	0.68	0.61	0.84	1.00			
Utah	0.64	0.15	0.80	0.64	0.74	0.71	0.67	0.70	0.70	0.70	0.73	0.79	0.74	0.77	0.66	0.77	0.38	0.57	1.00		
Wics.	0.62	−0.03	0.92	0.63	0.82	0.86	0.85	0.86	0.85	0.87	0.90	0.89	0.81	0.84	0.75	0.72	0.60	0.74	0.74	1.00	
Wyom.	0.59	0.10	0.80	0.64	0.75	0.77	0.69	0.70	0.70	0.74	0.71	0.75	0.75	0.77	0.65	0.66	0.48	0.62	0.75	0.71	1.00

prices, thus providing some deflation protection and a positive real return. During the latter designated deflationary period, only two states (Arizona and New York) provide a positive real return. In no case are positive nominal returns realized.

Varying returns across states suggests that there are potential gains from geographic diversification. Table 7 shows the correlation matrix for all return series. In particular, two results are worth mentioning. First, there is little correlation between the S&P 500 and any farmland returns, which indicates possible diversification gains between financial and real assets. Secondly, while diversification benefits are possible whenever the correlation coefficient is less than one, there is a strong positive correlation between all farmland return series.

Summary and conclusions

This paper has examined the effectiveness of U.S. farmland as an inflation hedge during periods of significant domestic inflation and deflation over the 1919–1988 period. Using S&P 500 stock prices for comparison purposes, it was noted that financial assets were inferior to farmland in hedging performance, especially in later periods. However, there were low correlation coefficients between the two asset types, indicating potential diversification gains for investment portfolios.

During the periods of significant inflation, farmland, in the aggregate, and on an individual state basis as well, generally performed well against inflation. The results were particularly encouraging during the 1968–1985 period. During the two periods of significant deflation, neither the real (farmland) or financial assets were effective hedges, although prices for the S&P 500 fell more drastically than those for farmland.

Unfortunately, during the most recent bout with inflation, negative returns were realized in both real and nominal terms. As inflation continues above the 3% level devel designated in this study as significant, it will be interesting to see whether farmland's effectiveness as an inflation hedge continues. Studies on the transmission mechanism from economic phenomena to appreciation of farmland are needed in order to predict future performance.

References

Fama, E. and G. Schwert. "Asset Returns and Inflation." *Jounral of Financial Economics* 5 (November 1977), 115–46.

Fogler, R., M.R. Granito, and L.R. Smith. "A Theoretical Analysis of Real Estate Returns." *Journal of Finance* 40 (July 1985), 711–721.

Gultekin, N. "Stock Market Returns and Inflation Forecasts." *Journal of Finance* 38 (June 1983), 663–74.

Hadaway, S. and B. Hadaway. "Inflation Protection from Multi-Asset Sector Investments: A Long-Run Examination of Correlation Relationships with Inflation Rates." *Review of Economic and Business Research* 16 (Spring 1981), 80–89.

Hartzell, D., J. Heckman, and M. Miles. "Real Estate Returns and Inflation." *American Real Estate and Urban Economics ASsociation Journal* 15 (Spring 1987), 617–637.

Ibbotson, R. and L. Siegel. "Real Estate Returns: A Comparison With Other Investments." *American Real Estate and Urban Economics Association Journal* 12 (1984), 219–244.

Ibbotson Associates. *Stocks, Bonds, Bills and Inflation: 1989 Yearbook*. Chicago: Ibbotson Associates, Inc., 1989.

Irwin, S., D. Forster, and B. Sherrick. "Returns to Farmland Revisited." *American Journal of Agricultural Economics* 70 (August 1988), 580–581.

Jaffe, J. and G. Mandelker. "The 'Fisher Effect' for Risky Assets: An Empirical Investigation." *Journal of Finance* 31 (May 1976), 447–58.

Kaplan, H. "Farmland as a Portfolio Investment." *Journal of Portfolio Management* 11 (Winter 1985), 73–78.

Kaul, G. "Stock Returns and Inflation: The Role of the Monetary Sector." *Journal of Financial Economics* 18 (1987), 253–276.

Kost, W. "Rates of Return for Farm Real Estate and Common Stock." *American Journal of Agricultural Economics* 50 (May 1968), 213–224.

Mandelker, G. and K. Tandon. "Common Stock Returns, Real Activity, Money and Inflation: Some International Evidence." *Journal of International Money and Finance* 4 (June 1985), 267–86.

Nelson, C. "Inflation and Rates of Return on Common Stock." *Journal of Finance* 31 (May 1976), 471–83.

Peel, D. and P. Pope. "Testing the Fisherian Hypothesis: Some Methodological Issues and Further Evidence for the UK." *Journal of Business, Finance and Accounting* 12 (Summer 1985), 297–311.

Reilly, F., R. Marquardt, and D. Price. "Real Estate as an Inflation Hedge." *Review of Economic and Business Research* 12 (Spring 1977), 1–19.

Rubens, J., M. Bond, and J. Webb. "The Inflation-Hedging Effectiveness of Real Estate." *Journal of Real Estate Research* 4 (Summer 1989), 45–56.

Stulz, R. "Asset Pricing and Expected Inflation." *Journal of Finance* 41 (March 1986), 209–24.

Webb, J. and J. Rubens. "Portfolio Considerations in the Valuation of Real Estate." *American Real Estate and Urban Economics Association Journal* 14 (Fall 1986), 465–495.

White, F. and R. Ziemer. "Farm Real Estate Pricing under Risk: An Empirical Investigation." *Southern Economic Journal* 49 (July 1982), 77–87.

9 PERFORMANCE MEASURES OF REAL ESTATE FIRM COMMON STOCK RETURNS

John L. Glascock and Wallace N. Davidson III

Introduction

According to investor folklore, real estate investments offer an above average rate of return and a hedge against inflation. Previous research on real estate returns suggests that investor folklore may have some basis of truth. The work of Brueggeman, Chen, and Thibodeau (1984), Ibbotson and Siegel (1984), Hartzell, Hekman, and Miles (1987), Kuhle, Walther, and Wurtzebach (1986), and Kuhle (1987) shows that real estate either earned excessive returns or provided a good hedge against inflation. In a review of the real estate return literature, Sirmans and Sirmans (1986–87) indicate that most studies find real estate returns exceed that of stock and bond investments.

Research on real estate returns is difficult because most real estate assets do not trade in a manner that provides repetitive price observations

---

* We wish to thank William T. Hughes, C.F. Sirmans and Jim Webb for comments on earlier versions. All remaining errors are ours. Financial support for this research was provided by the Louisiana Real Estate Commission.

on an organized exchange. This creates two difficulties for researchers. First, appraised (and sometimes index) values must be used to compute real estate returns. For example, Brueggeman, Chen, and Thibodeau (1984) and Ibbotson and Siegel (1984) used appraised values in their studies. Appraised values may overstate or understate appreciation for a particular period and may also misstate asset price variance (see Firstenberg, Ross, and Zisler, 1987–88; Geltner, 1989; and Giliberto, 1988). Second, real estate assets trade infrequently, and measuring real estate returns may be subject to non-synchronous data problems (see Scholes and Williams, 1977).

Pointing out these problems is not meant to imply that research in this area is hopelessly flawed. Instead, our intent is to suggest the necessity of comparing the previously obtained results from other procedures. For example, recent work by Alllen and Sirmans (1987), Titman and Warga (1986), Kuhle, Walther, and Wurtzebach (1986), and Kuhle (1987) has analyzed the stock market performance of REITs. The use of stock market data over similar time periods can provide a comparative analysis and help to overcome the previously mentioned problems.

Recently, other researchers have begun to investigate real estate related samples of exchange traded firms. For example, Gyourko and Keim (1990) used a set of samples that included REITs, general contractors, agent and managers, etc., that is similar to the set of firms in this research. Their purpose was to investigate the return/risk relationship of these samples with traditional market forces. They found, as in this research, that the returns of real estate related firms were dominated by a strong covariance with the stock market. This study is different in that it concentrates on the return characteristics, and not the explanatory relationship, as in Gyourko and Keim (1990).

This paper uses stock market data to examine the performance of 31 real estate related firms's common stock returns. Of the 31 firms, 15 are REITs; the remainder are divided among the areas of contractors, developers, and single-family housing builders, including mobile home builders, etc. The REIT group was tested separately and there was no significant difference from the overall results.

Research Hypothesis

The hypothesis is that if the market perceives real estate to be a good inflation hedge and/or investment, this perception will be impounded in the stock prices of real estate firms. These firms will have higher stock prices (and lower expected returns) because investors will bid up their stock prices. Therefore, real estate firms, in an efficient market, should earn normal risk-adjusted returns.

A variety of real estate related firms was tested to measure return and inflation hedging performance. While each set of these firms offers information about security exchange-traded real estate, each also provides limitations. REITs may pose problems in that they are essentially closed end mutual funds (see Ross and Zisler, 1991, for a discussion). Such funds for general assets (securities) have been shown to sell at a discount (see Copeland and Weston, 1988, pp. 387–390 for more detail). Thus, a REIT may provide information about the ownership form as well as real estate assets. Additionally, some of the sample firms are builders and developers whose returns may be similar to those of other manufacturing firms. While the sample is a diversified set of firms, analyzing such firms for performance and inflation protection can extend our knowledge of real estate (related) assets. It is possible that exchange related real estate is more similar to normal security assets than to non-exchange real estate. While the sample is limited in size, it does offer evidence about return performance over a ten-year period where other researchers have indicated that potential excess return exists for real estate investments.

Research Design

Sample

The sample includes the 31 real estate related companies that trade on either the American or New York Stock Exchanges for the entire ten-year period, 1977 to 1986. These companies are from the CRSP data file (Center for Research in Security Prices from the University of Chicago) by SIC code. There are 109 real estate related firms identified. Of these 109, only 44 are currently on the CRSP tape as of December 31, 1986. Of the 44, only 31 firms have complete information for the entire period 1977–86. In addition to the CRSP data list, the Standard and Poor's *Stock Market Encyclopedia*, Moody's *Handbook of Common Stock*, Standard and Poor's *Stock Guide*, and Valueline's *Investment Survey* are used to verify that each company is substantially real estate in nature. The composition is 15 REITs, 5 builders and contractors, and 11 other firms. The results do not qualitatively differ when only REITs are analyzed. A list of the 31 firms appears in Table 1.

Table 1. Real estate related firms: nominal returns 1977–86

		1977	1978	1979	1980	1981	1982	1983	1984	1985	1986
BRT	B R T RLTY TR	−.21430	0.90380	−.28570	0.46400	0.00000	0.81330	0.24860	−.31900	0.17620	1.21630
CTX	CENTEX CORP	0.13400	0.32720	0.88060	0.25710	−.39970	0.65590	0.06490	−.00570	0.12080	0.23910
EGP	EASTGROUP PPTYS	0.07670	0.27190	0.81290	0.68790	0.20460	0.11570	0.71970	0.12670	0.01520	−.02780
FNM	FEDERAL NATL MTG ASSN	−.06970	0.16160	0.07750	−.20480	−.25260	1.91290	−.05490	−.32360	0.69720	0.58160
FRT	FEDERAL REALTY INVT TR	0.34710	0.01650	0.07230	0.55430	0.02160	0.47650	0.38150	0.25430	0.33610	0.24240
FCY	FIRST CITY INDS INC	1.41620	0.27430	0.02680	0.05220	−.04986	0.05226	1.58960	0.40140	−.58220	−.21240
FUR	FIRST UN REAL EST EQ&MTG INVTS	0.15210	−.07880	0.56810	0.49860	0.14800	0.38350	0.26710	0.18640	0.07540	0.54090
HMG	HMG PROP INVS	0.47610	0.04360	0.20630	0.36630	0.30290	0.00310	0.15380	−.24710	−.04330	−.12790
HRE	H R E PPTYS	0.21060	0.00070	0.08480	0.10260	0.10610	0.27250	0.44010	0.17190	0.09470	0.19080
LOM	LOMAS & NETTLETON MTG INVS	0.42670	−.14350	0.39540	0.10320	0.25710	0.68260	0.08140	0.26820	0.32650	0.25620
MSW	MISSION WEST PPTYS	0.07670	0.99399	0.71400	−.14530	−.06590	0.65710	−.00900	0.11410	−.00220	0.45010
MYM	MONY REAL ESTATE INVS	−0.05170	−.14220	0.11120	0.02800	−.04580	0.49140	0.08030	0.21320	0.16580	0.30670
MRT	MORTGAGE & REALTY TRUST	0.23640	−.15490	0.19930	0.28430	−.03690	0.87130	0.17250	0.27250	0.12410	0.39480
MTG	MORTGAGE GROWTH INVS	0.13620	0.32530	0.38180	0.34030	0.23670	0.36570	0.12350	0.29890	0.05150	0.36500
NEI	NATIONAL ENTERPRISES INC	−.42860	−.24920	−.16670	0.19870	0.05520	1.72500	−.32590	−.37030	0.63620	−.05540
OH	OAKWOOD HOMES CORP	0.21060	−.02840	0.57750	0.54610	0.09130	1.21890	−.02340	0.20510	0.26280	−.11280
OHC	ORIOLE HOMES CORP	0.09240	0.11140	0.40750	1.28890	−.28990	1.21790	−.48260	−.10130	0.24920	−.00060
PEI	PENNSYLVANIA REAL EST INVT TR	0.16970	0.17510	0.57670	0.12670	0.07080	0.29140	0.48780	0.26770	0.36340	0.33170
PDL	PRESIDENTIAL REALTY CORP NEW	−.18180	0.33140	0.16630	−.12540	0.79040	0.63500	0.26280	0.27710	0.72380	−.16960
PDL	PRESIDENTIAL REALTY CORP NEW	−.22730	0.38010	0.14850	−.05130	0.15720	0.36500	0.94900	0.30350	0.55130	0.05420
PCT	PROPERTY CAP TR	0.11780	−.01270	0.64480	0.75730	0.13270	0.40220	0.09760	0.19620	0.12780	0.28740
RRF	REALTY REFUND TR	0.19870	−.30290	−.11180	−.06400	−.08820	0.65430	0.23520	0.33680	0.13030	0.27010
RPB	ROYAL PALM BEACH COLONY LP	0.23790	0.30610	0.00000	0.17530	−.24920	0.33140	0.29830	0.19130	0.77380	0.06880
RYN	RYAN HOMES INC	−.14590	0.01400	0.45710	0.18330	−.19810	1.50100	−.18190	−.22670	0.08030	0.74390
BFS	SAUL B F REAL ESTATE INVT TR	0.03020	0.52640	0.11510	0.23580	−.14660	0.41720	0.33840	0.26610	−.03350	0.03470
SKY	SKYLINE CORP	−.18790	−.26370	0.15630	0.19870	0.14550	0.65870	−.24410	−.06740	0.12190	−.13170
TUR	TURNER CORP	0.25950	0.02410	0.14960	0.70900	0.28960	0.19560	0.33710	0.22470	0.18270	−.15500
UAC	UNICORP AMER CORP NEW	0.26610	−.15740	−.31250	−.09060	−.44870	0.63280	−.22150	−.08310	0.09080	0.12670
WHI	WASHINGTON HOMES INC	−.52030	−.31360	−.16130	0.07650	−.14240	3.47250	0.58930	−.02320	1.07090	0.24000
WRE	WASHINGTON REAL EST INVT TR	0.09260	−.05200	0.42880	0.49540		0.31080	0.19160	0.44420	0.26490	0.26980
WFM	WELLS FARGO MTG & EQUITY TR	0.49350	−0.3770	0.33390	0.90420	0.07620	0.30420	0.18240	0.04120	0.02580	0.35720
						0.00870		0.39980			
EQUALLY	WEIGHTED INDEX RETURN	0.19330	0.24710	0.42020	0.38480	0.07620	0.33870	0.23320	0.00100	0.31640	0.18210
VALUE	WEIGHTED INDEX RETURN	−.04090	0.08530	0.22790	0.32620	−.04100	0.20110		0.04990	0.30670	0.16380

Methodology

The daily real estate returns of these 31 companies for the sample period are taken from the CRSP tapes. These returns are summed for each year for each company. Compounded daily returns are used to compute annual holding period returns. A summary of the returns by company appears in Table 1.

These returns are analyzed in a number of ways. First, they are compared to market indices to see how real estate firms performed relative to the market. Second, the Sharpe and the Treynor indices are computed for these firms and compared to Sharpe and Treynor indices for the market. These indices are defined below. Third, beta for these firms are computed. Finally, comparison of the companies' returns to the consumer price index is made.

Sharpe and Treynor Indices

In addition to nominal return measures of performance, Sharpe and Treynor ratios are computed for each company for each year and are compared to market measures of the same statistics. Elton and Gruber (1984) explain these ratios in detail, so they are only briefly discussed here.

The Sharp index adjusts returns by both the risk free rate of return and the standard deviation of the returns. This is shown below:

$$R_{is} = \frac{R_i - R_f}{\sigma_i} \tag{1}$$

where

R_{is} = the Sharpe index for company i
R_i = the return for company i
R_f = the risk-free rate of return
σ_i = the standard deviation of returns for company i.

The Sharpe index is a measure of reward-to-variability. The numerator measures the firm's risk premium, and the denominator measures the total variability of the returns. The Sharpe index may be appropriate for investors who have a non-diversified portfolio since it measures return per unit of total risk. A firm or portfolio performs better than the market portfolio when the firm's Sharpe index ratio is greater than the market's ratio $[(R_m - R_f)/c_m)$.

The Treynor index is appropriate for evaluating well diversified portfolios. It is a measure of reward-to-systematic risk. The Treynor index can be calculated as:

$$R_{iT} = \frac{R_i - R_f}{\beta_i} \tag{2}$$

where

R_{iT} = the Treynor index for company i
R_i = the nominal return for company i
R_f = the risk-free rate of return
β_i = the systematic risk for company i.

The market's Treynor ratio is $R_m - R_f$ since the market *beta* is one. Thus, a firm or portfolio performs better than the market when the firm's ratio is larger than $R_m - R_f$. This provides a measure of return-to-systematic risk (i.e., risk that an investor or the market cannot diversify away).

Results

Real Estate Firm Returns, 1977–1986.

Table 1 contains the summation of the daily analyzed returns for the real estate firms, as well as value-weighted and equally-weighted market portfolio returns for all NYSE and AMEX firms for each of the ten years. These returns are shown for each company.

Table 2 provides the number of times that an individual firm's return beats the equally weighted market index. Individual firm returns are classified as either better (a win) or worse than the comparison market index. There are no ties in this counting procedure. The binomial *t*-test is used to determine significance, with an expected outcome of 50 percent better than the market.

For the 31 firms, the range is from a low of only six wins in 1983 to a high of 22 wins in 1982. In five of the years (1978, 1979, 1980, 1983, and 1985) the *t*-test shows that the market index beat individual firm returns significantly more often than expected. In only two years, 1982 and 1984, the number of firms beating the index significantly beat random chance.

In the last column, out of a total of 310 chances (31 firms over 10 years), individual firms beat the market index significantly less often than pure chance would indicate. These results imply that when risk is ignored and return only is considered, the market in general performs better than real estate firms over this period.

Similar statistics are shown for the comparison between real estate firms and the value-weighted index of all AMEX and NYSE stocks.

Table 2. Statistical Comparison of Company Excess Return Equally Weighted Index Adjusted

	1977	*1978*	*1979*	*1980*	*1981*	*1982*	*1983*	*1984*	*1985*	*1986*	*Combined*
Number of positive	12	10	9	10	13	22	6	21	9	18	130
t-test	−1.26	−1.98*	−2.33**	−1.98*	−0.90	2.33**	−3.41***	1.98*	−2.3**	0.90	−2.83**

* significant at 0.10.
** significant at 0.05.
*** significant at 0.01.

In two years, 1977 and 1982, the real estate firms beat the market index significantly more often than chance. In only one year, 1985, did the real estate firms statistically underperform the market. For the total sample, there is no statistical difference between the number of times (167 of 310) the real estate firms beat the index and chance ($t = 1.36$).

These results could be consistent with the notion that real estate assets are inflation hedging. The lower return could be attributed to market participants bidding up the price of real estate assets to obtain the inflation hedging benefit. Additional tests are required to determine if this sample of real estate related firms under or over performed the market.

Sharpe and Treynor Results, 1977–1986

Table 3 contains the summary statistics for the Sharpe and Treynor indices. In most of the years, the market Sharpe index outperformed more than half of the real estate companies. The exception was 1984, when more than 50 percent of the real estate companies outperformed the equally-weighted market Sharpe index. These results are consistent with our earlier observations that our sample of real estate firms does not outperform the market average.

The Treynor index has similar results. The results for the entire 109 initial sample (not provided in detail) are qualitatively similar. For example, during the whole period, 1977–1986, only 34% of the real estate firm returns (each firm for each year is counted as one observation for this test) did better than the market using a Treynor index. A Jensen index test (detail not shown) provides similar results. Only in three years, 1981, 1982, and 1984, did more than half of the real estate firms outperform the market. In the remaining seven years, the market outperformed the majority of the real estate firms. Thus, on average, these real estate firms did not have risk adjusted returns equal to the market's returns.

Real Estate Firm Betas

A stock with a beta greater than one implies that, relative to the market, the security's price is volatile. A beta of less than one but greater than zero implies that the security's price is less volatile than the market. When a beta is less than zero, the stock's price moves inversely with the market.

Table 4 contains the annual beta averages for the 31 sample firms. The

Table 3. Sharpe and Treynor Indices Statistics

	1977	1978	1979	1980	1981	1982	1983	1984	1985	1986
Panel A: Sharpe Index Statistics										
Market Sharpe Index	6.22	7.91	15.60	14.12	−3.92	15.77	26.13	−9.48	30.97	19.41
Number of times company beat market	11	7	9	9	15	15	4	26	1	9
Panel B: Treynor Index Statistics										
Market Treynor Index	0.141	0.175	0.320	0.270	−0.065	0.232	0.313	−0.095	0.242	0.122
Number of times company beat market	12	9	12	13	26	23	13	21	16	20

Table 4. Beta Statistics

	1977	*1978*	*1979*	*1980*	*1981*	*1982*	*1983*	*1984*	*1985*	*1986*
Average Number	0.630	0.625	0.810	0.593	0.520	0.545	0.671	0.588	0.435	0.506
$B > 1$	8	8	9	5	4	6	8	6	4	4
$1 > B > 0$	18	22	22	25	25	22	21	23	24	26
$B < 0$	5	1	0	1	2	3	2	2	3	1

Table 5. Comparative Statistic Company Return versus CPI

	1977	*1978*	*1979*	*1980*	*1981*	*1982*	*1983*	*1984*	*1985*	*1986*
Number of position	21	13	19	20	12	30	23	21	25	22
t-test	1.98*	−0.90	1.26	1.62	−1.26	5.21***	2.69**	1.98*	3.41***	2.33**

* significant at 0.10.
** significant at 0.05.
*** significant at 0.01.

average annual beta (averaged across firms for each year) ranges from 0.435 in 1985 to 0.810 in 1979. This result of a below market (i.e., $\beta < 1$) beta is consistent with the recent work of Howe and Shilling (1990), and Chan, Hendershott, and Sanders (1990).

The number of betas greater than one range from four in 1981, 1985, and 1986, to nine in 1979. The number of betas less than zero ranges from zero in 1979 to five in 1977. The majority of the betas lie between zero and one.

Comparison of Returns to Inflation

Table 5 shows a comparison of real estate firm returns to the Consumer Price Index (CPI). In most years the number of firms beating the CPI is better than pure chance, but it is significant only in 1977 and in 1982 through 1986. Overal, out of 310 chances, the CPI was bettered 206 times. This number is significantly different from pure chance at the 10% significantly level.

To further examine the relationship between return and inflation, an equally weighted portfolio of the real estate firm returns is formed and regressed against the equally weighted market index and the inflation rate. Equation 3 shows this regression form.

$$R_p = \alpha + \beta(R_m) + \gamma(CPI) + e_r \tag{3}$$

where

R_p = equally weighted return on a 31-real estate firm portfolio
α = constant β = coefficient on market return
R_m = return on equally weighted market portfolio
γ = coefficient on inflation
e_r = error term assumed to fulfill the ideal conditions.

Table 6 contains the results.

This regression provides two outcomes. Firms, the sample of real estate firms do not provide a hedge against inflation. The coefficient for

Table 6. Real Estate Portfolio Return, Market Return, and Inflation (CPI)

Variable	*Coefficient*	*t Ratio*	*F*	R^2
Market index	0.86188	2.0976	2.374	0.4042
CPI	−1.7742	−1.2367		
Constant	0.12507	0.9728		

inflation is nominally negative but is not significant. Second, the only significant explanatory variable is the return on the market. A regression model where the standard deviation of the portfolio returns is added is also used. The returns do not change. Additionally, (3) for the entire large sample of 109 firms and the smaller set of 15 REITs is tested and similar returns are found. In general, this sample of real estate returns did not provide ex post inflation protection. It may be that observed inflation and unanticipated inflation are not well correlated, and thus our test for inflation hedging may be inappropriate. Rubens, Bond, and Webb (1989) provide an explanation for the poor inflation adjusted performance by indicating that assets performed well in terms of anticipated inflation, but poorly in terms of unanticipated inflation. Their study covers 1960 through 1986, a period similar to this research.

Conclusions

This research analyzes common stock returns for real estate related firms for the period 1977 through 1986. Real estate firms generally outperform the inflation rate, but do not perform as well as equally or value-weighted market portfolios. Thus, real estate investments through New York and American Exchange listed real estate companies do not offer unique inflation hedging ability.

The results are subject to two key limitations. First, the sample is somewhat small, because only firms with complete data are examined; it also includes a variety of real estate related firms. Second, actual inflation is used to proxy for unanticipated inflation.

Overall, the results provide three conclusions. First, real estate firms in the period 1977 to 1986 underperformed the market as a whole. Second, real estate firms performed less well on a risk adjusted basis than the market as a whole. Third, real estate firms did not provide unique inflation protection. The general market did a better job of providing positive returns in excess of inflation.

References

Allen, P. and C.F. Sirmans. "An Analysis of Gains to Acquiring Firm's Shareholders: The Special Case of REITs." *Journal of Financial Economics* 18, 1 (1987), 175–184.

Brueggeman, W.B., A.H. Chen, and T.G. Thibodeau. "Real Estate Investment

Funds: Performance and Portfolio Considerations." *AREUEA Journal* 12, 3 (Fall 1984), 333–354.

Center for Research in Security Prices. *CRSP Stock Files, Daily Returns*, 1987.

Chan, K.C., P. Hendershott, and A. Sanders. "Risk and Return on Real Estate: Evidence from Equity REITS." *AREUEA Journal* 18, 4 (Winter 1990), 431–452.

Copeland, T.E. and J.F. Weston. *Financial Theory and Corporate Policy*, 3rd ed. Reading, MA: Addison Wesley, 1988.

Council for Economic Advisors. "Economic Indicators." Various issues (1978–1987). Washington, DC: Superintendent of Documents.

Elton, E.J. and M.J. Gruber, *Modern Portfolio Theory and Investment Analysis*. New York: John Wiley and Sons, 1984.

Firstenberg, P.B., S.A. Ross, and R.C. Zisler, "Real Estate: The Whole Story." *Journal of Portfolio Management* 14, 3 (1987–88), 22–34.

Geltner, D. "Bias in Appraisal-Based Returns." *AREUEA Journal* 17, 3 (Fall 1989), 338–352.

Giliberto, S. "A Note on the Use of Appraisal Data in Indexes of Performance Measurement." 16, 1 (Spring 1988), 77–83.

Gyourko, J. and D.B. Keim. "The Risk and Return Characteristics of Stock Market-Based Real Estate Indexes." Working paper, Wharton University, January 1990.

Hartzell, D., J.S. Hekman, and M.E. Miles. "Real Estate Returns and Inflation." *AREUEA Journal* 15, 1 (Spring 1987), 617–637.

Howe, J.S. and J.D. Shilling. "REIT Advisor Performance." *AREUEA Journal* 18, 4 (Winter 1990), 479–500.

Ibbotson, R.G. and L.B. Siegel. "Real Estate Returns: A Comparison with Other Investments." *AREUEA Journal* 12, 3 (Fall 1984), 219–242.

Kuhle, J.L. "Portfolio Diversification and Return Benefits—Common Stock vs. Real Estate Investment Trusts (REITs)." *Journal of Real Estate Research* 2, 2 (1987), 1–9.

Kuhle, J.L., C.H. Walther, and C.H. Wurtzebach. "The Financial Performance of Real Estate Trusts." *Journal of Real Estate Research* 1, 1 (1986), 67–76.

Moody's *Handbook of Common Stocks*. Various issues (1978–1987). New York: Moody's Investment Service.

Ross, S.A. and R.C. Zisler. "Risk and Return in Real Estate." *Journal of Real Estate Finance and Economics* 4, 2 (1991), 175–190.

Rubens, J.H., M.T. Bond, and J.R. Webb. "The Inflation-Hedging Effectiveness of Real Estate." *Journal of Real Estate Research* 4, 2 (1989), 45–56.

Scholes, M. and J. Willians. "Estimating Beta for Nonsynchronous Data." *Journal of Financial Economics* 5, 3 (1977), 309–327.

Sirmans, G.S. and C.F. Sirmans. "The Historical Perspective of Real Estate Returns." *The Journal of Portfolio Management* 13, 3 (1986–87), 2–31.

Solt, M.E. and N.G. Miller. "Managerial Incentives: Implications for the Financial Performance of Real Estate Investment Trusts." *AREUEA Journal*, 13, 4 (Winter 1985), 404–423.

Standard and Poor's *Stock Guide*. Various issues (1978–1987). New York: Standard and Poor's Investment Service.

Standard and Poor's *Stock Market Encyclopedia*. Various issues (1978–1987). New York: Standard and Poor's Investment Service.

Titman, S. and A. Warga. "Risk and the Performance of Real Estate Investment Trusts: A Multiple Index Approach." *AREUEA Journal* 14, 3 (Fall 1986), 414–431.

Valueline's *Investment Survey*. Various issues (1978–1987). New York: Valueline.

10 A TUTORIAL ON PARTITIONING REAL ESTATE INVESTMENT CASH FLOWS USING THE INTERNAL RATE OF RETURN

Mark G. Dotzour and Donald R. Levi

Introduction

Much has been written on the use of the internal rate of return (IRR) as an investment decision-making criterion. In a 1977 survey article, Jaffe (1977) cited 1,188 IRR references and classified them into four categories: (1) tutorial, (2) calculations and multiple solutions, (3) alternative measures, models and computations, and (4) reinvestment, risk and discounting, and ranking. Because of the possibility of multiple solutions when cash flows turn negative, and of the inherent assumption that cash flows generated can be continuously invested elsewhere at the project IRR, the consensus is that the net present value investment decision-making criterion is superior, and that the IRR's principal use should be for ranking investment alternatives.[1]

At the same time, the IRR and its component parts may provide information about risks to real estate investors. At the outset, it should be recognized that investments in real estate are different from some other investment alternatives (e.g., certificates of deposit). In the simplest case, real estate returns may come from two distinct sources: (1) annual cash flow from rental income, and (2) the investment reversion[2] received at sale. Both are computed on an after-tax basis, and their respective contributions to the IRR calculated. In essence, these calculations partition cash flows contributing to the IRR into two parts, and investors may explicitly or implicity assess the risks associated with attaining projected returns from each component part. As an example, since price appreciation is an important determinant of the reversion, the risk associated with receiving the reversionary funds might be significantly different (likely higher) than the risk of achieving the estimated returns from annual cash flows.

The purpose of this paper is first to develop a generalized theoretical model for dividing real estate investment cash flows into additional component parts; second, to derive the first derivative of IRR with respect to each component part so that the impact of each component may be illustrated mathematically; and to show how the relative riskiness of each component of returns may be ranked using variances. Observations are offered on the potential impact of partitioning returns on investor wealth, and some further needs for research identified.

Previous work on partitioning returns

The idea of breaking an income stream into component parts and discounting each component part at an appropriate discount rate is not new, having been suggested by Modigliani and Miller (1963). They suggested that after-tax return was equal to the summation of (1) an uncertain stream, $(1\text{-}T)\bar{X}Z$, and (2) a sure stream, TR, where

T = tax rate
$\bar{X}$ = expected value
Z = random variable
R = interest charges.

Arditti (1974) showed that Modigliani and Miller's partitioning was "appropriate only where a stream is broken up into two substreams, one certain and the other uncertain." This is readily possible for real estate investment cash flows by partitioning each cash flow into pre-tax (uncertain) and tax (certain) substreams.[3]

In 1978 Valachi (1978) suggested a three-way "partitioning of the IRR."[4] He partitioned annual cash flows into two parts, cash flow before taxes and tax shelter, retaining the reversion as the third component. *Given* a particular set of tax deductibility rules, he recognized that the contribution of tax shelter to IRR is less risky than other components of the IRR.[5]

Zerbst (1980) "partitioned the IRR" into six parts. Cash flow before taxes, growth in cash flow before taxes over the investment holding period, and tax shelter were viewed as the three components of annual cash flows, while "net" price appreciation,[6] return of initial investment, and loan amortization were the three component parts suggested for the reversion.

A difficulty with some previous IRR partitioning processes is that they may bias the relative contributions of cash flow and price appreciation to total return. As an example, depreciation has both positive and negative impacts on the IRR. As a deduction, depreciation reduces annual taxable income and provides tax shelter for annual cash flows. On the other hand, depreciation reduces the investor's adjusted basis, thereby increasing the amount of taxable gain and taxes at sale. Given a constant marginal tax bracket,[7] and the tax rules established in the 1986 Tax Reform Act, the net impact of depreciation is simply the time value of money for income taxes deferred, as subsequently will be shown mathematically. The treatment of depreciation in previous IRR partitioning methods has overstated the total contribution of depreciation enhancing annual cash flow by the immediate tax savings and understated by an equal amount the apparent contribution of price appreciation to returns.[8]

In a similar manner, the principal portion of mortgage loan payments has biased the apparent contributions to IRR of cash flow and price appreciation (in the Valachi (1978) and Zerbst (1980) partitioning methods) in the opposite fashion to depreciation. Principal payments reduce annual cash flow returns but are returned at sale via loan amortization, thereby overstating the returns due to price appreciation. In reality, the net impact of principal payments/loan amortization also is reflected by the time value of money.[9]

One- and two-period models for partitioning investment returns

Pro forma income statements for real estate investments often assume increases (or decreases) in both rental income and operating expenses. Thus, different cash flows may result for each year that a real estate investment is held. Conceptually, a pro forma income statement for a real estate project might be influenced by:

- initial effective gross income;
- growth in effective gross income;

- initial operating expenses;
- growth in operating expenses;
- mortgage interest payments;
- mortgage principal payments; and
- depreciation deductions.

Note that effective gross income and growth in effective gross income, taken alone, will have an associated tax cost. On the other hand, all other pro forma items listed, except mortgage principal payments, provide tax sheltering benefits. Thus, clearly both tax rules and marginal tax rates influence real estate investment annual returns.

From the standpoint of the reversion, sales expenses technically reduce taxes, price appreciation leads to tax liability, and the return of initial investment and loan amortization are tax neutral. Both the annual cash flow and reversionary items can all be expressed in the following one-period IRR model:[10]

$$CF_0 = \frac{ATCF_1}{1 + IRR} + \frac{ATCF_R}{1 + IRR} \qquad (1)$$

where

CF_0 = initial investment, or cash flow at time zero
$ATCF_1$ = after tax cash flow for year one
$ATCF_R$ = after tax reversion from sale
IRR = internal rate of return.

Then

$$CF_0\,(1 + IRR) = ATCF_1 + ATCF_R; \qquad (2)$$

$$1 + IRR = \frac{(ATCF_1 + ATCF_R)}{CF_0} \qquad (3)$$

and

$$IRR = \frac{ATCF_1 + ATCF_R}{CF_0} - 1. \qquad (4)$$

Since

$$ATCF_1 = [EGI_1 - OE_1 - INT_i - PRIN_i] - [EGI_1 - OE_1 - INT_i - D_i][T] \qquad (5)$$

and

$$ATCF_R = (PP + PA)(1 - SE) - [(PP + PA)(1 - SE) - (PP - D_i)](T) - [(PP)(LTV) - PRIN_i] \quad (6)$$

where

EGI_1 = effective gross income for period one
OE_1 = operating expenses for period one
INT_i = mortgage interest payments for the ith period
$PRIN_i$ = mortgage principal payments for the ith period
PP = purchase price
PA = price appreciation for period one
SE = sales expenses as a percentage of sales price
D_i = depreciation deduction for the ith period
T = marginal tax rate
LTV = loan to value ratio
CF_0 = initial investment, or PP (1-LTV).

Then (4) may be expanded into its component parts:

$$\begin{aligned} IRR = [\{[(EGI_1 - OE_1 - INT_i - PRIN_i)] \\ - [(EGI_1 - OE_1 - INT_i - D_i)(T)] \\ + [(PP + PA)(1 - SE) - [(PP + PA)(1 - SE) \\ -(PP - D_i)](T) - [PP(LTV) - PRIN_i]\}/PP(1 - LTV)] - 1 \end{aligned} \quad (7)$$

In a one-period model, under current tax laws, tax shelter from depreciation may be fully recaptured by taxes due from sale,[11] and principal payments are fully recovered upon disposition. Therefore, the one-period model may be written:

$$IRR = \frac{(EGI_1 - OE_1 - INT_1)(1 - T) + (PP + PA)(1 - SE)(1 - T) + PP(T) - PP(LTV)}{PP(1 - LTV)} - 1. \quad (8)$$

A two-period IRR model may be written:

$$CF_0 = \frac{ATCF_1}{1 + IRR} + \frac{ATCF_2 + ATCF_R}{(1 + IRR)^2} \quad (9)$$

where

$ATCF_2$ = after tax cash flow in period two.

Then

$$CF_0(1 + IRR) = ATCF_1 + \frac{ATCF_2 + ATCF_R}{1 + IRR}; \quad (10)$$

$$1 + \mathrm{IRR} = \frac{\mathrm{ATCF}_1}{\mathrm{CF}_0} + \frac{(\mathrm{ATCF}_2 + \mathrm{ATCF}_\mathrm{R})}{\mathrm{CF}_0(1 + \mathrm{IRR})} \tag{11}$$

and

$$\mathrm{IRR} = \frac{\mathrm{ATCF}_1}{\mathrm{CF}_0} + \frac{\mathrm{ATCF}_2 + \mathrm{ATCF}_\mathrm{R}}{\mathrm{CF}_0(1 + \mathrm{IRR})} - 1. \tag{12}$$

Equation (12) may be expanded as follows by replacing the IRR in the right-hand side of (10) with IRR as defined by (8).

$$\begin{aligned}\mathrm{IRR}_2 = {} & \frac{(\mathrm{EGI}_1 - \mathrm{OE}_1 - \mathrm{INT}_1)(1 - \mathrm{T}) - \mathrm{PRIN} + \mathrm{D(T)}}{\mathrm{PP}(1 - \mathrm{LTV})} \\ & + \frac{(\mathrm{EGI}_1 + \Delta\mathrm{EGI} - \mathrm{OE}_1 - \Delta\mathrm{OE} - \mathrm{INT}_2)(1 - \mathrm{T}) - \mathrm{PRIN}_2 + \mathrm{D}_2(\mathrm{T})}{\mathrm{PP}(1 - \mathrm{LTV})\left[\dfrac{(\mathrm{EGI}_1 - \mathrm{OE}_1 - \mathrm{INT}_1)(1 - \mathrm{T}) - \mathrm{SE}(\mathrm{PP} + \Delta_1\mathrm{PP})}{\mathrm{PP}(1 - \mathrm{LTV})} \dfrac{(1 - \mathrm{T}) + \Delta_1\mathrm{PP}(1 - \mathrm{T})}{\mathrm{PP}(1 - \mathrm{LTV})} + 1\right]} \\ & + \frac{\begin{array}{c}(\mathrm{PP} + \Delta_1\mathrm{PP} + \Delta_2\mathrm{PP})(1 - \mathrm{S}) - [(\mathrm{PP} + \Delta_1\mathrm{PP} + \Delta_2\mathrm{PP})(1 - \mathrm{S}) - (\mathrm{PP} - \mathrm{D}_1 - \mathrm{D}_2)](\mathrm{T}) - \\ {[\mathrm{PP}(\mathrm{LTV}) - \mathrm{PRIN}_1 - \mathrm{PRIN}_2]}\end{array}}{\mathrm{PP}(1 - \mathrm{LTV})\left[\dfrac{\begin{array}{c}(\mathrm{EGI}_1 - \mathrm{OE}_1 - \mathrm{INT}_1)(1 - \mathrm{T}) - \mathrm{SE}(\mathrm{PP} + \Delta_1\mathrm{PP})(1 - \mathrm{T}) - \\ \Delta_1\mathrm{PP}(1 - \mathrm{T})\end{array}}{\mathrm{PP}(1 - \mathrm{LTV})} + 1\right]}\end{aligned} \tag{13}$$

Impact of partitioned components on returns

If we let (14) be a shorthand representation of (13) such that

$$\mathrm{IRR}_2 = \frac{\mathrm{CF}_1}{\mathrm{PP}(1 - \mathrm{LTV})} + \frac{\mathrm{A}}{\mathrm{B}} \tag{14}$$

where

A = second-period after-tax cash flow from rent and reversion; and
B = second-period discount factor = $(\mathrm{IRR})^2$,

then the partial derivatives with respect to each component part of the IRR may be taken and interpreted.

The partial derivative of IRR with respect to EGI_1 (15) shows that IRR will increase monotonically with increases in EGI, and that the increase will come from three factors. First, an unexpected increase in period one EGI will increase the first-year cash return after taxes and be discounted at the IRR for the first year (PP(1 – LTV)). The second source of change in IRR results from the fact that the second-year cash flow will be based upon an appreciated/depreciated value from the first-year EGI. Holding other factors constant, an increase in EGI_1 will result in an increase in EGI_2, which will be discounted at the (B) second-period discount rate. The third component with a negative sign indicates that the increased return in the first period will increase the overall IRR and cause an increase in the second period discount rate (B). This influence is a natural consequence of the IRR calculation that discounts all cash flows at the same discount rate. An increase in first-period cash flow will increase the IRR, which results in a reduced present value at (A) second-period cash flows:

$$\frac{\partial IRR_2}{\partial EGI_1} = \frac{1 - T}{PP(1 - LTV)} + \frac{1 - T}{B} - \frac{A(1 - T)}{B^2}. \tag{15}$$

The partial derivative of IRR with respect to changes in the growth rate in annual EGI (16) shows that an unexpected increase in the rate of growth of EGI for the second period will increase the second-period cash flow and increase IRR by a magnitude determined by the marginal tax rate and (B), the second period discount rate:

$$\frac{\partial IRR_2}{\partial \Delta_1 EGI_1} = \frac{1 - T}{B}. \tag{16}$$

The partial with respect to OE_1 (17) shows that an unexpected increase in first-period operating expenses will cause IRR to decline because of the same three reasons enumerated in the partial with respect to EGI, only in reverse fashion. Since $T < 1$, then higher operating expenses will reduce the first-period cash flow and (holding all else constant) will reduce second-period cash flow because the base level of expenses increased:

$$\frac{\partial IRR_2}{\partial OE_1} = \frac{T - 1}{PP(1 - LTV)} + \frac{T - 1}{B} - \frac{A(T - 1)}{B^2}. \tag{17}$$

Equation (18) shows that an increase in the growth rate of operating expenses causes IRR to fall. Holding all other factors constant, an unexpected increase in the rate of growth of OE will not affect first-year cash flow, but will reduce the second-year cash flow net of taxes:

$$\frac{\partial IRR_2}{\partial \Delta_1 OE_1} = \frac{T - 1}{B}. \tag{18}$$

Equation (19) illustrates the impact of loan amortization on IRR. The interpretation is that principal payments reduce IRR in period one but are offset by their return via loan amortization for a sale in year two, and the effect of principal payments for previous years is reflected by the time value of money as previously suggested:

$$\frac{\partial IRR_2}{\partial PRIN_1} = \frac{-1}{PP(1 - LTV)} + \frac{1}{B}. \tag{19}$$

When expanded to an n = period model, (20) illustrates that year n principal payments have no effect on the IRR:

$$\frac{\partial IRR_2}{\partial PRIN_2} = 0. \tag{20}$$

The impact of depreciation, illustrated in (21) shows that an increase in the first-period depreciation allowance will have two effects on IRR. First, the increased allowance in the first period will increase tax shelter and have a positive impact on IRR. The second effect will be an increased tax due on the resale of the property by an equal amount due to the decreased tax basis in the property. The second effect will be smaller than the first because of the time value of money.[12] Consequently, under the Tax Reform Act of 1986 and a constant marginal tax rate, the value of depreciation is due entirely to the ability to defer taxes into the future:

$$\frac{\partial IRR_2}{\partial D_1} = \frac{T}{PP(1 - LTV)} - \frac{1}{B}. \tag{21}$$

The partial derivative with respect to the depreciation allowance in the second period (22) shows that changes in second-period depreciation will have no impact on IRR. This happens because the tax shelter generated by the deduction is completely recaptured by the taxes due when the property is sold.

$$\frac{\partial IRR_2}{\partial D_2} = 0. \tag{22}$$

Equation 23 shows that the impact on IRR of a change in the first-period interest expense will be negatively correlated (net of the effects of tax deductibility). The second term in the derivative shows the impact on IRR due to a reduction in the second-period discount rate. This second effect will mitigate the influence of the first but will not completely offset it:

$$\frac{\partial IRR_2}{\partial INT_1} = \frac{T - 1}{PP(1 - LTV)} + \frac{A(1 - T)}{B^2}. \tag{23}$$

The partial with respect to second-period interest expenses (24) illustrates the impact of adjustable rate mortgage loans on real estate investments. The change in interest rate in the second year will not affect first-period returns. Consequently, the change in interest rate will inversely affect the second-period cash flow (net of tax effects):

$$\frac{\partial IRR_2}{\partial INT_2} = \frac{T - 1}{B} \tag{24}$$

Equation (25) illustrates that an increase in price appreciation in year one will lead to an increase in IRR due to higher after tax reversion in period two. The second term suggests a negative influence on IRR because the second-period discount rate has increased, due to the increased return in the first period:

$$\frac{\partial IRR_2}{\partial \Delta_1 PP} = \frac{(1 - S)(1 - T)}{B} - \frac{A(1 - SE + SE(T))}{B^2}. \tag{25}$$

The partial derivative with respect to second-period price appreciation (26) shows a positive correlation between appreciation and IRR, subject to the mitigating impact of increased sales expenses and income taxes:

$$\frac{\partial IRR_2}{\partial \Delta_2 PP} = \frac{(1 - S)(1 - T)}{B}. \tag{26}$$

Equation 27 measures the changes that occur with IRR when a change in sales expenses occur. IRR will be negatively correlated with changes in sales expenses, and mitigated somewhat by the marginal tax rate ($T < 1$). Hence, the impact of changing sales expenses will be determined by the level of price appreciation in each year of the holding period, as well as the marginal tax rate.

$$\frac{\partial IRR_2}{\partial S} = \frac{-A(PP + \Delta_1 PP)(T - 1)}{B^2}. \tag{27}$$

A change in the loan-to-value ratio (holding all other factors equal) has three impacts on IRR. The first influence illustrated in (28) occurs because an increase in LTV means less equity invested in the project, which reduces the discount rate for first-period cash flow. The second term is negatively correlated with IRR because an increase in LTV means a higher loan balance to be repaid in the terminal period. The third term is positively correlated with IRR, because the increased LTV means decreased equity contribution which reduces the second-period discount rate:

$$\frac{\partial IRR_2}{\partial LTV} = \frac{[EGI_1 - OE_1 - INT_1](1 - T)PP}{[PP - PP(LTV)]^2} - \frac{PP}{B} + \frac{A(PP)}{B^2}. \tag{28}$$

The derivative of two-period IRR with respect to marginal tax rates is presented in (29). Virtually all components of IRR are shown to be correlated with tax rates.

$$\frac{\partial IRR_2}{\partial T} = EGI_1 - \Delta_1 EGI_1 + OE_1 + \Delta_1 OE_1 + INT_2 + D_2 - \frac{(\Delta_1 PP + \Delta_2 PP)(1 - S) - S(PP) + D_1 + D_2}{B} - \frac{A[-EGI_1 + OE_1 + INT_1 + S(PP + \Delta_1 PP) - \Delta_1 PP]}{B_2}. \quad (29)$$

Sources and uses of the IRR

Items which positively contribute to the IRR may be thought of as sources of the IRR, and those items which contribute negatively to the IRR may be thought of as uses of the IRR.[13] The sources of IRR are:

- initial level of effective gross income
- growth in effective gross income
- depreciation
- price appreciation
- return of initial investment at sale.

The percentage contribution of each component source of the IRR may be computed by dividing the present value of each component by the total present value of all IRR sources, thereby providing a relative measure of each source's contribution to IRR.

Similarly, the uses of the IRR are reflected by the negative present value of:

- initial level of operating expenses
- growth in operating expenses
- mortgage interest payments
- mortgage principal payments
- sales expenses
- taxes.

The percentage contribution of each component use of the IRR likewise may be computed by dividing the present value of each component use by the total present value of the investment.

The advantages of fully partitioning real estate investment cash flows by using the internal rate of return in the manner suggested include:

1. the relative contribution of sources and uses of the IRR are not biased as with some previous cash flow partitioning methods which utilized the IRR; and
2. different risks may be associated with achieving each component return in the IRR.

While real estate investors may intuitively evaluate the risk associated with attaining the magnitude of each projected IRR source and use, the challenge to researchers is to develop appropriate risk premiums so that various IRR sources and uses may be discounted at appropriate discount rates.[14] For those cash flows that can be considered to possess a high degree of certainty (e.g., fixed mortgage interest, mortgage principal, depreciation and tax rates), the appropriate discount rate may be at or near the rate for risk-free investments.

Ranking return sources by risk levels

Partitioning real estate investment returns may result in higher investment values. The component returns have varying degrees of risk associated with their expected return. Property owners may be able to increase the value of their investment if they can sell (1) the low-risk return sources to investors seeking low-risk assets and (2) the more risky return sources to investors seeking additional return potential.[15] When one investor owns all component returns, he receives a total return that is a weighted average of the component returns, accepting the low-risk components along with the higher risk expected return sources.

The suggested method of partitioning real estate investment cash flows allows investors to evaluate the risk associated with each component return and rank these return sources according to risk.

If the expected return is a function of the component returns previously enumerated, then:

$$E(R) = E(R_{EGI}) + E\,(R_{\Delta EGI}) + E(R_{PA}) + E(R_{AMORT}) - E(R_{OE}) - E(R_{\Delta OE}). \qquad (30)$$

and the variance of the real estate returns is:

$$Var(R) = V(R_{EGI}) + Var(R_{\Delta EGI}) + V(R_{PA}) + V(R_{AMORT}) + V(R_{OE}) + V(R_{\Delta OE}). + \text{covariance terms} \qquad (31)$$

Note that the calculated variance may be used to rank the riskiness of each component return.

The variance associated with price appreciation appears to be the largest because it requires accurate forecasts of future rent levels, and required rates of return in future years. In addition, the return from price appreciation is correlated with EGI, ΔEGI, INT, PRIN, DEP, LTV, and T, as shown in (25) and (26).

The variance associated with the return from changes in EGI appears to be slightly less than returns from price appreciation. Variability exists because investors must forecast future economic/market rent conditions, and the covariance term includes the marginal tax rate and other second-period cash flows as shown in (16) for the two-period model.

The variance associated with the return from initial levels of EGI is determined by the investors ability to correctly assess current market rent conditions and supply/demand relationships. In addition, (15) reveals that the covariance term includes only the marginal tax rate and the second-period cash flows. Consequently the variance of the return from initial EGI should be less than the variance of returns from future changes in EGI.

The variance associated with returns from depreciation deductions is relatively low because the depreciation allowance is scheduled by known tax laws based upon a known purchase price. Variability derives from the uncertainty of the land value used to calculate the depreciable basis and from the possibility of changes in tax laws.

The variance associated with principal reduction due to loan amortization is negligible, because the principal reduction is scheduled by loan contract and (19) shows no covariance with other return sources.

Concluding comments

The purpose of this paper has been to demonstrate how real estate investment returns may be partitioned according to the component returns of the IRR model. Such partitioning may be useful in evaluating riskiness and ranking alternative projects with highly similar IRRs.

Mathematical models of the one-period and two-period IRR for real estate investments were derived. The proposed partitioning of the component returns eliminates biases that are inherent in partitioned IRR literature. Specifically, in earlier partitioning models the treatment of depreciation caused returns from annual cash flows to be overstated. Similarly, the treatment of annual principal reduction through loan amortization has been shown to understate annual cash flow returns and to overstate returns from price appreciation.

Interpretations of changes in each component part in investment returns were demonstrated mathematically by taking the first derivative of each component part with respect to IRR. Although these interpretations may be intuitive to the veteran teacher, they may be an aid to understanding for mathematically competent graduate students with minimal exposure to real estate investment analysis.

Using the two-period IRR model, the variance for each component of return was evaluated and the associated covariance terms were mathematically derived. Returns from price appreciation and gross rental income are expected to have higher variance, when compared to returns from tax benefits or loan amortization.

Total overall return of a real estate investment may be viewed as a weighted average of the component returns. It has been proposed that individuals could maximize the value of real estate assets by partitioning the component returns and selling the individual components to other investors, matching the risk-return opportunity of each component to the risk-return preference of individual investors. Recently, Webb and Rubens (1988) have empirically found that a measurable difference exists in the variance of returns from annual income and price appreciation. A logical next step for researchers is to use simulation techniques to quantify and rank the variance of the other components of real estate returns, and then to empirically estimate the risk premiums demanded by investors for each source of return.[16, 17]

Appendix

In this appendix we demonstrate how real estate investment cash flows may be partitioned into multiple components. We begin with the following project information:

Wildfire Apartments estimates first-year potential gross income of \$324,000. Rents are projected to increase 5% annually. The apartment complex generates no other income.

Vacancy and collection allowances are 5% of potential gross income. Operating expenses for the first year are projected to be \$129,600. These expenses will increase at a 4% annual rate after the first year.

This project may be purchased for \$2,024,000. The land has been appraised at \$400,000. The project is expected to increase in value at an annual rate of five percent. A $1,600,000 loan mortgage loan is available at a 9.5% fixed interest rate amortized into monthly payments over a 30-year term.

The apartment complex is projected to be sold at the end of a four-year holding period. Sales expenses are projected to be 7% of the sales price. The investor has stable (non-capital gain) income of $500,000, so you may safely assume that income from this project will be subject to the highest marginal tax bracket (1988 rules were used in this example; the instructor may wish to update the relevant tax rates).

(*Note to Instructor*: To familiarize students with pro forma income statements and spreadsheets, and to ensure understanding of the underlying investment decision-making tools, weekly homework assignments can be made. For example, a series of weekly homework assignments might be:

First week: Prepare a four-year pro forma income statement by hand, without using a computer.

Second week: Complete the same assignments, except this time use spreadsheets. Also include in this assignment the calculation of any decision-making criteria that utilize only annual income and which you choose to cover in class, such as gross rent multipliers, return on investment, cash on cash return, return on equity and payback period.

Third week: Add the calculation of the reversion to the spreadsheet, and calculate both the net present value (at a given discount rate) and the internal rate of return.

Fourth week: Partition investment cash flows into a specified number (e.g., 17) of component parts (discounted at the IRR), and aggregate such component parts into sources and uses of returns. Also, the students might be asked to explain how the division into component parts potentially may be useful to investors in evaluating the risks associated with alternative investments.)

Table 1 contains the four-year pro forma income statement for this property, and Table 2 shows the cash proceeds realized from selling at the end of the holding period. Table 3 shows one way to partition real estate investment cash flows under the procedures described in this article. In partitioning, note that the component cash flows are discounted at the project IRR. Discounting at the IRR assumes that all sources and uses of returns are equally risky, which clearly is an unrealistic assumption. Thus,

Table 1. Projected Annual Cash Flows, 1988 Tax Rules

(1)	Potential gross income	$324,000	$340,200	$357,210	$375,072
(2)	Less: vacancies & collection	−16,200	−17,010	−17,860	−18,752
(3)	Effective gross income	307,800	323,190	339,350	356,320
(4)	Less: operating expenses	−129,600	−134,784	−140,176	−145,782
(5)	Net operating income	178,200	188,406	199,174	210,538
(6)	Less: mortgage interest	−151,576	−150,600	−149,524	−148,340
(7)	Less: depreciation	−59,056	−59,056	−59,056	−59,056
(8)	Taxable income	−32,432	−21,250	−9,406	880
(9)	NOI (from line 5)	178,200	188,406	199,174	210,538
(10)	Less debt service	−161,444	−161,444	−161,444	−161,444
(11)	Cash flow before taxes	16,756	26,962	37,730	49,094
(12)	Taxes (Line 8 × tax rate)	−9,080	−5,952	−2,634	1,760
(13)	Cash flow after taxes	25,836	32,914	40,364	48,214

Table 2. Projected Sales Proceeds, 1988 Tax Rules

Calculation of tax due:	
Gross sales price	$2,460,184
Less: selling expenses	−172,212
Net sales price	2,287,972
Less: adjusted basis	−1,787,780
Gain on sale	500,192
Tax due on sale	140,054
Calculation of sales proceeds:	
Gross sales price	$2,460,184
Less: selling expenses	−172,212
Less: income tax due	−140,054
Less: unpaid mortgage balance	−1,554,260
Cash proceeds from sale	593,658

as additional research permits better quantification of the risks associated with each real estate investment cash flow source and use, this assumption should be relaxed and different discounts employed that are appropriate for the risks associated with each investment cash flow component.

The present value of all investment cash flow components are shown in Table 4. Table 5 sets out the sources of investment returns (those components with positive present values). Similarly, Table 6 sets out the uses

Table 3. Partitioning Annual Cash Flows

EGI	307,800	307,800	307,800	307,800	857,332
EGI growth	0	15,390	31,550	48,520	58,035
Operating expenses	(129,600)	(129,600)	(129,600)	(129,600)	(360,982)
Operate expenses growth	0	(5,184)	(10,576)	(16,182)	(19,440)
Net operating income	178,200	188,406	199,172	210,538	
Interest	(151,576)	(150,600)	(149,524)	(148,340)	(418,390)
Depreciation	(59,056)	(59,056)	(59,056)	(59,056)	
Taxable income	(32,432)	(21,250)	(9,408)	3,142	
Net operating income	178,200	188,406	199,172	210,538	
	(151,576)				
Interest	(9,868)	(150,600)	(149,524)	(148,340)	
Principal	16,756	(10,844)	(11,920)	(13,104)	(31,288)
BT cash flow		26,962	37,728	49,094	
Tax savings:					
Interest	42,440	42,168	41,866	41,536	117,148
Depreciation	16,536	16,536	16,536	16,536	46,058
Operating expenses	36,288	36,288	36,288	36,288	101,076
Growth OE	0	1,452	2,960	4,530	5,442
Taxes paid:					
Effect gross income	(86,184)	(86,184)	(86,184)	(86,184)	(240,054)
Growth EGI	0	(4,310)	(8,834)	(13,586)	(16,260)
AT cash flow	(25,836)	(32,916)	(40,364)	(48,214)	

Partitioned Cash Flow From Sale

Initial purchase price	2,024,000	
Price appreciation	436,184	238,996
Sales expenses	(172,212)	(94,360)
Mortgage balance	(1,554,260)	
Taxes due on sale	(140,052)	(76,758)
Reversion cash flow	593,660	

Table 4. Present Value* of Investment Cash Flow Components

PV effective gross income	857,332
PV taxes on EGI	−240,054
PV EGI growth	58,070
PV taxes on EGI growth	−16,260
PV operating expenses	−360,982
PV tax saved on OE	101,076
PV OE growth	−19,440
PV tax saved on OE growth	5,442
PV mortgage interest	−418,390
PV tax savings on mortgage interest	117,148
PV tax depreciation tax savings	46,058
PV of disposition taxes	−76,758
PV of sales expenses	−94,360
PV Price appreciation	238,996
PV of principal paid	−31,288
PV of principal returned	25,060
PV return of initial equity	232,320
Total present value	423,970
less initial investment	−424,000
NPV	30**

* Discounted at project IRR
** Does not total to zero due to rounding

Table 5. Present Value of Cash Flow Sources of IRR

ITEM	*PV**	*% OF TOTAL*
Effective gross income	857,332	51.0
Growth EGI	58,070	3.5
Tax shelter OE	101,076	6.0
Tax shelter growth OE	5,442	0.3
Tax shelter mortgage interest	117,148	7.0
Tax shelter depreciation	46,058	2.7
Price appreciation	238,996	14.2
Loan amortization	25,060	1.5
Return of initial equity	232,320	13.8
Total positive PV	1,681,502	100%

* Discounted at projected IRR

Table 6. Present Value of Cash Flow Uses of IRR

ITEM	*PV**	*% OF TOTAL*
Tax cost for EGI	−240,054	19.1
Tax cost for growth EGI	−16,260	1.3
Operating expenses	−360,982	28.7
Growth in operating expenses	−19,440	1.5
Mortgage interest	−418,390	33.3
Disposition taxes	−76,758	6.1
Sales expenses	−94,360	7.5
Principal payments	−31,288	2.5
Total negative PV	−1,257,532	100%
Initial investment	−424,000	
Total PV (including initial investment)	−1,681,532	

* Discounted at project IRR

of investment returns, and is composed of components with negative present values.

As an example of how component sources and uses of returns may be reaggregated for analytical purposes, note that all tax-related components may be reaggregated into one figure for analytical purposes (i.e., a negative $63,348). Note that this reaggregation of taxes avoids the bias in returns attributable to annual cash flow and the reversion under some previous partitioning procedures referred to in the main body of this paper.

References

Arditti, Fred D. "A Note on Discounting the Components of an Income Stream." *Journal of Finance* 29 (June 1974), 995–999.

Cassidy, Thomas C. "Breaking Down the IRR." *Commercial Investment Real Estate Journal* 5 (Spring 1986), 26–30.

Dorfman, Robert. "The Meaning of Internal Rates of Return." *Journal of Finance* 36 (December 1981), 1011–1021.

Dotzour, Mark G. and Donald R. Levi. "Partitioning the After-Tax IRR for Better Analysis." *Real Estate Appraiser and Analyst* (Spring 1989), 60–66.

Jaffe, Austin J. "Is There a 'New' Internal Rate of Return Literature?" *Journal of American Real Estate and Urban Economics Association* 5 (Winter 1977), 482–502.

Messner, Stephen D. and Byrl N. Boyce. "Partitioning Real Estate Yields." *Commercial Investment Journal* 4 (Summer 1985), 24–28.

Modigliani, Franco and Merton H. Miller. "Corporate Income Tax and the Cost of Capital: A Correction." *American Economic Review* 53 (June 1963), 433–443.

Pellatt, Peter G.K. "The Analysis of Real Estate Investments Under Uncertainty." *Journal of Finance* 27 (May 1972), 459–471.

Valachi, Donald J. "The Three Faces of IRR." *Real Estate Review* 8 (Fall 1978), 74–78.

Webb, James R. and Jack H. Rubens. "The Effect of Unbundling Asset Returns on Restricted Mixed-Asset Portfolios." Working paper presented at American Real Estate Society's annual meeting, 1988.

Robert H. Zerbst. "Partitioning the Internal Rate of Return." *Real Estate Review* 9 (Winter 1980), 80–84.

Notes

1. On IRR interpretation, see Pellatt (1972).
2. Sales price less sales expenses, disposition taxes, and mortgage balance.
3. As one reviewer suggested, although the tax substream is certain at any point in time, it may be uncertain over time because of the external risk that income tax laws and rates may change.
4. As noted in Messner and Boyce (1985), "partitioning cash flows with the IRR" may be more appropriate terminology than "partitioning the IRR."
5. For example, if rents fall or operating expenses increase, the level of tax shelter will increase.
6. Price appreciation less sales expenses and disposition taxes.
7. Not all taxpayers will be subject to a 28% marginal tax bracket, but this assumption is reasonable for many. The 1991 tax rates for married taxpayers filing jointly are: 15% from $0 to $34,000 taxable income, 28% on taxable income between $34,000 and $82,150, and 31% on taxable income exceeding $82,150. Capital gains are subject to a 28% cap. Tax brackets are now indexed to the inflation rate, and can be expected to change in the future. The assumption of constant marginal tax rates is a simplifying assumption for the generalized model presented in the next section, and arguably is a reasonable assumption for a generalized model being used to derive mathematically the impact of each component part on total investment returns.
8. By taxes due on sale resulting from the depreciation-induced reduction in basis. The correct treatment of depreciation was recognized in Messner and Boyce (1985), but this article did not fully partition all cash flows.
9. As recognized in Cassidy (1986). Our suggested partitioning procedure will demonstrate this mathematically.
10. As noted by one reviewer, the generalized model ignores loss carry-over rules because the inclusion of such rules is not essential to show how a given component of the IRR is influenced by other sources and uses of returns. Loss carry forward can be incorporated when cash flows from a specific project are partitioned by modifying the procedure suggested in Dotzour and Levi (1989). (Also see note 13.)

11. Recall our assumption of a constant marginal tax bracket, and the discussion of capital gains and tax brackets in note 7.

12. *Ibid.*

13. An empirical application of a multiple-partitioning model is found in Dotzour and Levi (1989), and in the appendix to this article which illustrates partitioning into return component sources and uses, and demonstrates how such sources and uses may be re-aggregated in various ways for analytical purposes.

14. See Modigliani and Miller (1963) for a discussion of the Monte Carlo sampling technique to evaluate real estate investments under conditions of uncertainty.

15. This is similar to the special allocation concept familiar to tax practitioners. Whether component investment parts may be sold separately after the Tax Reform Act of 1986 was not researched, but prior law made special allocations subject to a "substantial economic effects" test and the sole effect of the special allocation could not be to simply reduce taxes.

16. For example, a comparison of returns on a gross lease contract (where the owner pays all operating expenses) could be compared with the returns of a net lease (where the risk of changing operating expenses is transferred to the tenant) on other similar buildings to estimate the risk premium associated with the uncertainty associated with changes in operating expenses.

17. Historically, some syndication offerings have divided operating returns, tax savings, and potential returns from price appreciation to various classes of general and limited partners using special allocations. Analyses of these investments vehicles may yield information about risk premiums associated with each of these sources of returns. Moreover, variances may be used to rank component return riskiness, and to determine whether such riskiness is compatible with calculated risk premiums.

11 STATISTICAL INFERENCE IN EVENT STUDIES USING MULTIPLE REGRESSION

John J. Glascock and Imre Karafiath

Introduction

The use of financial price data to measure the impact of corporate events has become common in real estate and finance. For example, Henderson (1990) indicates that during 1987 and 1988 20 event studies were published in the *Journal of Finance* and *Journal of Financial Economics*. In the real estate literature, event studies have covered primarily corporate restructuring topics.[1]

Given the extensive and growing use of the event study technique, we advocate a convenient alternative (the "event parameter approach") to the traditional two-step event study procedure.[2] This procedure relieves the investigator of many programming chores, as event study results can be obtained using standard multiple regression procedures. By using standard regression packages, the investigator can obtain test statistics consistent with the wide body of accepted econometric theory.

This paper is a review and extension of Karafiath (1988). In the next section we present an alternative demonstration of the equivalence between the two-step and multiple regression procedures. In the third section we illustrate an application of the technique, using a sample of firms that had sold real estate assets. The final section is a summary.

The event parameter approach

Assume that for any day t in a non-event period (consisting of T observations) the underlying security return generating process is completely described by the single index market model [SIMM]:

$$R_{jt} = \alpha_j + \beta_j R_{mt} + e_{jt},\ \mathrm{t} \in \{\mathrm{T}\} \tag{1}$$

In the event parameter approach, it is assumed that for any day s in the event period (of S observations) the security return generating process can be described by equation (1) with the addition of an abnormal return δ_{js}:

$$R_{js} = \alpha_j + \beta_j R_{ms} + \delta_{js} + e_{js},\ \mathrm{s} \in \{\mathrm{S}\} \tag{2}$$

In the traditional event methodology the estimated coefficient $\hat{\delta}_{js}$ is a prediction error, defined as actual minus predicted value $\hat{\delta}_{js} = \mathrm{R}_{js} - \hat{\mathrm{R}}_{js}$, where $\hat{\mathrm{R}}_{js} = \hat{\alpha}_j + \hat{\beta}_j \mathrm{R}_{ms}$. In this paper we advocate the use of a dummy variable regression that facilitates the direct calculation of abnormal returns and test statistics.

To clarify the exposition of the dummy variable regression, we use the subscript $s = 1, \ldots, S$, to denote the event window. The t subscript denotes all observations $t = 1, \ldots, T, T+1, \ldots T+S$, where T is the number of observations normally used to estimate the market model. The alternative procedure adds dummy variables and event window observations to the right-hand side of (1). The number of dummy variables must equal the number of observations (S) in the event period; the coefficient on each dummy is a daily abnormal return. The following equation is estimated in a single step over the $T + S$ days in the estimation and event periods:

$$R_{jt} = \hat{\alpha}_j + \hat{\beta}_j R_{mt} + \sum_{s=1}^{S} \hat{\delta}_{js} D_{st} + \hat{e}_{jt},\ t = 1, \ldots, T + S. \tag{3}$$

where R_{jt}, R_{mt}, $\hat{\alpha}_j$, and $\hat{\beta}_j$ follow the usual definitions, and,

D_{st} = a dummy variable equal to one on observation $T+s$ only and zero elsewhere. Dummy variables are assigned to observations which are normally not used to estimate α and β

$\hat{\delta}_{js}$ = the coefficient on the dummy variable D_{st}, or abnormal return to security j on day $T+s$

$\hat{e}_{jt}$ = the residual on day t. This residual is zero for any observation where a dummy variable is equal to one.

The results obtained from (3) are identical to the results obtained from the traditional two-step procedure. One way to demonstrate this equivalence is to derive OLS estimators of α_j, β_j, and δ_{js}, in the usual way, i.e., by minimizing the sum of squared errors for (3). The function to be minimized is:

$$SSE = \sum_{t=1}^{T+S} \{R_{jt} - \hat{\alpha}_j - \hat{\beta}_j R_{mt} - \hat{\delta}_{j1} D_{1t} \ldots - \hat{\delta}_{jS} D_{St}\}^2. \tag{4}$$

Taking the partial derivatives of (4) with respect to $\hat{\alpha}$, $\hat{\beta}_j$, and each of the $\hat{\delta}_{js}$ yields the following set of least-squares normal equations:

$$\sum_{t=1}^{T+S} 2\{R_{jt} - \hat{\alpha}_j - \hat{\beta} j R_{mt} - \hat{\delta}_{j1} D_{1t} \ldots - \hat{\delta}_{jS} D_{St}\}(-1) = 0 \tag{5}$$

$$\sum_{t=1}^{T+S} 2\{R_{jt} - \hat{\alpha}_j - \hat{\beta} j R_{mt} - \hat{\delta}_{j1} D_{1t} \ldots - \hat{\delta}_{jS} D_{St}\}(-R_{mt}) = 0 \tag{6}$$

$$\sum_{t=1}^{T+S} 2\{R_{jt} - \hat{\alpha}_j - \hat{\beta} j R_{mt} - \hat{\delta}_{j1} D_{1t} \ldots - \hat{\delta}_{jS} D_{St}\}(-D_{1t}) = 0 \tag{7}$$

$$\vdots \qquad\qquad\qquad\qquad \vdots$$

$$\sum_{t=1}^{T+S} 2\{R_{jt} - \hat{\alpha}_j - \hat{\beta}_j R_{mt} - \hat{\delta}_{j1} D_{1t} \ldots - \hat{\delta}_{jS} D_{St}\}(-D_{St}) = 0 \tag{8}$$

In (8) the dummy variable D_{St} takes on a value of one for only one observation—the last observation in the event period—and is zero elsewhere. For this one observation, all the other dummies are equal to zero. Thus, (8) simplifies to:

$$\{R_{jt} - \hat{\alpha}_j - \hat{\beta}_j R_{mt} - \hat{\delta}_{jS} D_{St}\} = 0,\ t = T + S. \tag{8b}$$

It immediately follows that:

$$\hat{\delta}_{jS} = R_{jt} - \hat{\alpha}_j - \hat{\beta}_j R_{mt},\ t = T + S \tag{9}$$

where R_{jt} and R_{mt} are the values of the security return and market return corresponding to the last observation in the event window. Applying similar reasoning to the remainder of the dummy variables and the appropriate least squares normal equations, it follows that:

$$\hat{\delta}_{js} = R_{jt} - \hat{\alpha}_j - \beta_j R_{mt},\ s = 1, \ldots, S;\ t = T + s \tag{10}$$

where R_{jt} and R_{mt} are the return to security j and the market return corresponding to observation $T+s$.

To complete the demonstration of the equivalence between the dummy variable and two-step procedures, it is necessary to show that the S observations of the event period do not influence the OLS estimates of the intercept $\hat{\alpha}_j$ and slope $\hat{\beta}_j$.

The dummy variables are all zero over the first T observations; thus, equation (5) may be rewritten as:

$$\sum_{t=1}^{T} 2\{R_{jt} - \hat{\alpha}_j - \hat{\beta}_j R_{mt}\}(-1) +$$
$$\sum_{t=T+1}^{T+S} 2(\{R_{jt} - \hat{\alpha}_j - \hat{\beta}_j R_{mT} - \hat{\delta}_{j1} D_{1t} \ldots - \hat{\delta}_{jS} D_{St}\}(-1) = 0. \quad (5b)$$

Expanding the second term of (5b):

$$\begin{aligned} &R_{j(T+1)} - \hat{\alpha}_j - \hat{\beta}_j R_{m(T+1)} - \hat{\delta}_{j1} D_{1(T+1)} + \\ &R_{j(T+2)} - \hat{\alpha}_j - \hat{\beta}_j R_{m(T+2)} - \hat{\delta}_{j2} D_{2(T+2)} + \\ &\cdot \qquad\qquad\qquad\qquad\qquad\qquad \cdot \\ &\cdot \qquad\qquad\qquad\qquad\qquad\qquad \cdot \\ &\cdot \qquad\qquad\qquad\qquad\qquad\qquad \cdot \\ &R_{j(T+S)} - \hat{\alpha}_j - \hat{\beta}_j R_{m(T+S)} - \hat{\delta}_{jS} D_{S(T+S)}. \end{aligned} \quad (5c)$$

Substituting (10) for $\hat{\delta}_{js}$ in (5c) reveals that expression (5c) is equal to zero. (Recall that each of the D_{st} is equal to one in the expansion (5c).) A similar expansion can be applied to (6.) Thus, (5) and (6) can be reduced to:

$$\sum_{t=1}^{T} \{R_{jt} - \hat{\alpha}_j - \hat{\beta}_j R_{mt}\}(-1) = 0 \quad (11)$$

$$\sum_{t=1}^{T} \{R_{jt} - \hat{\alpha}_j - \hat{\beta}_j R_{mt}\}(-R_{mt}) = 0. \quad (12)$$

Equations (11) and (12) are the least-squares normal equations for α_j and β_j. The values of $\hat{\alpha}$ and $\hat{\beta}$ are determined by the first T observations only; the S observations in the event period do not influence the estimated slope or intercept.

The primary advantage of the dummy variable technique is that any standard regression package will directly calculate market model prediction errors as the estimated $\hat{\delta}_{js}$ coefficients. In addition, many regression packages can be programmed to provide a t-test on the sum of the δ coefficients, i.e., a t-test of the cumulative abnormal returns. In this section, we discuss three applications of the dummy variable technique. These applications illustrate (1) the common event date (e.g., regulatory events); (2) obtaining a t-test according to the cross-sectional standard deviation, as discussed in Brown and Warner (1985); and (3) the Z test presented in Mikkelson and Partch (1988).

The dummy variable method has been most widely used to examine the impact of common (calendar) events, (e.g., regulation, the international debt crisis, or the 1986 Tax Reform Act) on a portfolio of securities. In this application, both abnormal returns and test statistics can be conveniently obtained from one multiple regression. As shown by Binder (1985b, pg. 373, equation 4 and the following paragraph), given a common calendar event the prediction error for an equally weighted portfolio is exactly the prediction error averaged across the individual securities. Further, the t-test on the prediction error from the equally weighted portfolio is exactly the same as a test across securities, provided that cross-sectional dependence in security returns is properly taken into account.[3]

If there is a different event date for each firm, (3) must be estimated separately for each firm via OLS. To calculate the cross-sectional standard error as presented by Brown and Warner (1985), only the prediction errors (i.e., the $\hat{\delta}_{js}$ coefficients) need be saved in the regression package. In the Appendix we provide a sample of SAS code to implement this test; the SAS MACRO option is required.[4]

The dummy variable procedure can also be used to replicate the test statistic recently implemented by Mikkelson and Partch (1988). The advantage of the test used by Mikkelson and Partch is that serial correlation in prediction errors is properly taken into account.[5]

For firm-specific events, assuming cross-sectional independence, Karafiath and Spencer (1991) suggest the following procedure:

1. Estimate (3) via OlS for each firm j.
2. For each firm j, program the statistical package to calculate a t-test for the specified daily or cumulative prediction error. Note that with sufficient degrees of freedom (not a problem with daily return data) the t-distribution is asymptotically standard normal.
3. Denote this firm-specific test statistic as Z_j. Aggregating across firms, form the test statistic as $Z = (1/\sqrt{J})\Sigma Z_j$. This test will be asymptotically standard normal.

In Figure 1 we present a sample computer printout for step 1 above. The coefficient on the variable RMT1 (market return) is the security beta; we have verified that it is identical to the beta obtained from a market model regression over the first T (110) observations only. In this example we used 131 observations with 21 dummy variables, i.e., an

Table 1. Sample Computer Printout Using the Event Parameter Approach

SAS

19:32 WEDNESDAY, JUNE 10, 1992

DEP VARIABLE: FIRM1

ANALYSIS OF VARIANCE

SOURCE	DF	SUM OF SQUARES	MEAN SQUARE	F VALUE	PROB > F
MODEL	22	0.009327527	0.00423978	2.297	0.0026
ERROR	108	0.01993785	0.00184610		
C TOTAL	130	0.02926538			
ROOT MSE		0.01358712	R-SQUARE	0.3187	
DEP MEAN		0.001271236	ADJ R-SQ	0.1799	
C.V.		1068.811			

PARAMETER ESTIMATES

VARIABLE	*DF*	*PARAMETER ESTIMATE*	*STANDARD ERROR*	*T FOR HO: PARAMETER = 0*	*PROB > |T|*
INTERCEP	1	0.000711	0.001303613	0.546	0.5861
RMT1	1	1.02257	0.16772788	6.097	0.0001

DUM01	1	−0.001948	0.01376253	−0.142	0.8877
DUM02	1	−0.01469	0.01366521	−1.075	0.2847
DUM03	1	−0.004892	0.01369412	−0.357	0.7216
DUM04	1	−0.009176	0.01364910	−0.672	0.5028
DUM05	1	−0.008151	0.01369100	−0.595	0.5528
DUM06	1	−0.000396	0.01373416	−0.029	0.9770
DUM07	1	0.009722	0.01370931	0.709	0.4798
DUM08	1	−0.008959	0.01365772	−0.656	0.5132
DUM09	1	−0.003102	0.01367839	−0.227	0.8210
DUM10	1	−0.002354	0.01365627	−0.172	0.8634
DUM11	1	0.006692	0.01371631	0.488	0.6266
DUM12	1	−0.01448	0.01365027	−1.061	0.2910
DUM13	1	0.01058	0.01365074	0.775	0.4399
DUM14	1	−0.005580	0.01375094	−0.406	0.6857
DUM15	1	0.002507	0.01370709	0.183	0.8552
DUM16	1	−0.006069	0.01366843	−0.444	0.6579
DUM17	1	0.01477	0.01365151	1.082	0.2815
DUM18	1	0.01043	0.01380889	0.756	0.4513
DUM19	1	−0.000701	0.01370884	−0.051	0.9593
DUM20	1	−0.002118	0.01366454	−0.155	0.8771
DUM21		−0.003629	0.01371786	−0.265	0.7918
TEST:		NUMERATOR:	1.1E-05 DF:	1 F VALUE:	0.0578
		DENOMINATOR:	1.8E-04 DF:	108 PROB >F:	0.08104

Table 2. Sample event study results using the event parameter approach interval −05 to 05

FIRM NAME	*DATE*	*CAR*	*F(1,108)*	*Z-SCORE*
AETNA LIFE & CAS CO	841113	−0.0115	0.0578	−0.2404
AMERICAN BAKERIES CO	730328	0.0297	0.1176	0.3429
BENDIX CORP	810128	0.1173	3.8593	1.9645
BOISE CASCADE CORP	810527	−0.0132	0.0612	−0.2474
BORMANS INC	711105	0.1308	2.2234	1.4911
CARROLS CORP	811016	−0.0123	0.0092	−0.0959
CASTLE & COOKE INC	760910	0.0254	0.3735	0.6111
CHRIS CRAFT INDS INC	810924	−0.0745	2.1821	−1.4772
CHRYSLER CORP	800804	0.2805	3.8926	1.9730
CITIZENS FINANCIAL CORP	741008	−0.0198	0.0116	−0.1077
CLUETT PEABODY & CO INC	761210	−0.0579	0.4948	−0.7034
COMBUSTION ENGINEERING INC	811006	−0.0185	0.0906	−0.3010
CONTINENTAL STEEL CORP DE	711230	0.0230	0.0414	0.2035
CRYSTAL OIL CO	770228	−0.0270	0.0897	−0.2995
DART INDUSTRIES INC	720308	−0.0591	2.1601	−1.4697
DAYTON HUDSON CORP	820107	−0.0049	0.0121	−0.1100
ELTRA CORP	711220	0.0257	0.3010	0.5486
G A C CORP	720106	0.1351	1.2806	1.1316
HOSPITAL CORP AMER	821019	−0.0207	0.1299	−0.3604
LUCKY STORES INC	801125	−0.0003	0.0000	0.0000
NATIONAL HEALTH ENTERPRISES INC	750120	0.0164	0.0031	0.0557
NATIONAL TEA CO	760213	−0.0255	0.0651	−0.2551
OCCIDENTAL PETROLEUM CORP	830324	0.0236	0.1421	0.3770
PUROLATOR COURIER CORP	760309	−0.0135	0.1031	−0.3211
(OVERALL)		0.0187		0.5532

event window spanning from day −10 to +10. The abnormal return on the event date (DUM11) is 0.67 per cent, not statistically significant at the 5% level. At the bottom of the exhibit, the F test reveals that the cumulative abnormal return over the −5 to +5 interval is also not significant; this is programmed as test that the sum of DUM06 through DUM16 is zero. (Source code is provided in the Appendix.)

Both the R^2 and regression F are misleading when the dummy variable technique is used; adding additional dummies to the right hand side will progressively increase the R^2, as the additional dummies will explain 100% of the variance in the additional observations. (Note the decline when the R^2 is "adjusted.") Similarly, in the absence of a significant cumulative abnormal return the regression F tends to diminish with additional dummies; in Figure 1, the F statistic for a regression estimated separately over the first T observations only (and no dummies) is 37.17, the square of the t-test on RMT1.

In Figure 2 we present event study results from steps 2 and 3 above. For each firm in the sample we present the event date, the cumulative abnormal return and the F-test for the interval −5 to +5. The Z-score in the last column is the square root of the F and given the same sign as the CAR. The Z-test for the −5 to +5 interval is 0.55, calculated according to step 3 above.

Summary

The event study has become a standard tool of real estate research. In this paper, a convenient and accurate procedure for obtaining event study results has been presented. Two specific applications have been illustrated: one for the case of common calendar (i.e., tax reform) events and one for the case of firm-specific events (i.e., corporate restructuring). This paper is pedagogical. This procedure has been discussed elsewhere by Binder (1985a and 1985b), Malatesta (1986), and Thompson (1985) with an alternative exposition found in Karafiath (1988). However, it is hoped that by clarifying the details of this methodology, this paper will encourage the use of an efficient and accurate method of obtaining event study results.

Notes

1. Allen and Sirmans (1987) investigated the impact of acquisition by REITs; Glascock,

Davidson, and Sirmans (1989 and 1991) and Owers and Rogers (1986) analyzed the acquisition and disposition of real estate assets; Hite, Owers, and Roger (1984) examined the spinoff of real estate operations; McIntosh, Officer, and Born (1989) examined REIT Merger activity; Rutherford and Nourse (1988) analyzed the formation of real estate units by parent firms. This short list is intended only to suggest the importance of the event methodology and is by no means exhaustive.

2. The "event parameter approach" advocated in this paper was developed by Binder (1985a and 1985b), Dufour (1980), Malatesta (1986), and Thompson (1985). Sections of the present exposition rely heavily on Karafiath (1988), Karafiath, Mynatt, and Smith (1990), and Karafiath and Spencer (1991).

3. This is proved in Thompson (1985) and Hughes and Ricks (1984).

4. One OLS regression is required for each firm in the sample. The most convenient way to estimate these regressions is to select a package that will allow the programmer to place the regressions inside a loop.

5. The serial correlation in prediction errors is not due to serial correlation in stock returns or disturbance terms. Rather, prediction errors will be serially correlated due to measurement error in the base period regression that was used to estimate α and β. For each firm, security returns in the event period are forecast using the same estimates of α and β; thus, the prediction errors for each firm have a common source of error, leading to serial correlation. For details, see Karafiath and Spencer (1991); Sweeney (1991); Salinger (1992); and Mitchel (1989).

References

Allen, P.R. and C.F. Sirmans. "An Analysis of Gains to Acquiring Firm's Shareholders: The Special Case of REITs." *Journal of Financial Economics* 18 (1987), 175–184.

Binder, John. "Measuring the Effects of Regulation with Stock Price Data." *Rand Journal of Economics* 16 (Summer 1985), 167–183.

Binder, John. "On the Use of the Multivariate Regression Model in Event Studies." *Journal of Accounting Research* (Spring 1985), 370–383.

Brown, Stephen J. and Jerold B. Warner. "Using Daily Stock Returns: The Case Of Event Studies." *Journal of Financial Economics* 14 (1985), 3–31.

Dufour, Jean-Marie. "Dummy Variables and Predictive Tests for Structural Change." *Economics Letters* 6 (1980), 241–247.

Glascock, J., W. Davidson, and C.F. Sirmans. "An Analysis of the Acquisition and Disposition of Real Estate Assets." *Journal of Real Estate Research* 4, 3 (Fall 1989), 131–140.

Glascock, J., W. Davidson, and C.F. Sirmans. "The Gains from Corporate Selloffs: The Case of Real Estate Assets." *Journal of American Real Estate and Urban Economics Association* 19 (Winter 1991).

Henderson, G. "Problems and Solutions in Conducting Event Studies." *Journal of Risk and Insurance* 17 (June 1990), 282–306.

Hite, G., J.E. Owers, and R.C. Rogers. "The Separation of Real Estate Operations by Spin-Off." *Journal of American Real Estate and Urban Economics Association* 12 (Fall 1984), 318–332.

Holthausen, R.W. and R.W. Leftwich. "The Effects of Bond Rating Change on Common Stock Price." *Journal of Financial Economics* 6 (1986), 57–58.

Hughes, J.S. and W.E. Ricks. "Accounting for Retail Land Sales: Analysis of a Mandated Change." *Journal of Accounting and Economics* 6 (August 1984), 101–132.

Karafiath, Imre. "Using Dummy Variables in the Event Methodology." *Financial Review* 23 (August 1988), 351–358.

Karafiath, Imre, R. Mynatt, and K.L. Smith. "The Brazilian Default and the Contagion Effect Hypothesis. "Journal of Banking and Finance (June 1990).

Karafiath, Imre and David E. Spencer. "Statistical Inference in Multi-Period Event Studies." *Review of Quantitative Finance and Accounting* 1 (1991).

Malatesta, Paul. "Measuring Abnormal Performance: The Event Parameter Approach Using Joint Generalized Least Squares." *Journal of Financial and Quantitative Analysis* 21 (March 1986), 27–38.

McIntosh, W., D.T. Officer, and J.A. Born. "The Wealth Effects of Merger Activity: Further Evidence from Real Estate Investment Trusts." *Journal of Real Estate Research* 4 (Fall 1989), 141–155.

Mikkelson, Wayne H. and Megan Partch. "Withdrawn Security Offerings." *Journal of Financial and Quantitative Analysis* 27 (March 1988), 119–134. (Note the correction in the December issue.)

Mitchell, Mark L. "The Impact of External Parties of Name Brand Capital: The 1982 Tylenol Poisonings and Subsequent Cases." *Economic Enquiry* 27 (October 1989), 601–618.

Owers, J.E. and R.C. Rogers. "The Diverstiture of Real Estate Assets by Sell-Offs." *Real Estate Issues* 11 (Spring/Summer 1986), 29–35.

Rutherford, R.C. and H.O. Nourse. "The Impact of Corporate Real Estate Unit Formation on the Parent Firm's Value." *Journal of Real Estate Research* 3 (Fall 1988), 73–84.

SAS Institute Inc. *SAS® User's Guides, Version 5 Editions*. Cary, NC: SAS Institure, Inc., 1985.

Salinger, Michael. "Standard Errors in Event Studies." *Journal of Financial and Quantitative Analysis* (March 1992), 39–53.

Sweeney, Richard. "Levels of Significance in Event Studies." *Review of Quantitative Finance and Accounting* 1 (1991), 373–382.

Thompson, Rex. "Conditioning the Return Generating Process on Firm Specific Events: A Disussion of Event Study Methods." *Journal of Financial and Quantitative Analysis* 20 (June 1985), 151–186.

Appendix: A

Source Code for Sample Event Study

In the following program, it is assumed that the security returns have been stored in FILE8; the corresponding market returns have been stored in FILE9. In the sample printout following the code, the variables CPE1 through CPE24 are the individual firms cumulative prediction error over the −5 to +5 interval. The variable CPEBAR is the mean CPE over this interval. The SAS function STDERR was used to calculate the standard error of the mean and the *t*-test.

```
OPTION LINESIZE = 79;
DATA AAA; INFILE FILE8; INPUT PIRM1-FIRM24;
DATA BBB; INFILE FILE9; INPUT RMT1-RMT24;
DATA CCC; MERGE AAA BBB;
ARRAY ONE(24) FIRM1-FIRM24;
ARRAY TWO(24) RMT1-RMT24;
DO J = 1 TO 24;
IF (ONE(J) < −1) THEN ONE(J) = .;
END;
ARRAY DUMMY(21) DUM01-DUM21;
DO J = 1 TO 21;
 IF (_N_ = J + 110) THEN DUMMY(J) = 1; ELSE DUMMY(J) =0;
END;
%MACRO EVENT;
%DO K = 1 %TO 24;
PROC REG NOPRINT DATA=CCC OUTEST=DDD;
MODEL FIRM&K=RMT&K DUM01-DUM21;
   TEST DUM06 + DUM07 + DUM08 + DUM09 + DUM10 +
      DUM11 + DUM12 + DUM13 + DUM14 + DUM15 + DUM16;
DATA LAST&K; SET DDD;
CP&K = SUM(OF DUM06-DUM16);
KEEP CPE&K;
%END;
DATA EEE;
%DO K = 1 %TO 24;
MERGE LAST&K;
%END;
CPEBAR = MEAN(OF CPE1-CPE24);
STDHAT = STDERR(OF CPE1-CPE24);
TTEST = CPEBAR/STDHAT;
PROC TRANSPOSE; PROC PRINT DATA=DATA1;
%MEND;
%EVENT;
```

Sample Printout

SAS
19:41 WEDNESDAY, JUNE 10, 1992

OBS	*_NAME_*	*COL1*
1	CPE1	−0.01145
2	CPE2	0.02972
3	CPE3	0.11733
4	CPE4	−0.01322
5	CPE5	0.13076
6	CPE6	−0.01227
7	CPE7	0.2541
8	CPE8	−0.07454
9	CPE9	0.28052
10	CPE10	−0.01982
11	CPE11	−0.05790
12	CPE12	−0.01849
13	CPE13	0.02298
14	CPE14	−0.02697
15	CPE15	−0.05905
16	CPE16	−0.00485
17	CPE17	0.02571
18	CPE18	0.13506
19	CPE19	−0.02071
20	CPE20	−0.00030
21	CPE21	0.01637
22	CPE22	−0.02551
23	CPE23	0.02364
24	CPE24	−0.01351
25	CPEBAR	0.01871
26	STDHAT	0.01584
27	TTEST	1.18071

INDEX